# THE SECRET WAR AGAINST DOPE

*Also by Andrew Tully*

Novels

Nonfiction

# THE

# SECRET WAR

# AGAINST DOPE

*by*

## ANDREW TULLY

With an Introduction by

## VERNON  D.  ACREE
### COMMISSIONER OF CUSTOMS

Coward, McCann & Geoghegan, Inc.
New York

This book is for
Douglas Larsen and Richard Mullens

232456

# PREFACE

There is no single hero in this book, just a relatively few hard-working U.S. Customs agents. They do not come on with the blazing gun, the bulging bicep, or the sexual stare of the television screen. Their heroism—and they would snort at the term—is in their patient, dogged, thinking pursuit of the twentieth century's Merchants of Death. Most of them probably have never fired a gun in anger, although they are armed twenty-four hours a day, because you don't fight narcotics traffickers with bullets but with intelligence and a kind of ingrained stealth. It is a hard job because the pusher at all levels lives by his wits, sustained by the evil wisdom of the breed. Besides, violence is illogical except as a last resort. The dead trafficker can't talk; he cannot lead his interrogators to the executive suites of the death-dealing international industry.

This book, quite simply, is about good guys and bad guys. The author is on the side of the good guys. The reader will search in vain for social worker asides about the pusher driven to his vicious trade by poverty or by an unsympathetic parent or because he couldn't get along with his teddy bear. He has no redeeming virtues. He deserves only our cold, fearful contempt. He is killing our children.

ANDREW TULLY
Washington, D.C.

# INTRODUCTION

The problems inherent in and growing out of the high-priority task assigned to the Customs Bureau by the President and Congress—to prevent the illegal entry of narcotics into the United States—are painted in graphic colors and with grim reality on these pages by a leading craftsman of our times, Andrew Tully.

Mr. Tully has researched his chronicle with meticulous care and patience, reviewing extensive reports, judicial reviews, millions of words of evidence, interviewing suspects and investigators, all adding to the totality and credibility of his remarkable story. Although he undertook this challenging assignment sometime before my appointment as Commissioner, I regard this book as a long-overdue tribute to the dedicated men and women of Customs.

But this book reflects more than a journalist's literary skill: What emerges, literally leaping out of the pages, is the deep concern of an American parent over the searing dangers of the drug epidemic which has afflicted our country.

The book mirrors the determination of a public-spirited citizen to help arouse sentiment in support of strengthened laws, greater cooperation between the people and their government, to the end that this cancer on our society be extirpated.

President Nixon, who has taken a strong position of leadership in this escalating effort, said in a nationwide radio address on March 10, 1973: "We have already made encouraging progress in the war against drug abuse. Now we must consolidate that progress and strike even harder."

As head of the Customs Bureau, which was designated by the President as the country's "first line of defense" against the drug trafficker, I want to reaffirm our pledge that there will be no relaxation of effort, no abridgment of responsibility, no diminution of our resolve to make things tougher for the smugglers until they either are behind bars or are driven out of business.

We have reason to believe that they are getting the message. Thanks to the cooperation of many friendly governments, we are making very significant seizures of illicit drugs at our borders, thus keeping hundreds of millions of doses from reaching the users and the pushers and sparing many thousands of our youth the misery of drug addiction.

In the words of President Nixon in his State of the Union address of March 14, 1973: "No single law enforcement problem has occupied more time, effort and money in the past four years than that of drug abuse and drug addiction. We have regarded drugs as 'public enemy number one,' destroying the most precious resource we have— our young people—and breeding lawlessness, violence and death."

Despite our progress, we are still far from victory . . . there is still a lot of work to be done. The government cannot do it alone. We need the total dedication of an aroused citizenry. This book by Mr. Tully, whose opinions are his own and not necessarily those of the Customs Bureau, is an important contribution to that objective.

VERNON D. ACREE
United States Commissioner of Customs

# CONTENTS

# THE CRIME AND THE LAW

# 1

# Cloak, Dagger, and Horse

Newspapers at the time would have called it a "routine search." But Customs Inspector Lynn Pelletier, a comely twenty-two-year-old redhead, knew what she was looking for when she peeked into an imported Volkswagen camper at Port Elizabeth, New Jersey, on the gray morning of April 5, 1971. In her mind was a bulletin issued in January by Andrew Agathangelou, director of the United States Customs Bureau's Division of Intelligence, calling attention to the increased use of campers and microbuses by dope smugglers around the world. Moreover, the Customs Commissioner, Myles J. Ambrose, had ordered periodic inspection of every automobile entering an American port.

Miss Pelletier was looking for hashish. As she went over the camper, trying to remember all the lessons her training instructors had taught her, she noticed there was a screw loose in a panel under the right side of the dashboard. She tugged the panel open, put a hand in the opening, and drew out a plastic bag containing a quantity of white powder. Forthwith, she called upon Inspector Harry Dittmyre to assist her in a further search of the respectably bourgeois vehicle. They found fifteen more plastic bags filled with white powder inside the roof liner. Inspector Daniel Sheehey took the bags to Shed No. 321 and conducted a field test of the powder. He got a positive reaction for heroin.

The camper had arrived the day before on the M/S *Atlantic Cognac* and was consigned to Roger Xavier de Louette, care of the Sheraton Hotel in New York. After De Louette came to claim the camper, Customs Inspector Larry Harris assigned Miss Pelletier to examine the "subject vehicle." When the field test revealed that the plastic bags contained heroin, De Louette was arrested on the spot.

Eventually, Miss Pelletier and other inspectors discovered a total of eighty-eight packages of heroin concealed in various parts of the camper—nineteen of them in a plastic water tank. ("Dumb," snapped Miss Pelletier about that hiding place.)*

A little less than seven months later, a top official of the French counterpart of America's espionage shop, the Central Intelligence Agency, was indicted by a United States grand jury in Newark on three counts of conspiring to smuggle and smuggling 96 pounds of heroin, worth $12,000,000 at the addict's level, into the country. The indictment set off a diplomatic tizzy that rocked France and set the American intelligence community to reappraising the security of its secrecy-shrouded relationship with the French Service of Exterior Documentation and Counterespionage (SDECE).

Undoubtedly, diplomatic considerations were one of the two reasons the seizure was not announced until May 11, when a federal grand jury handed down a two-count indictment against De Louette. The other reason was that Customs' detectives were doing some more digging in the United States and abroad, meanwhile lending interested ears to De Louette's story. It was this digging and listening that led, on November 14, 1971, to the three-count indictment of Colonel Paul Fournier, a supervisory agent in SDECE.

On that April morning when she found the first plastic bag of white powder, Lynn Pelletier told reporters that nothing exciting had come her way since she began working for the Customs Bureau the previous July. "And this happened," she said. "It was a shock."

After he was arrested, Roger de Louette was taken to the office of the special agent in charge at 201 Varick Street, New York City, to be photographed and fingerprinted. He was also duly informed that he had the right to a lawyer and was not obliged to answer any questions. "But of course right now it looks like you're gonna be the patsy," an agent told De Louette. "Maybe you'd like to tell us what

---

* In January, 1973, Customs officials were astonished to read that at least 261 pounds of heroin and 137 pounds of cocaine, seized by a city-federal strike force in 1962 and valued on the street at $74,000,000, had disappeared from a New York City police vault. All narcotics seized by Customs are kept in vaults in various cities under supervision of the bureau's Inspection and Control arm and are guarded around the clock by armed security personnel. Keys are carried on the person of the Custodian of Customs Seizures, who may release narcotics required in court as evidence only under subpoena from the United States Attorney who has jurisdiction. As of February, 1973, Customs had never lost an ounce of contraband drugs.

you know." De Louette asked for a definition of the word "patsy." The agent, Paul Boulad, told him, "It means you'll go to jail while your bosses go free." De Louette said he'd "cooperate."

Meanwhile, at Washington's insistence, De Louette was also questioned by a French policeman, Commissaire Daniel Hartwig.

With Hartwig's approval, the agents escorted De Louette to the Park-Sheraton Hotel at Seventh Avenue and 56th Street in an attempt to make contact with De Louette's receiver. The party remained there for two days in adjoining rooms, waiting for the phone to ring or a knock on the door. Then they gave up, and De Louette, who insisted he had no idea who the receiver was, was arraigned in Newark before a United States magistrate, who held him in the whopping bail of $500,000.

For a reason he could not immediately explain, Customs Special Agent Paul Boulad found the name De Louette familiar. He had heard or seen the name somewhere. Something, he thought, in connection with Cuba or Cubans. Boulad had a check made of Customs intelligence files in Washington.

The result of the check was interesting rather than spectacular. An informant in Havana had mentioned the name De Louette only in passing as a member of a French agricultural mission in the Cuban capital which might prove a source of information on the personalities of various Cuban officials. It was the informant's expert guess that the mission was an intelligence cover.

Boulad turned to the French file. He also had the name De Louette tossed into the Customs Automatic Data Processing Intelligence Network (CADPIN). The file contained raw, unverified reports that certain French bureaucrats believed to be undercover operatives for various French intelligence groups were involved in currency manipulations and maintained contacts with known narcotics traffickers. An analyst's comments suggested that perhaps France's espionage organizations were not above engaging in extralegal activities to obtain funds for their operations. CADPIN disgorged the information that De Louette had been seen in the company of one Colonel Paul Fournier, whose last name was also reported to be Ferrer. The French file identified Fournier-Ferrer as an "operations agent" for SDECE. Customs' attachés at the American Embassy in Paris apparently had got around some.

From these small but significant morsels of intelligence gossip, the New York and Washington offices, with assists from their operatives in France, were able to draw a rough outline of De Louette's background and his probable higher-up connections. De Louette himself filled in assorted blank spaces so that Customs had enough information to put before a second federal grand jury in Newark. That information, which fingered Colonel Fournier as the mastermind of the conspiracy, was viewed as so sensitive that United States Attorney Herbert J. Stern flew to Paris on November 5 to confer with French government officials on the case. Stern returned with word that the officials had rejected his request to talk to Colonel Fournier, although Fournier had allegedly agreed to "open his file on the case completely" to French authorities.

The three-count indictment against Fournier painted this story, replete with the kind of small detail that gives authenticity to testimony:

On December 15, 1970, Fournier met with De Louette and asked whether the latter would be interested in a profitable mission—smuggling heroin into the United States. De Louette, a forty-eight-year-old World War II veteran who had been awarded the Croix de guerre for gallantry in action, had been dismissed some months earlier by the Bureau for Agricultural Development, which was believed to be an espionage cover organization. De Louette agreed to be recruited.

Fournier then arranged for De Louette to meet a man, never identified, at the Café de Paris in Paris, and the two of them negotiated an agreement to smuggle 96 pounds of heroin into the United States. For his services, De Louette was told he would receive $1,200 per kilogram (2.2 pounds), or a total of $50,000.

The unnamed conspirator instructed De Louette to obtain an American visa, to buy a Volkswagen camper in which the heroin would be concealed, and to make arrangements for shipping the camper to the United States. At a second meeting, also arranged by Fournier, De Louette received the equivalent of $5,500 in French currency to buy the VW and to meet other expenses of his mission.

De Louette bought the camper from the Garage Michel-Ange V.W. in Paris on February 25, 1971. No fool, De Louette avoided the French sales tax by paying for the camper with a check for 14,079 Swiss francs drawn on the Crédit Suisse in Geneva, where he had account No. 195-715. The next day, De Louette flew to Geneva to deposit enough money to cover the check.

On March 15, Fournier contacted De Louette again. This time the colonel told De Louette to drive the Volkswagen to Pontchartrain, about 25 miles from Paris, and rendezvous with another unidentified man, who would be driving a green Simca and would identify himself through the use of a code word, which De Louette later confessed he had forgotten.

From this man De Louette took delivery of the 96 pounds of heroin, which he and the nameless one secreted in wall panels, behind the dashboard, under the floorboards and in the plastic water tank of the camper. Then De Louette drove the Volkswagen to the French port of Le Havre, where he watched as the vehicle was loaded aboard the *Atlantic Cognac*, bound for Port Elizabeth. Fournier ordered De Louette to proceed to the United States on April 4, and De Louette did so, arriving at Kennedy International Airport on TWA Flight 803.

After his arrest and subsequent cooperative conversations with Customs investigators and the French commissaire, Hartwig, De Louette was vanned off to the Somerset County Jail in New Jersey, where he continued to talk whenever he could find someone to talk to.

As early as April 6, the day after De Louette's arrest, France's Central Office for the Suppression of Illicit Drug Trafficking turned over an official inquiry to Investigating Magistrate Gabriel Roussel. A week later Roussel wrote U.S. Attorney Stern that under French law he could not proceed against Fournier without a statement from De Louette. Whereupon Stern obtained permission to appoint an official of the Bureau of Narcotics and Dangerous Drugs to ask De Louette the questions that Roussel wanted asked—and to ask them in the presence of a French narcotics policeman, Claude Chaminadas, who was assigned to the French consulate in New York.

"Over my dead body," interjected De Louette's court-appointed counsel, Donald A. Robinson of Newark. Robinson demanded assurances that De Louette's answers and any testimony he might give to a grand jury would not be used against him in France. He noted that the Fifth Amendment to the Constitution protected De Louette from self-incrimination. Stern wrote Roussel again, asking him to immunize De Louette from prosecution in France. Immediately, French government spokesmen insisted that Roussel lacked the power to grant immunity.

So the waltz went on until September 14, when Stern met with French law enforcement officials in New York and proposed that De Louette take a lie detector test. If De Louette should refuse to take the test or fail it, Stern said he would prosecute him and recommend the maximum sentence for conspiring to import narcotics—twenty years. Stern wrote to Roussel later, explaining that the French officials at the meeting agreed that if De Louette passed the test, they would "proceed with an appropriate prosecution" of Fournier.

Chaminadas bet Stern a meal in a French restaurant that De Louette wouldn't take the test. But De Louette did so on September 21, and Stern reported that the results of the test showed De Louette had been telling the truth. Among other questions, De Louette was asked if Fournier had given him a contact in the French consulate in New York. His answer was yes, and De Louette named a middle-level official—not Chaminadas. The results of the test were dispatched to Paris.

Thus far, all the information linking Fournier to the heroin conspiracy had come from De Louette's conversations with American interrogators. Then came November and the second indictment, this one naming Fournier as well as De Louette. The next day, De Louette was arraigned before Judge Frederick B. Lacey in U.S. District Court in Newark.

De Louette pleaded guilty and told the court what he had told his interrogators and what was reflected in the indictment: to wit, that he had been recruited into the conspiracy by Fournier. Judge Lacey went to extraordinary lengths to assure himself—and presumably the French government—that De Louette knew exactly what he was doing. He examined De Louette for two hours, as the defendant stood before him in impeccable haberdashery, a petite French interpreter at his side. Finally the judge accepted De Louette's confession as having been made free of any pressure or promises and thus gave his judicial stamp to the charges in the indictment naming Fournier.

In Paris, Fournier finally surfaced to shrug off the indictment. In a statement authorized by Defense Minister Michel Debré, the intelligence official told U.S. Attorney Stern: "If I am guilty, Mr. Stern, prove it. And justice will follow its course."

Stern replied: "If you are innocent, Mr. Fournier, come to this country and stand trial. If you are innocent, you have nothing to fear. You are assured of a fair trial under our system of justice. Don't hide behind an anonymous service [SDECE] and an international border."

Fournier's statement also expressed surprise that he was indicted in the United States, "since I have never set foot in that country." Stern informed him that "you were not charged with setting foot in the United States; you were charged with illegally shipping 96 pounds of pure heroin into the United States." Fournier also said he was surprised that Stern "should oppose de Louette's being questioned by a representative of justice of our country." But Stern noted that Magistrate Roussel had refused to agree to the condition that De Louette's words not be used to incriminate him, as the American Constitution decreed.

Fournier appeared to be on safe ground in his native land. U.S. officials finally learned that he had been cleared in a four-day investigation. His statement said he had given French officials "all the explanations that were asked of me," and "without seeking to hide behind professional secrecy." However, he said his duty to SDECE and France "requires me to remain anonymous." At the same time, official French sources issued a series of denunciations of both De Louette and Stern, even as Stern wrote to Roussel, suggesting that the magistrate was putting "primary emphasis on the arrest and extradiction of de Louette rather than the arrest and prosecution of Fournier."

At De Louette's arraignment, the prosecution had put into the record a statement that De Louette had a contact in the French consulate in New York, but the name of the contact was not disclosed. That evening, the French narcotics policeman, Claude Chaminadas, dismissed the findings of the lie detector test taken by De Louette and called De Louette a liar. "He's been lying all along," the New York *Times* quoted Chaminadas as saying. "He who only hears one bell only hears one sound."

However, a subpoena issued for the consulate "contact" on October 21 to appear before the grand jury had been refused on the ground that the individual in question had diplomatic immunity.

Within days of De Louette's arraignment, the pot bubbled more furiously. Colonel Roger Barberot, director of a French government foreign aid agency, declared in a radio interview that he believed narcotics traffic had been organized by French secret service agents.

Referring to *"L'affaire de Louette,"* Barberot said, "My conviction is—and some will tell you so officially—that the operation was mounted by a certain number of SDECE agents in Paris itself. De Louette had to be got rid of in the United States to get rid of a very heavy past. It is the sequel of that operation that is coming out now." Barberot also said, in a casual footnote, that he believed the real name of Paul Fournier was Paul Ferrer, a former Air Force master sergeant who had risen to the rank of colonel in SDECE.

Magistrate Roussel immediately demanded the tape of the interview, and the French government issued a statement reiterating that it would pursue any charge filed against Fournier, or Ferrer, and that the French consulate official accused by De Louette would "make his deposition before the American judiciary in conformance with Article A20 of the Franco-American Consular Convention of 1966, which provides notably for a deposition in writing."

Undeterred by criticism, Colonel Barberot, a former French ambassador to Uruguay and the Central African Republic, charged in further radio and newspaper interviews that a former operating chief of SDECE had been dismissed in 1970 on suspicion of high treason. The accused official, Colonel René Bertrand, with the cover name of Colonel Jean Beaumont, announced that he would sue Colonel Barberot for libel and ask damages of one million francs ($180,000).

Subsequently, Barberot spent an hour and a half with Roussel, emerging to tell reporters that he had shed no new light on smuggling. But he called for a thorough investigation and housecleaning of SDECE. Fournier, or Ferrer, made no immediate comment.

Paris was in a minor uproar, with newspapers joining in criticism of SDECE. Defense Minister Michel Debré sought to calm the storm by pooh-poohing the importance of the De Louette case. "A former occasional employee of the service seems to me to have fallen into deplorable operations in recent months," Debré said. "To lighten the sentence that awaits him, the accused has hurled grave charges. That's in the nature of things, just as it's in the nature of things that imaginations quickly build up fictional serials."

But Debré could not dilute the curiosity of the French newspapers. Reporters were sent scurrying to pick up intelligence on Fournier-Ferrer, and Paris editions identified him "positively" as a man of fifty-two who had joined General de Gaulle's Secret Service in 1940 after the fall of France and had risen to become the director of research, or operating chief, of SDECE. Fournier-Ferrer was credited with having bugged Arab embassies in Berne during the Algerian war.

According to the right-wing newspaper *L'Aurore*, the colonel "did not hesitate to use information amiably communicated to him by certain services of eastern countries," and "talked of drug routes, of the collusion of Central Intelligence Agency members in these rackets, etc." Other newspapers reported that at least three men arrested on drug charges in past years had worked for SDECE. The highly respectable and authoritative *Le Monde* spoke sadly of the huge quantities of heroin passing through France and remembered that the kidnapping of the Moroccan left opposition leader, Mehdi Ben Barka, in 1965 had disclosed a tie-in between at least lower ranks of SDECE and underworld operations in drugs and prostitution.

Parisian newspapers seemed to be wondering between the lines whether the American drug seizure signified that this tie-in between police and the gangster element still existed despite the exposures of the Ben Barka case, which had forced a reorganization of the SDECE. There was colorful speculation that the SDECE had risen from the ashes of its 1965 disgrace to become again an autonomous empire whose higher-ups were untouchable.

But the most spectacular story was published by the London *Daily Express*, which quoted Fournier-Ferrer as "revealing" a power struggle between the CIA and SDECE.

"Only a few weeks ago," said the *Express* story, "Colonel Fournier was one of SDECE's top agents operating in the U.S. attached in a low capacity on the periphery of the French Embassy in Washington. He told his chiefs in SDECE that American CIA agents had stumbled onto his activities and were eager to settle an old score with him and have him expelled from the U.S.

"The perfect opportunity came when Mr. de Louette fell into the hands of American authorities by bungling the heroin smuggling. Colonel Fournier believes that Mr. de Louette was approached by CIA men and told that it would do him a lot of good if he were to incriminate Colonel Fournier in the drug scandal.

"Since then, Colonel Fournier said, he has been questioned about the affair by American detectives investigating the case. He said that at his own request he was given truth drugs, but that the Americans were even then unable to corroborate their version of his role. But now he has told his bosses he is ready to testify again to the French authorities under the influence of truth drugs."

So far as is known, Fournier-Ferrer never gave further testimony to any French tribunal. But De Louette told his story—168 transcript pages' worth—to Magistrate Roussel during a three-day interrogatory in March, 1972, in the presence of U.S. agents, prosecutor Stern and De Louette's counsel.

De Louette, who had been indicted in France, renounced all his rights under French law—a condition Roussel had demanded. His story filled in all the nooks and crannies in his earlier confession to American agents and named Fournier-Ferrer as the "mastermind" of the smuggling scheme. De Louette also testified that the SDECE at times resorted to "irregular means," including drug trafficking, when there was not enough money in the agency's budget to finance operations.

". . . I have sometimes heard of operations that were not above-board," De Louette told Roussel. "One example of which comes back to me: In 1953 in Indochina a helicopter which was available to the service transported several times opium in order to obtain money for operations about which I didn't know anything." De Louette said he heard this from the chopper's pilot, but he refused to name the pilot.

The transcript also disclosed that the French policeman stationed in New York, Daniel Hartwig, who was present at De Louette's first interrogations by United States agents, told De Louette he "should never have said this to the Americans." Another section of the transcript showed that Hartwig made a phone call to someone in Paris during that questioning period and that this led to an immediate visit to Fournier-Ferrer by the chief commissioner of the Police Judiciaire in Paris. No written report on the conversation had been filed with Magistrate Roussel at the time of the March interrogatory.

"I was absolutely astonished," De Louette said. He explained that he had expected his charge against Fournier-Ferrer to be pursued in "a discreet investigation." But, said De Louette, "Once they went to see him, that was it. I never thought he would know that I had talked."

Excerpts from the transcript had the feel and atmosphere of a paperback spy novel, with emphasis on cloak-and-dagger maneuverings and the sad and sordid overtones of marital and money troubles. As De Louette told his tale, it was rich in detail:

He had been introduced to Fournier-Ferrer at a time when he was struggling to make ends meet after the collapse of an intelligence mission in Cuba. Fournier-Ferrer promised to help him find employment which would enable him to provide 3,000 francs a month to his estranged wife for the support of their five children and still have enough to live on himself. At the time, De Louette was trying to make do on 600 francs a month as a bureaucrat. As he put it, he also had certain obligations to his mistress and their child, with whom he lived.

Sometime in June, 1970, Fournier-Ferrer phoned De Louette and asked "if I would be willing to make a short trip towards the Italian border for a small special matter." De Louette agreed to do so, and Fournier-Ferrer arranged an appointment for him at a Paris café with "a man whom I had already met from the service." The man asked De Louette to smuggle $17,000 in counterfeit American money into Italy. But although De Louette traveled to the rendezvous, a small town on the Italian border, the deal was canceled and he was instructed to return to Paris. The next day, he got a phone call from Fournier, who suggested that since he (De Louette) was going to Algeria on business, he could carry the $17,000 in bogus cash to that country.

But, said De Louette, "Having learned the severe police action against counterfeiting in Algeria [the death penalty, in some cases], I did not accept." Fournier-Ferrer asked De Louette to keep the money for the time being—that perhaps during one of his subsequent trips he could deliver the cash in another country.

Then in December, 1970, Fournier-Ferrer phoned De Louette to ask if he would accept an assignment—"a very special assignment which included certain risks. This was at a time when my personal situation was at its worst and I would have accepted anything." At any rate, Fournier-Ferrer set up a meeting at the Café de Paris on the Champs-Élysées with a man unknown to De Louette. "He told me this man would be alone at a table and that he would have a *Paris-Match* magazine with a pair of gloves placed on top of the magazine."

De Louette showed up at the café at the appointed time and found waiting for him a man of about thirty, "dark complected, distinguished looking and dressed in a very elegant manner and a very conservative manner. . . . He had a navy-blue overcoat with a small velvet collar . . . first I understood that he also belonged to the service. That is to say, when he referred to the service he said 'we' or 'us.' " At that meeting, arrangements were made for De Louette to buy the Volkswagen camper, to ship it to the United States by sea and to fly to New York to claim it. Since the relatively vast sum of $50,000 in wages was involved, there was the suggestion that De Louette rationalized the venture as a service to SDECE.

A few weeks later, Fournier-Ferrer phoned De Louette to ask if the arrangements were proceeding satisfactorily. Assured that they were, Fournier-Ferrer instructed De Louette to meet with a second man at the Café Le King on the Rue François to fill the man in on the petty details. De Louette did so, giving the unidentified man the date on which he would receive delivery of the camper, the date on which the vehicle would be shipped and the probable date of the ship's docking in Port Elizabeth, New Jersey. The camper was due to arrive on a Saturday, and De Louette would not be able to clear it through customs until the following Monday. De Louette was told that an unidentified man would contact him at his hotel in New York to take delivery of the heroin on Monday or Tuesday.

De Louette was nervous. "I remember in fact telling him I hope this won't happen [a Tuesday delivery] because I don't want to be in possession for too long a period of time of the merchandise."

At any rate, De Louette was not surprised by the explanation given him for SDECE's little flyer in drug trafficking. His contacts told him that municipal elections were soon to be held in France and "some irregular means" had to be found to obtain funds for politicians friendly to SDECE. Presumably, SDECE could not be expected to sponsor a series of snail suppers.

To De Louette, the *raison d'être* behind the French espionage agency's interest in merchandising counterfeit United States money in Algeria also apparently seemed logical. The aim of that operation, he was told, was to plant the bogus money on an American living in Algeria and then alert the Algerian police in order to secure the "elimination" of the American via legal capital punishment. De Louette recalled that on a previous occasion he had observed intelligence agents at the SDECE headquarters in Paris walking on counterfeit Guinean currency to give it a "used" look. Subsequently, the counterfeit money was put into circulation in Guinea and "the operation was a success."

After De Louette's arrest at Port Elizabeth, De Louette said, Commissaire Hartwig "gave me his word" that if he supplied the name of his mistress, Marie Jose Robert, then twenty-two and pregnant, "nothing would be done against her." But, according to De Louette, Mademoiselle Robert subsequently was indicted in France for possession of the $17,000 in counterfeit American currency, which De Louette had unaccountably left in her apartment but of which she was "totally unaware." Mademoiselle Robert was jailed for three months and released only two days before giving birth. De Louette also charged that, at Roussel's request, police interrogated a son by his marriage for seven and a half hours when the boy arrived in the university compound at Bordeaux to look for a room.

Not surprisingly, De Louette's three-day interrogation did little to improve Franco-American relations, already severely strained by the disclosure of SDECE's alleged involvement in drug trafficking. To American officials, the sensational transcript belied French assurances that Paris was giving the United States its "fullest cooperation" in the war against the illicit narcotics trade. The French examining magistrate, Roussel, meanwhile was in turn sarcastic and outraged by some of De Louette's replies to inquiries about his familiarity with SDECE's operations.

Once, indeed, Donald Robinson of De Louette's defense team objected strenuously to what he called Roussel's harassment of his client.

Turning to the interpreter, Robinson said quietly, "Please tell Judge Roussel . . . that he do his best not to shout, not to throw things like his glasses, and that he perhaps be more calm in asking his questions."

Given the translation, Roussel snapped, "I am *not* getting angry."

Meanwhile, release of the interrogation transcript tied up a loose diplomatic end. It showed that during De Louette's earlier questioning by Customs agents he had identified Donald McNabb, a middle-level official at the French Consulate in New York, as the man Fournier-Ferrer had told him to contact in the event of unforeseen difficulties unrelated to the smuggling operation. De Louette said Fournier-Ferrer described McNabb as "one of our own"—an employee of the SDECE.

At his sentencing session before a federal court judge in Newark in April, 1972, De Louette was rewarded for one of the most detailed exercises in cooperation in Customs' annals. He drew only the minimum five-year term in a federal penitentiary and received credit for time already served as the *chef de cuisine* at New Jersey's Somerset County Jail. He also received fulsome praise from Judge Frederick B. Lacey, who imposed the sentence, and United States Attorney Stern. But one of De Louette's attorneys, Donald A. Robinson, was unimpressed by this leniency. "I figure De Louette will spend at least three more years in prison," he told reporters after the sentencing.

Vernon D. (Mike) Acree, who had succeeded Myles Ambrose as Commissioner of Customs on May 2, 1972, saw the case in broader and more spectacular terms. In an official statement, Acree declared: "It would not be easy to identify a case so charged with high drama and intrigue as the story of Roger de Louette and Paul Fournier, high-ranking French intelligence officers, who were indicted on charges of conspiring to smuggle $12 million worth of heroin into the United States. The case contained all the elements of a fast-moving cinematic scenario, which dwarfed the movie, *French Connection,* in terms of plot development, power and excitement. The result is now history, but it is a chronicle to which finis has not yet been written. When, on some unknown date in the future, the final chapter in the war on the narcotics drug trafficker is written, the de Louette case is certain to be reckoned as one of its turning points."

# 2

# The Rat Catchers

Ahmed said he was a Lebanese and he had a passport to prove it. Swarthy, grim-looking men who wore badges of the Syrian National Police claimed he was a Turk wanted in Istanbul for the murder of a prostitute, but they couldn't prove it. At any rate, Ahmed's visible means of support was innocuous enough; he owned and operated a cargo-carrying camel caravan in a little village outside the Syrian city of Homs.

Then Ahmed made a mistake. He started to spend lots of money, conspicuously. At about the same time, a cable from the United States Customs Bureau's Harold F. Smith, Assistant Commissioner for Investigations, arrived at police headquarters in Damascus. The cable said that substantial amounts of crude morphine, from which heroin is processed, had been crossing the border into Lebanon from the vicinity of Homs by camel caravan. Could the Syrian police be of any assistance?

A squad of Syrian drug constables jumped Ahmed's caravan a few days later as it was wending its way to the Lebanese border. They searched the cargo. Nothing. They undressed Ahmed and his camel drivers. Nothing. The caravan was permitted to proceed. But Lebanese authorities were asked to put Ahmed under surveillance.

Possibly the surveillance was too casual. In any event, it was not until several weeks later that a conscientious—and imaginative—Lebanese cop, poking about the area in which the camels were tethered, smelled a curious odor. He couldn't quite put his mind's finger on it, but it was definitely not a camel odor.

The cop hung around for three hours, watched nervously by Ahmed and his helpers. He took idle note that one of the camels was about to evacuate its bowels—and solved the case. Out onto the sand with the fecal matter plopped a sealed bag smaller than a man's hand, made of a kind of oilskin. The bag contained crude morphine.

26

For sixteen months, as he confessed later, Ahmed had been force-feeding bags of morphine to his Biblical beasts of burden in Syria, then recovering the bags from the camels' dung in Lebanon.

Back in Washington, Harold Smith was fascinated but not exactly surprised. As the official charged with guarding America's 290 ports and thousands of miles of coastline and land boundaries against dope smugglers, he had learned something about the smugglers' wily ingenuity.

They hide the junk everywhere—in artificial limbs, in stuffed iguanas and boa constrictors, behind the backs of paintings and inside religious icons, in automobile tires and gasoline tanks, inside chair seats, in the stuffing of children's dolls and teddy bears, in the lavatories of commercial airliners. Ostensibly respectable business-men earn as much as $1,000,000 a year as receivers of smuggled narcotics. One importer dealing in oscilloscopes—a device using a cathode tube to depict on a screen periodic changes in electric voltage—received shipments of heroin from France concealed in these devices. Heroin was shipped from Spain in cans of paella, a seafood dish, and from Italy and South America in wine jugs with two compartments—wine in the top compartment, junk in the bottom. Cheap dishes from Nepal were made of hashish; they were broken up into small pieces for street sale. A bricklayer was arrested in California when the 123 bricks in his truck were found to be made of marijuana. A cache of 4.8 pounds of heroin, worth almost $500,-000 at the addict level, was found in the air tanks of scuba diving equipment.

Given the vicious atmosphere of the drug traffickers' world, it was inevitable that they should descend to the nadir in macabre ingenuity. In December, 1972, Customs agents revealed that they were investigating an international ring of smugglers who for eight years had been smuggling heroin into the United States inside the bodies of dead American servicemen, shipped from Indochina for burial (Chapter 20).

Most of the stuff is still brought in by the professional courier, who as a beginner is paid $1,000 per kilo for his services but who usually buys a piece of the action after several successful carries and eventually can expect to earn $500,000 a year if he is both prudent and skillful. But one of the results of the drug explosion of the sixties, when a permissive attitude toward the use of drugs became fashionable and singers like Arlo Guthrie poked sordid fun at Customs officials, was the emergence of the amateur dope-runners.

A majority of these were—and are—students of the hippie persuasion, out both for a fast buck and to nourish their rebellion against the system. But Customs also has put the arm on smugglers whose appearance and avocations would seem to shield them from suspicion. One of these arrests followed by several days the arrival at New York's Kennedy International Airport in the fall of 1970 of a BOAC airliner whose point of origin had been Pakistan.

One piece of luggage on the flight, a trunk, went unclaimed. It carried instructions to hold the trunk until called for. When an associate professor at a New York college appeared at the BOAC baggage counter to claim the trunk, he was taken into custody. A search had shown the trunk contained 55 pounds of hashish with a value of about $85,000. The professor confessed he had found his academic salary inadequate to his needs and had decided to run one smuggling mission, then quit and move to California. He got two to ten years in prison.

"Five years ago, that professor probably would have got away with it," said Commissioner of Customs Myles Joseph Ambrose. "In the sixties, everybody talked about the problem but nobody did a goddamn thing about it."

Ambrose, a New York lawyer and a former assistant to the Secretary of the Treasury for Law Enforcement under President Eisenhower, had a point. Indeed, there is considerable validity to the claim advanced by many Customs people that the launching of America's total war against drug trafficking coincided with Ambrose's arrival to take over the bureau. When he was appointed Commissioner by President Nixon in August, 1969—at forty-three, the youngest ever to hold the office—the Customs Bureau had the same number of employees it had in the Coolidge administration and was operating on an annual budget of $123,000,000. The bull-like and persuasive Ambrose begged, wheedled and demanded more money, more people and more cooperation from the government's highest levels, and he got almost as much as he asked. Within two years, the budget had been increased to $189,000,000 (for the fiscal year ending July 1, 1972) and Ambrose had managed to boost his force from 9,000 to more than 14,000 bodies.

In 1969, Customs had one single-engine airplane and three boats, the latter operating exclusively in the Caribbean. By the late winter of 1972 the bureau had eleven fixed-wing aircraft, four of them twin-engine models, eight helicopters, and twenty-eight qualified pilots. At the same time, Customs had acquired a flotilla of twenty-four boats, including six 36-foot Uniflites, and a fleet of 1,320 automobiles, many of them confiscated from convicted smugglers and thus of small initial burden to the taxpayers. In 1971 the bureau started using dogs to sniff out marijuana and hashish in mail, cargo, unaccompanied baggage and vehicles. During their first year in service, the dogs detected 13,000 concealed pounds of marijuana, 650 pounds of hashish, 4,000 marijuana cigarettes, 35 pounds of opium, and 300 grams of heroin.

By 1972 Customs had also increased the number of its representatives abroad from fifteen during the previous year to twenty-nine; these representatives are attached to United States embassies.

As the Vietnam War wound down, Customs also hired a number of tough Green Berets and U.S. Marines for training as special agents in the crack Customs Agency Service, the field force of Harold Smith's Office of Criminal Investigations. And late in 1970, the bureau broke with tradition—and probably with some veteran Customs hands—by hiring women for the first time as special agents.

Lest pressure groups seize the occasion to crow, Commissioner Ambrose explained the precedent-shattering move in a brief statement after swearing in the first five new agents in New York City. First, he said it was President Nixon's idea, then added: "We don't want to get involved in women's lib, or male chauvinism, but it hasn't been easy to break the tradition of so many hard-nosed guys against the idea of women agents. I want to make it clear that these girls are not female agents, not junior agents, not assistant agents, not assistants to special agents, or anything else. They are special agents, who will be required to perform the same functions as male special agents."

Such functions, of course, include search-and-seizure arrests and the arts of self-defense in handling prisoners, male and female. The girls took the future in stride. "I'm not afraid of anything, really," said Geraldine Rose Baker, twenty-five, of New York, a former track star at the University of Wisconsin. "I'm almost foolish in that sense." If any old-timers scoffed, they did so privately.

In the war against dope, most of these new recruits became part of the United States' first line of defense against the smugglers of controlled or illicit narcotics. In that role, it is Customs' statutory job to try to keep dope from entering the country. Once dope is smuggled in, the battle is taken over by the Justice Department's Bureau of Narcotics and Dangerous Drugs (BNDD), although Customs agents have the authority to continue their investigation and pursuit of smugglers within the United States in cases where the delay involved in turning over their evidence to another agency would pose obvious difficulties. The FBI has no jurisdiction in narcotics cases but frequently turns over to the appropriate agency information developed in the course of its investigations of other crimes.

Thus it can be seen that the burden of winning the war against dope addiction in the United States rests most heavily on Customs' bureaucratic shoulders. Although Richard Nixon pronounced narcotics "America's Public Enemy Number One" during his 1968 campaign and his administration in its first three years increased by 1,000 percent the amount of money spent on the antidrug campaign, the illicit flow of narcotics into America sometimes seemed endless.

Despite heroic efforts by Customs on the barricades and BNDD in the interior, a government report in August, 1972, frankly acknowledged that the situation remained critical. The 111-page *World Opium Survey 1972* was compiled by the State Department, the Central Intelligence Agency, the Customs Bureau, the BNDD and the Treasury Department. It gloomily concluded that international drug traffickers were still assured of "adequate supplies in the foreseeable future."

For example, the survey estimated that ten tons of heroin entered the United States each year, and it noted that despite greatly increased surveillance, authorities were able to seize only about 8 percent of this almost incredibly huge cargo. The report put drug trafficking in the category to which it belonged—big business. Some estimates of its bigness ran as high as $5 billion a year, which seemed reasonable in light of the fact that heroin seizures in 1971 had a street value of more than a half billion dollars. Moreover, the profit margin was so astronomical that the risks run by the smuggling syndicates seemed negligible. An investment of $300,000 for 100 kilograms of heroin in Europe or Asia was bringing the smugglers a gross of $1,000,000 upon delivery in New York, and 100 kilograms of heroin, sold pure, cost about $22,000,000 on the street in the United States. In fact, that is a minimum figure because all heroin is adulterated before being sold to dealers.

Faced with the seemingly insurmountable task of breaking up this multibillion-dollar business, Customs lucked out when the dynamic Myles Ambrose left its helm to head the new Office of Drug Abuse Law Enforcement. Ambrose was considered virtually irreplaceable by the men and women he worked like galley slaves, but there was rejoicing when President Nixon named as Ambrose's replacement a career law enforcement officer, Vernon D. (Mike) Acree, an assistant commissioner of the Internal Revenue Service.

Like Ambrose, a hard-driving, no-nonsense professional, Acree had made his mark as chief of the IRS intelligence division. In that post, he had personally dispatched hundreds of tax crooks and numerous corrupt IRS employees to jail, and at the time of his appointment he was recognized by most experts in the field as the top investigative officer in government.

Indeed, six months after taking over at Customs, Acree was named on November 13, 1972, a recipient of a $10,000 tax-free Rockefeller Public Service Award, established in 1952 and considered the highest form of recognition by the private sector of a federal career servant. His award was in the field of administration, where his innovative management methods had become prototypes for programs used widely throughout the federal government and in more than a dozen foreign countries.

A native of Washington, D.C., Acree began his federal career as a clerk in the Treasury Department. During World War II, he was a master sergeant with the Army's Criminal Investigation Division (CID) and directed a successful campaign against black marketing and profiteering in the American and British zones of occupied Germany. Later, he headed security forces charged with combating graft and corruption in the operation of the Marshall Plan and during the Korean War. But he was most widely known for his hard-nosed crackdown on corruption within the IRS during the fifties, when the service had been shaken by scandals and its prestige had hit rock bottom. Under Acree's leadership, there was effected a strict separation between the fact-finding and action-taking processes within IRS's security operations, and the job he did there became a blueprint for internal auditing and security in other government agencies.

Acree, fifty-two at the time of his appointment, took over as Customs chief on May 2, 1972, and announced that he would continue Ambrose's policies of modernizing the bureau's operations and tightening up procedures. In pursuit of those goals, he had a long way to go, but he also was the legatee of the start Ambrose had made in streamlining Customs' investigative techniques and broadening its global contacts. Among other developments, Customs had gone electronic.

In the old days, a Customs inspector stuck a suspect's name in his hat and hoped he could remember it. The bureau has made that picturesque system obsolete with CADPIN (Customs Automatic Data Processing Intelligence Network), which became operational on March 15, 1970. CADPIN comprises two Burroughs high-speed data-processing computers located in San Diego, California, and linked by leased telephone lines to Washington, to all posts along the Mexican border, and to other selected Customs offices, international airports and Canadian crossings. By the fall of 1972 the system had been linked to 290 of these terminals.

CADPIN's role is the swift, almost instantaneous identification of known and suspected smugglers. A name is entered, by numbered code, at a primary inspection area and a yes or no reply is received in less than six seconds. Simultaneously, the complete record on the individual whose name received a yes reply is printed out at the secondary inspection post and will be there before the suspect arrives for further inspection. In short, if John Doe is a known or suspected smuggler, Customs will be waiting for him with a stern welcome, the more so if CADPIN warns that he is "dangerous" or may be armed.

Once a record is entered, it is available immediately to every CADPIN station in the country. One day a lookout resulted in a productive "hit" and the seizure of three ounces of heroin less than five minutes after the record was entered. On another occasion, the "remarks" line of the entire CADPIN file was searched for records containing any of the following: Corsica, Corsican, France, French, Fn. or Fr. Two hundred and ninety-eight records were found that carried one or more of these terms. Queries can be made on a vehicle license number, a person's name, a social security, passport or other identifying number.

CADPIN was an immediate success. During its first twenty months of operation the lookout system registered more than 300 productive hits, resulting in the seizure of two airplanes and 114 other vehicles, 119 arrests and 43 referrals to other agencies, chiefly the Immigration and Naturalization Service. Drugs seized during that period, which almost surely would have gone into the illicit market in pre-CADPIN days, included 5,687 pounds of marijuana, 5 pounds of cocaine and more than 270,000 illegal pills. Agents also picked up 15 pounds of peyote, 16 peyote plants, assorted narcotics injection paraphernalia, 1,000 pieces of undeclared jewelry and 6 handguns.

Not all of CADPIN's hits were smugglers. At San Ysidro, California, inspectors using the computer caught a man accused of abducting a little girl from Portland, Oregon. At El Paso, Texas, a man wanted on a murder charge was turned over to state authorities.

Numerous stolen cars were recovered. If an individual was known to police for any reason and came to CADPIN's attention, his chances of crossing over into, say, Mexico were slim to nonexistent.

Unfortunately, many dope smugglers have no previous criminal records. In the summer of 1970, a boom year for traffickers, the Customs Bureau made a check of the carriers arrested after making three times as many seizures of drugs as during the corresponding period in 1969. The great majority of offenders were youthful amateurs—individuals in the twenty- to twenty-five-year age group who had never run afoul of the law in even a minor way. Many of them were one-timers, bringing in a "key"—a kilogram—to pay for a vacation abroad. Moreover, after a courier has run several missions, some international syndicates shift him to another run—to Canada, say. When he is shifted back to the American run, Customs has nothing on him.

Moreover, the chances of being caught are lower than Customs officials like to think about. In the words of Harold Smith, the smugglers "have the automatic protection of being hidden in an awful big haystack." More than 250,000,000 travelers and their baggage and more than 2,500,000 cargo shipments must be cleared by the Customs Bureau every year. At the same time, Customs guards must patrol 7,500 miles of land border and 50,000 miles of coastline.

There are also the foreign diplomats. Protected from search of their persons or luggage by international law, they are ideal prospects for drug syndicates seeking respectable couriers. Cognizant of the petty niceties of foreign relations, Customs people refuse to discuss any suspicions they may harbor about diplomats regularly entering the United States, but the bureau's records show that elsewhere in the world diplomats have been caught moving narcotics.

Other government sources get down to specifics. For example, a number of Latin-American diplomats allegedly have been nabbed abroad, including ambassadors from Mexico, Guatemala and Uruguay. Italian police in 1970 arrested a Pakistani ambassador on narcotics charges. There is a long list of diplomats around the world who are "being watched." Personnel of various international agencies with diplomatic privileges are under suspicion in Southeast Asian countries. The Army is reportedly involved in the opium business in Laos, with Royal Lao Air Force planes used to transport the drug.

Sometimes a foreign official will forget himself and fall into a trap. For several months an official of Panama's civil aviation authority named Joaquín Him had been suspected of collusion with dope smugglers. In his official position, Him—a Panamanian of Chinese extraction—allegedly neglected to order the examination of baggage belonging to certain well-placed individuals on the smuggling black list, a considerable annoyance to the United States because so much junk was entering this country from Panama. American authorities finally apprehended Him when he appeared in the Canal Zone, administered by the United States, to watch a softball game. Washington turned a deaf ear to Panama's formal protest that Him's person was inviolate.

Meanwhile, Customs got a helping hand from its parent, the Treasury Department. In January, 1972, Assistant Treasury Secretary Eugene T. Rossides announced that a new investigative program had been launched against 328 suspected drug traffickers aimed at prosecution for income tax evasion. The campaign was entrusted to the same army of Internal Revenue Service agents who put such criminal bigwigs as Al Capone in jail in the 1930's and '40's.

The object of the probe was to make sure that the suspected dealers in illicit dope could not make a thin dime of income without accounting for its source. Such dealers usually are big spenders, and the IRS agents were poised to ask some embarrassing questions of them if their records showed they were spending more money than they reported to the tax collector. Thus the program would concentrate on what Rossides called the "middle and upper echelon" dope salesmen, whose individual profits from the traffic ran into millions of dollars a year.

Just before he left office Myles Ambrose addressed himself to the subject of heroin stockpiles in the United States. "I don't know how much heroin is sitting around this country," he said. "The stockpiles may be enormous. I suspect they are." Two factors supported Ambrose's suspicions: (1) Heroin seizures were so much bigger than they used to be and (2) narcotics smugglers operated during the drug explosion of the sixties with little official interference.

Veteran fighters in the war against drugs shared Ambrose's suspicions. They pointed out that, despite record seizures by both Customs and the Justice Department's Bureau of Narcotics and Dangerous Drugs, heroin remained in plentiful supply. Two yardsticks are used to measure whether heroin is hard or easy to get—price and purity. The price of a shot had not increased measurably, and the heroin sold was no less pure than it was before the record seizures. If the heroin was stockpiled across the country, it was in the hands of the middlemen, one step away from the importer and two steps away from the smuggler. Those dealers are the responsibility of local police, but the cops hadn't made any big hits.

Presumably, this situation was the reason President Nixon established the Office of Drug Abuse Law Enforcement, headed by Ambrose, as "a major new program to drive drug traffickers and pushers off the streets of America." The program was built around a nationwide network of investigative and prosecuting units, using special grand juries established under the Organized Crime Act of 1970. It also went to work assisting state and local agencies in detecting, apprehending and convicting drug traffickers, with federal monies available to cooperating law enforcement groups.

Abroad, Customs has mutual assistance pacts with local authorities in every country but the Soviet Union, Communist China and their satellites, and is a cooperating member of Interpol—the International Criminal Police Organization. Formed in 1956 and built up to a strength of 111 member countries by 1972, Interpol provides a liaison office for its member nations, assisting in criminal investigations and in such public service activities as locating missing persons.

Interpol will not undertake any intervention of activity in connection with cases which have a political, military, religious or racial character; its business is law enforcement cooperation within what its constitution describes as "the respective limits of the laws existing in the different countries." It is thus free of politics and barred from taking part in an investigation that conflicts with the laws of any country involved in a criminal case. Unlike the United Nations, for instance, Interpol may not impose sanctions on a member nation or take an official stand critical of a country's law enforcement procedures.

Each member of Interpol has a National Central Bureau (NCB), which provides information to the organization's General Secretariat in Paris, requests assistance from the General Secretariat and other NCB's, and processes requests received directly from other members. In the United States, the NCB is located in the Treasury Department, which traditionally had been involved in or had jurisdiction over such international crimes as counterfeiting, the narcotics trade, smuggling and financial crimes. It is staffed by Customs and Secret Service agents on detail from their agencies.

Interpol Washington has direct Telex communication with forty-one NCB's, including Britain's Scotland Yard, the Italian Questura, and the French Sûreté, and cable connections to the others. The

United States is also part of Interpol's international radio network, which provides virtually instantaneous communication among members around the world. Interpol maintains the most extensive file in history on international crimes and criminals; a criminal is "international" if he crosses an international border or if the effects of his crime spread across a border. The Interpol file in 1972 consisted of more than a million photographs, fingerprints and dossiers of individuals with international police records, fugitives and missing persons.

The system works. In calendar year 1971, 716 persons were arrested in various parts of the world as a result of information furnished by the Interpol network. Information dispatched from Interpol in Damascus, Syria, led to the seizure by U.S. Customs of 200 pounds of hashish in Los Angeles. Acting on a request from Iran, Customs agents recovered a Moslem holy book that had been stolen from a mosque in Teheran and smuggled into the United States.

But Customs continued to be the United States' first line of defense against drug abuse. Ninety percent of the marijuana used in the United States still comes from abroad, 85 percent of it from Mexico. More than 90 percent of the hard drugs—heroin, opium and cocaine —comes from overseas. Thus a case can be made that while Customs' job may not be the most dangerous or glamorous, it is far and away the most important, and probably the toughest.

At least 80 percent of the world's illegal heroin originated as Turkish opium up to 1972, when the Turkish government outlawed the growing of opium poppies. Considerable amounts of opium come from Thailand, Burma and Laos and some from Communist China, most of it passing into and through Hong Kong, where clandestine laboratories turn it into heroin. Wholesalers in Vietnam who sold to pushers dealing with American servicemen got their heroin from smaller laboratories in Thailand, Laos and Nationalist China. Most authorities agree that only about 5 percent of Red China's exports reach the United States, although in late 1971 Justice Department intelligence reports said that many of the 4,000-odd aliens who sneak into the United States from mainland China every year are involved in the heroin racket. In recent years, Iran has become another source of concern among international lawmen. The Iranian government banned all opium growing in 1955 because of a serious addiction problem in that country, but ten years later it reinstituted the lucrative crop of "legal" opium in what officials called "self-defense" against Turkey.

From the productive Middle East, opium is moved as morphine base to Marseilles, either by boat or overland by truck through Bulgaria or Greece and Yugoslavia. Most smugglers try to avoid the overland route because it passes through Communist countries, where authorities are tough, penalties are severe and punishment is not delayed by a lot of democratic due process. It is in Marseilles that the morphine base is converted into heroin, although some illicit laboratories have sprung up in Italy, notably in Naples. In recent years West Germany has become an important staging area for morphine base shipments.

Sometime around 1968, South American hoodlums began to muscle in on the heroin-smuggling racket theretofore the almost exclusive field of Corsicans, Frenchmen and the international Mafia. Indeed it sometimes seemed to Customs men in the field that the Latin Americans had become dominant because of the numerous and substantial seizures made by both Customs and the Bureau of Narcotics and Dangerous Drugs in Miami and New York City, main terminal points for most travelers coming from south of the border.

In South America, Spanish-speaking criminals developed routes for both heroin and cocaine, moving the junk to the United States from Chile, Argentina and Brazil, and to a lesser extent from ports in Central America, particularly Panama. They hired *contrabandistas*, soldier-of-fortune pilots who will fly any cargo anywhere if enough money is involved. In the United States, they recruited couriers and narcotics distributors in Cuban, Puerto Rican and other Spanish-speaking colonies in New York, Miami and Chicago.

After the fall of the Fulgencio Batista regime in Cuba and the installation of Fidel Castro's puritanical Communist government, hoodlums fled the island in hordes—along with doctors, lawyers and academicians. Hundreds of these hoods emigrated to Spain, where they set up shop across from Marseilles and its heroin labs, and from Barcelona and other Spanish ports dispatched heroin concealed in assorted legitimate cargo by ship to the United States.

Meanwhile, Corsican "organization" people, fleeing the official heat in Europe or merely shifting their bases of operations for greater profit, reversed the emigration from South America. Beginning in the sixties, there was a minor flood of Corsicans and Frenchmen allied with the Corsican "Mafia" to Latin-American countries. There they joined fellow countrymen who had preceded them to the New World in the fifties and were formed into the Grupo Francés (French Group) under the leadership of Auguste Ricord.

Grupo Francés quickly became a tightly controlled syndicate of international drug smugglers which maintained contact with smuggling organizations in France, Italy, Spain, Switzerland and Germany and operated from Buenos Aires, Argentina; Montevideo, Uruguay; Santiago, Chile; Asunción, Paraguay; and Rio de Janeiro, Brazil.

Finally, there was the Mafia—the Cosa Nostra of vicious song and story. It requires enormous financial resources to handle the tons of illicit junk, notably heroin, flowing into the United States, but the profits of these receivers—wholesalers and distributors—also are enormous. The street-level cost to addicts for one kilo of pure heroin averages $225,000. That one kilo is produced from 10 kilos of raw opium sold by Turkish farmers to smugglers for a mere $350. By the time the heroin reaches the United States the big receiver is assured of a profit of at least 1,000 percent.

The Mafia had the financial resources, derived from gambling, labor and waterfront racketeering, prostitution, and other profitable "businesses." But for a long time the big families such as the Bonanno, Luchese, Genovese and Gambino gangs shunned dope trafficking as "too dirty." As younger, greedier and less "sentimental" leaders rose to eminence and power, however, they succumbed to the lure of the big money to be made in peddling junk. Accordingly, by the mid-sixties the Mafia had become the ultimate bankroll of the dope racket. A few independents continued to prosper in New York, Miami, Chicago and Los Angeles, but it was the Mafia that dealt with the major syndicates operating out of Europe and South America. Its bankroll, its efficiency and its underworld supremacy were so great that in 1971 two French gangsters could "sell" a Mafia buyer named Louis Cirillo to a French syndicate for a lifetime pension of $500 for every kilo Cirillo bought from the syndicate (Chapter 5).

Customs made its share of hits in its twenty-four-hour-a-day battle of wits—and manpower—with both Grupo Francés and the traveling salesmen from Europe, but the bureau frequently was frustrated by the enormous financial resources of the various intertwined syndicates. That is to say, the syndicates always managed to get up bail money for its more important people no matter how high it was set. Then the suspect simply jumped bail and fled the country. In 1972 Customs was trying to track down for extradition more than a score of fugitives in various parts of the world who had forfeited bond as high as $400,000.

One of these was Hovsep Caramian, a Uruguayan national living in Buenos Aires, who jumped bail of $300,000 even as a New York City grand jury was deliberating his case.

Once narcotics violators flee the country, it's hard to get them back even if they're arrested abroad, because many of the extradition treaties the United States has with foreign countries do not cover narcotics charges. Mexico refuses to extradite its nationals even if they have never stepped foot into that country until they are wanted elsewhere in the world. Under Mexican law, if a parent was born there, the son automatically becomes a Mexican citizen—which is particularly handy for offenders working in neighboring California, Arizona, New Mexico and Texas. Customs also finds it virtually impossible to penetrate the secrecy of the numbered Swiss bank accounts in which most big wheelers deposit their loot. Swiss law demands a mountain of incriminating evidence against a depositor before a bank may reveal his name and the size of his account.

The bureau spends more than $2,000,000 a year to buy information and has always regarded such expenditures as an exercise in economizing. Dope syndicate security is so tight and the penalty for treason is so harsh that buying information in this sordid marketplace often is the only way agents can crack a big case. During the strained relations between American and French narcotics authorities in 1971–72, French officials scoffed at the idea of buying informers.

"Just because you people have a lot of money you think you can buy a lot of information," one French official complained. "As far as we are concerned, we automatically suspect any paid informer. His aim is generally highly immoral: greed, revenge or rivalry with a competing gang."

"Yeah," replied Customs' Harold Smith. "We know all that. We suspect our informers, too. We know they're not the stuff archbishops or Eagle Scouts are made of. But we're trying to get information; we're not running a Salvation Army or a seminary. And we don't introduce those guys to our families."

In trying to persuade prisoners to sing, Customs officially prescribes three approaches. As Commissioner Acree described them, "There's the religious-moral approach, the sociological approach and the self-interest approach. As might be expected, the third approach is the most successful."

In any event, the first approach involves trying to convince the individual that smuggling dope is morally wrong, and since he's been caught in the act, he might like to make amends to society by coming clean and telling all he knows. As Acree put it wryly, "The market for this approach is extremely limited; very few Sunday School teachers go in for dope pushing." The agent then might turn even

more solemn and describe the crime and decadence permeating
American cities and the disgusting, wasted lives led by American
addicts. This approach usually is unsuccessful, too, simply because
most couriers and dealers don't know any addicts and indeed may
never have encountered one. Moreover, many suspects arrested by
Customs come from countries that have no significant drug problem.

So Customs falls back on the argument of what's in it for the
offender. That is to say, the agent seeks to persuade the suspect that
if he talks, the court might look more kindly upon his case. Moreover, the offender is guaranteed protection from the drug syndicate if
he sings; at any given time Customs has anywhere from a dozen to
fifty informants established in obscure jobs or in minimum-security
prisons, where their persons are relatively safe from vengeance seekers and where they are—not so incidentally—available for periodic
questioning as other cases they may know something about are developed. Customs officials take pains to emphasize that they cannot
and do not guarantee a deal, which is as may be. However, the
official line is that the United States Attorney involved will be "made
aware" of the assistance the defendant has given the prosecution's
case, and at the time of sentencing that officer of the court may
choose to make such information available to the judge.

Agents usually try to buttress a feeling of mutual friendship and
confidence by providing the informant with little amenities while he's
in jail—toothpaste, cigarettes, razor blades, reading matter, perhaps
some extra outdoor exercise time, and, more rarely, a private visit
with a wife or girlfriend. Special Agent Irwin Weinstein of Washington headquarters once nabbed a man who he believed would talk if
the approach was right. The man was something of a fop. He complained that he probably would never be able to wear a new $150
suit he'd bought the day before his arrest. Weinstein brought the new
suit to the prisoner's cell so he could wear it during all his interview
sessions and court appearances.

"I couldn't have done more for him," Weinstein recalled. "That
dude was in seventh heaven. He sang—long and clear."

In addition to those who have hide to save as a result of being
caught in a bust, there are numerous paid informers, whose moon-
lighting profession is to sell what they know. Customs keeps the
names on this list a closely guarded secret, except in the rare instances when an informer's testimony in a public trial is needed to
add the last knot in tying up a case. In such cases, the bureau gives
the informer all the protection its resources can command; usually he

is moved to another community as far as possible from revenge seekers, and sometimes he is even flown to a foreign country. Wherever he is secured, Customs finds him a legitimate job, although he remains on tap for questioning. Moreover, no informer is forced to testify; he must agree in writing to do so.

Cultivating paid informers is both an art and a tedious, time-consuming chore. It can take weeks and more often months and even years to land a reliable informant. The assignment of digging up these informers is the job of the undercover agents, many of whom spend most of their law enforcement careers underground. Their field of operations is the "interesting" neighborhood, usually located in a big-city slum, but often enough in more respectable areas and sometimes in high-rent, fashionable sections lived in or frequented by so-called Beautiful People. Several foreign diplomats have been trapped in smuggling operations, as will be seen, as a result of evidence gathered by Customs undercover men living it up in the more expensive stratum of society.

The undercover man's primary job is to get to know well as many people as possible in the haunts to which he is assigned. The idea is that if he is accepted in these neighborhoods as a right guy, people will pour confidences into his ear—people who are themselves drug-trafficking suspects or who are acquainted with others known or believed to be involved in the racket. Some of the individuals cultivated may have criminal records and accordingly may be susceptible to a little pressure—as a last resort. That is to say, if all else fails, such people may find themselves hauled regularly to assorted police stations for questioning or otherwise subjected to legitimate methods of harassment. Given the choice between such habitual harassment and making an untidy dollar by selling information, the individual is almost sure to choose self-interest.

The question as to how far such informers can be trusted probably can never be answered. Reliability is never taken for granted. However, over a period of time the record separates the trustworthy from the phonies. If an informer's information is accurate more often than not, he gets high marks. If it becomes obvious he is fabricating stories to stay on the payroll, he is given the gate and usually winds up in jail for perjury or finds himself being prosecuted for plying his own illegal trade. A new informer is tested on a minor case or asked to confirm false information. If he passes that first test, he is slowly, step by step, assigned to more important and legitimate cases.

But even the most valuable informer can expect no protection from Customs' Rat Catchers if he becomes involved in a crime within the jurisdiction of other law enforcement agencies. At his trial, the court may be informed that he has lent a hand to Customs' investigations; otherwise, he's on his own.

# 3
# A Child and the Problem

They found the body of the twelve-year-old boy under a flight of stairs in a Harlem tenement house one cold night in March, 1972. His arms were punctured with hypodermic needle marks. He had died of an overdose of heroin. The boy's neighborhood was located in the territory served by pushers whose distributors got their heroin from a man who lived in a luxurious Park Avenue apartment house and who wintered on the French Riviera. Customs and federal narcotics agents knew this, but they hadn't a shred of evidence that would hold up in a courtroom.

If the boy was this man's victim, he was also the victim of mankind's 4,000-year dalliance with opiates, known today as opium, morphine, codeine, and heroin. Had he lived in Asia in 2000 B.C. he might have been, or become, an opium smoker. In the eighteenth century he would have been addicted to morphine. Ironically, he died of an opium derivative once hailed as a "cure" for morphine addiction.

Heroin, named for the Greek god Heros, was discovered in 1874 by a German doctor, Heinrich Dreser, who announced that the new drug, properly used, would solve both the morphine and opium problems. However, he soon learned heroin could not be *properly* used. It was, in fact, more dangerous than either opium or morphine. It made addicts more easily, and the addiction was harder to cure because heroin was four to eight times more powerful than morphine when used as an analgesic. Used to relieve coughs, heroin caused severe respiratory depression and fearsome withdrawal symptoms.

The heroin that killed the boy had its origin in the sweet-smelling poppy plant as an oozing brown seepage, opium. It almost surely came from Turkey, where for many years farmers had raised opium legally, under a government monopoly which supervised the crop and paid a standard price for it. Under pressure from the United States,

Turkey agreed in June, 1971, to ban opium growing at the end of 1972, but when they found the boy's body, the Turkish and American governments were negotiating for American aid to finance substitute projects.

In Turkish fields, a local entrepreneur had bought up surplus bags of opium balls, grown illegally by the farmers for fatter profits. He delivered these balls, probably by night, to his buyer across the border in Syria. Then the chemist took over. In a huge caldron set up outdoors in some wilderness laboratory, he boiled the opium with lime, water and ammonium chloride, then filtered it to produce crude morphine, or morphine base. The morphine crystals, packed in waxed paper bags, then were shipped surreptitiously through Lebanon to a French freighter lying just outside the harbor of Beirut. Someone aboard the freighter—a seaman, a cook, an engineer—smuggled the morphine into the French port of Marseilles, headquarters for the heroin processing and distribution racket.

A few miles outside Marseilles, a respectable French chemist, who was often away from home on business, converted the morphine into heroin. In a secret laboratory, he emptied the morphine into enamel basins and mixed it with acetone to remove remaining impurities and to separate the morphine from opium's other alkaloids. He then filtered the relatively pure morphine and proceeded to the chore of turning it into heroin.

By this time the chemist had been joined by two assistants, and all donned rubber gas masks to avoid being drugged into unconsciousness by the morphine fumes. They used carbon black to bleach the milk-chocolate-colored morphine base white. For six long hours, they boiled the morphine with a salt called acetic anhydride, a chemical also widely used in making perfume and textiles. This, in turn, was blended with hydrochloric acid to transform the still insoluble heroin into a salt that could be easily mixed with water for injection.

That was the dangerous stage. The mix had to be heated to a temperature no higher than 215 degrees Fahrenheit; if it becomes hotter than that, it is almost certain to explode and blow the laboratory and its occupants to useless pieces. Records on such blowups are understandably incomplete, but between them French and American authorities have evidence that six persons died between 1967 and 1972 because the heroin mix got too hot. The whole process takes more than twenty-four hours, involves seventeen separate steps, and cannot be interrupted once it is begun.

Customs officials tend to snicker at the use of the word "laboratory" to describe the setups used to convert morphine base to heroin. If necessary, the procedure could be performed in a fair-sized truck. Marcel Morin, a French policeman with a PhD who was dispatched to Marseilles in August, 1971, to break up the laboratories, is fond of telling journalists that most labs can be packed into the trunk of a small car. And in fact all that is needed, according to experts, are a few pots and pans, a source of heat and power and running water. One laboratory busted by French authorities had a mixer set on a metal tripod made from bedstead supports and was powered by an old washing machine engine. Two propane gas heaters had been installed in a couple of stripped-down refrigerators to create a drying oven.

Because the electric current required for the process could tip off nosy cops who go around reading electric meters, most chemists simply hook onto a power line. That is what a retired seaman named Joseph Cesari* did when he operated a laboratory which set what is believed to be a world's heroin production record in 1964. At a farmhouse in the countryside outside Marseilles, Cesari processed 17½ pounds of morphine at a whack, compared with the average 6 pounds. Moreover, using a barely literate handwritten formula, Cesari produced heroin that was, amazingly, 98 percent pure. It is chemists such as Cesari who have given French heroin the reputation of being the "champagne" of the product.

Beginning in the late sixties, most chemists switched from the more elaborate processing establishments to small, mobile labs that could be dismantled, packed into a truck or a car and shifted to new locations in less than eighteen hours. If American estimates that there are at least ten labs in operation in the Marseilles neighborhood at any one time are accurate, that means they are producing about 440 pounds a week, since the conversion cycle is twenty-four hours. In other words, every week of the year the labs turn out heroin with a street value in America of almost $50,000,000. That is big business in a volume that might make General Motors envious.

Most of the chemists are free lances, although in recent years European syndicates have taken their heroin makers into the organization and given them a piece of the action. The free agents earn an

---

* Cesari, who was arrested by French police after they seized a secret laboratory near Marseilles and found 264 pounds of pure heroin on the premises, hanged himself in his prison cell in April, 1972. In a letter to his wife, Cesari wrote: "My dearest, I love you. Excuse what I did. I could not do otherwise."

average of $3,000 per pound of heroin, and most of them tend to view their trade as slightly on the heroic side.

One chemist, who was arrested by Customs and later turned state's evidence, explained the perils of his profession. "You cops don't realize what terror seizes one," he said dramatically. "One must work very carefully. There must be no distractions. It is impossible to work in a noisy, jolting city. For making 20 kilos of heroin [44 pounds] I was paid only $14,000. That is not much for risking one's life."

Perhaps not. But the chemist's audience was unsympathetic. They had seen too many victims of his skill.

At any rate, the heroin that killed the child in Harlem was now a fluffy white powder that looked like baby talc. It was packed into double plastic bags, sealed with Scotch tape, and stowed in metal canisters for shipment to the United States. How this particular shipment was smuggled in was unknown, but it could have arrived concealed beneath the floorboards of a new French car. Or someone might have persuaded a returning American student or schoolteacher to deliver a suitcase packed with gifts for an aunt in New York—a suitcase with a false bottom.

There followed a succession of adulterations. The 90-percent-pure heroin was cut with milk sugar to reduce it to 75 percent pure. Then it was cut with mannite, a white children's laxative, to make it only 55 percent pure. Finally, the dealer reduced the heroin further by mixing it with more mannite and a quantity of quinine. It was then ready to be peddled in the streets—subject of course to whatever further cutting the pusher might figure he could get away with.

Fat profits had also been made all the way down the line to the street pusher. Customs people believed that the heroin used by the dead boy had originated as part of an illicit "collection" of 200 kilograms of pure heroin that cost the smugglers about $600,000 in Europe. The heroin had been processed from raw opium for which syndicate collectors paid Turkish farmers a paltry $4,000.

The syndicate sold the pure heroin to a wholesaler or wholesalers in New York City for a total of $2,000,000, a gross profit of $1,-400,000. As adulterated heroin fixes, the 200 kilograms were sold to addicts on the street for a total of more than $45,000,000. Put another way, if an addict could afford a kilogram of pure heroin, the tab would be $225,000. Proceeding through channels to the wholesaler, the distributor, the retailer and finally the street pusher, the 200 kilograms were split and resplit and then split again any number of times to give everybody a monumental profit.

In this particular case, the profit to the wholesaler or group of wholesalers amounted to a tidy $400,000. The principal distributor bought 20 kilos of relatively pure heroin for $13,000 a kilo and sold an adulterated 33 kilos to smaller distributors for $20,000 a kilo. These distributors in turn took down a profit of $30,000 each at the then current state of the market. The street pushers paid $500 per ounce for adulterated heroin and put it up in 5-grain packets which they peddled to addicts for $5 per packet. There are 437½ grains to the ounce.

Whatever the state of the market—prices are lower when the supply is plentiful, higher when there is a temporary shortage—heroin addiction is always expensive. The average cost of what the experts call a "moderate" habit is estimated at $40 a day. But an addict supporting a habit that requires 100 capsules, or shots, every twenty-four hours must spend about $150 a day merely to escape the pains of withdrawal. In 1972 there were an estimated 400,000 to 500,000 heroin addicts in the United States. If the lower figure is accepted, these addicts spent a total of $6 billion on heroin during 1972 even if they nourished only a "moderate" $40-a-day habit. The actual cost probably was closer to $8.5 billion.

Even the supplier of heroin paraphernalia can make big money. The New York State Commission of Investigation estimated that the owner of a small Harlem variety store and his partner made a gross profit of at least $135,650 selling such gear as glassine envelopes during a period of only four months. Officials of the commission said the gross profit accruing from the sale of the envelopes to package heroin and the chemicals to cut it represented a whopping 782 percent return on the two men's original investment.

They call it stuff, smack, horse. For the addicts, heroin is "the king of the cop-outs." It takes them out of their aimless, often miserable world with its frustrations and its constant challenges. It produces a feeling of exhilaration known as a rush. And then, as the elation wears off, there is the "nod-out" produced by the drug's narcotic effect, which sends the addict into a drowsy and tranquil state for several hours—at least in the beginning. Later, as the body develops tolerance, the victim finds he needs a new fix every few hours.

The beginner sniffs his horse. But as he pursues his habit, he notices he's not getting the kick he needs. So he turns to the needle. This is more complicated. The heroin has to be cooked; the addict puts some horse and some water in a spoon or bottle cap and holds a lighted match under it until the drug dissolves. He then draws the solution into a hypodermic syringe and injects it, either just under the skin (skin popping) or into a vein (mainlining). Usually the skin-popper graduates to mainlining, which produces an immediate rush, whereas the effect of skin popping is not felt for three to five minutes—a long time in the addict's life.

Some addicts inject only half the drug at a time to avoid taking an overdose. They wait to "see how it feels" before injecting the other half. After mainlining for a long time, the addict often discovers his veins have sunken into the tissue and he can't find them. Then he shoots in another part of his body—the hands, usually, the legs, the neck.

Wherever he shoots, if he shoots long enough, he courts side perils. Abscesses form as the skin rots, and if the addict shoots into the back of his hand, the hand eventually can swell to twice its normal size. Dirty or rusty needles can cause blood poisoning, hepatitis and tetanus. Many addicts seek help only because their bodies have become too wounded to continue shooting, and as a last resort they go to doctors or clinics in an attempt to stave off the horrors of withdrawal.

The best description of these horrors was given to the magazine *U.S. News and World Report* by a girl who withdrew "cold turkey," that is, without medication:

"It's like a terrible case of the flu. Your joints move involuntarily—that's where the phrase 'kick the habit' comes from. You jerk and twitch and you just can't control it; you throw up; you can't control your bowels, either, and this goes on for four or five days. And afterwards, for 15 days afterwards, you can't sleep and you're gagging all the time and you cough up blood because if you're on drugs you don't eat and that's all there is to cough up."

An autopsy, along with what a policeman called "the awful goddamned mess around the body and the stink," showed that the twelve-year-old boy who died under the staircase in Harlem had suffered all these horrors before death mercifully intervened.

On the other side of the coin is the addict's rapid descent into utter poverty because of the constant need to spend more and more on his habit. The habit turns addicts into criminals—shoplifters, muggers, burglars, murderers. "Yes, I would have killed to get a fix," a teenager who had kicked the habit told the police. "You don't understand—you have to have it, regardless. If there's no other way to get it, then you have to kill."

In the late sixties, a number of American cities opened rehabilitation centers where heroin addicts could undergo the controversial methadone treatment for their addiction. Dr. Robert L. Dupont, of the District of Columbia Narcotics Treatment Administration, told the New York *Times* that nearly 4,000 persons were taking continuing treatment for drug addiction, 60 percent of them in the methadone program. Of the rest, 20 percent were being helped to abstain totally from drugs and 20 percent were gradually withdrawing from the use of heroin.

"These are about 25 percent of the total heroin addicts in the city, who will probably not be committing crimes," Dr. Dupont said. "For them we have unhooked the iron link between addict and pusher. For the first time, the addict in this city has an alternative." Unfortunately, there were other addicts using the program who were taking methadone regularly only until they could raise enough money to go back on heroin.

In any case, methadone seemed merely to be scratching at the surface of heroin addiction in the United States. In 1965 there were an estimated 150,000 addicts in the country. By the spring of 1972 this total had increased to between 400,000, according to the Bureau of Narcotics and Dangerous Drugs, and 500,000 according to Congressman Seymour Halpern, Republican of New York, who spent several months on a comprehensive study of drug abuse for the House Foreign Affairs Committee.

All this was despite the impressive fact that in 1971 law enforcement authorities confiscated $920,000,000 worth of narcotics—three times the amount seized during the previous year. Moreover, Halpern claimed that the purity level of heroin had increased in smaller cities and towns, indicating "a calculated attempt by traffickers to hook more victims and quickly open new markets." Such new markets, of course, produced an upsurge in the crimes of theft—robbery, burglary and larceny—because there was no way for most of the addicts to support their habits except by turning to thievery.

Yet heroin is cheap compared with cocaine. No matter how much they stole, heroin addicts probably could not have afforded cocaine —coke, Charley, snow—which sells for more than $12,000 a pound to the wholesaler in New York City. Thus cocaine has come to be known as the millionaire's drug; before the word became outmoded by the times and its transparent phoniness, they called cocaine the society drug. It comes from the leaf of the coca bush, which grows almost exclusively in the mountains of South America, and has been used legitimately since 1880 as a local anesthetic. The coca leaf is also the source of nonnarcotic flavoring extracts for cola drinks.

For centuries, the Indians in the Andes region of Bolivia and Peru have chewed the coca leaf. It tastes good, in a pungent sort of way, it warms the body, or seems to, and it puts the stomach under anesthesia. Doctors, not entirely in jest, have said that chewing the coca leaf is the easiest way to eliminate the pangs of hunger and thirst. A Peruvian millionaire planter whose peons were found peddling the leaf in illicit traffic explained why he didn't pay them enough to buy a couple of square meals a day. "They have the coca leaf," he said. "You don't need as much food in your stomach if you're a coca chewer. My people don't really *want* more food."

The traffic in coca leaves is regulated by the International Narcotics Control Board of the United Nations, stationed in Geneva. All legitimate movements of the drug are recorded. But Peru and Bolivia together produce upwards to 35,000 tons of coca a year. The demand for coca leaves for medicine and cola drinks is estimated generously at 500 tons a year. The surplus is gobbled up by the junk peddlers. Illicit traffickers hire peasants to macerate the bulky leaves at the source of supply, then extract the cocaine in clandestine laboratories in the hills to cut down the cost of transportation. Usually, the paste is adulterated with boric acid, tartaric acid and sodium bicarbonate to fatten profits.

Most cocaine addicts sniff the stuff. It gives them a quick kick, banishes fatigue, and for an hour or two increases mental powers. But it also causes hallucinations, and a strong dose can cause convulsions by overstimulating the spinal cord. Many longtime addicts suffer from sleeplessness, morning nausea and severe headaches. A speedball is a blend of cocaine and heroin which is injected into the bloodstream. The cocaine and heroin equalize each other, one giving a boost and the other a numbing effect that wards off the jitters. Drinking black coffee laced with whiskey is much safer—and immeasurably less expensive.

Least expensive of all, of course, are marijuana, the pop name for the leaves of the cannabis plant, and hashish, which is the solid yellow resin from the plant. A marijuana cigarette, or joint, can be bought on the street for $1 or often less. Hashish is only a little more costly at the retail level. A smuggler can buy marijuana in Mexico for anywhere from $1 to $4 a pound, depending on the state of the market. In the Middle East, hashish is purchased initially for from $2.50 to $15 a pound.

Marijuana is smoked; hashish, which is the cannabis drug in concentrated form, is both smoked and eaten. Both distort the senses, giving the user a feeling of euphoria and the delusion that he has suddenly become a kind of superman. Although *Cannabis sativa* will grow anywhere (it has been found in stunted form in the Arctic Circle), 90 percent of the marijuana entering the United States comes from the interior of Mexico. Most of the hashish, or resin, on the other hand, has been smuggled in from the Middle East via assorted European points. The cannabis leaves are pressed into one-kilo bricks and packed into glassine bags, and because of their bulk they present a considerable transportation problem. Thus the smugglers are forced to use trucks, cars, boats and private airplanes to get the stuff across the border. Most hashish, which is the concentrated form of the drug and looks like dark oatmeal, is brought in by "travelers" in their luggage.

A Gallup Poll in February, 1972, reported that marijuana use and that of hallucinogenic drugs continued to increase in colleges and universities. According to Gallup, more than half the students interviewed said they had tried marijuana at least once, and 18 percent said they had tried a "mind-expanding" drug once. (Hallucinogenic drugs such as LSD are of only peripheral interest to the Customs Bureau, since most of such mind blowers are manufactured within the United States and thus escape border surveillance and inspection. Less than 10 percent of these drugs find their way into the United States from Mexico and Canada, although unknown quantities are smuggled into both countries and then smuggled back across the border.)

In mid-fall of 1972, a New York *Times* survey of college campuses in New York, New Jersey and Connecticut revealed that heroin had "virtually disappeared and the popularity of most other hard drugs is fading rapidly." But, said the *Times*, "the sale and use of soft drugs—marijuana, hashish and pills—is common, casual and virtually institutionalized, with large numbers of students turning on and school authorities turning the other way." The *Times* called most colleges "virtual sanctuaries for soft-drug users" and added that despite "stern anti-drug policies, school officials are reluctant to call in the police and have adopted motherly attitudes toward soft-drug use, so pills are popped and marijuana is smoked openly in dormitories and lounges."

The big marijuana dealers in Mexico and the United States sell and buy in ton lots; one Mexican supplier has boasted that he sends an average of six tons a week to or across the border. After buying the leaves for $12,000 a ton, he delivers the lot to clients in Tijuana for $25,000 a ton. He will deliver it to San Diego for $65,000 a ton, to Los Angeles for $100,000 a ton, and to San Francisco for as high as $200,000 a ton. "I can afford to lose half of what I ship," he told an American who was trying to buy him out.

In their turn, the heroin racketeers look down on the marijuana-hashish crowd as bush league. Although smuggling cannabis is profitable, it is Hoboken to the heroin crowd. Cannabis is just not worth the time and the risk to the Corsican hoodlum or the Mafia godfather. He can buy a pound of heroin in France for, say, $3,000, and sell it in New York wholesale for $9,000. A pound of marijuana bought for $4 in Mexico will bring him $100 tops in Los Angeles.

Except in an academic, after-hours way, the Department of the Treasury's Bureau of Customs is not interested in the social pecking order among dope smugglers. Chatting with a reporter in early 1972, Commissioner of Customs Myles Joseph Ambrose put it in the lawman's perspective.

"They're all creeps to me," said Ambrose. "We don't go in for sociological round tables. Our job is to confiscate the junk and throw the pushers in jail. But I'm afraid no matter how hard we work at the job, or how smart our successors are, smuggling will always be a problem for law enforcement agencies. It always has been. I wouldn't be surprised to learn that Cain did a little smuggling on the side before he murdered Abel."

Ambrose came close to the recorded truth. Customs duties are mentioned in the Old Testament, in Ezra 7:24, wherein King Artaxerxes proclaims that "it shall not be lawful to impose toll, tribute, or custom upon the priests and Levites, the singers, porters or ministers." Custom was the tribute levied on traveling merchants by the early kings—that is, it was the customary fee exacted by the king for permitting the merchant to sell his wares in the king's land. Because there were opium smokers and hashish eaters long before King Artaxerxes' day, there undoubtedly were smugglers of dope. And it is significant that in the United States there was a Customs Service before there was a Treasury Department to operate it—because smugglers were robbing the weanling nation's meager treasury.

After the adoption of the Constitution on March 4, 1789, the second act passed by the new Congress was the Tariff Act of July 4, 1789. Four weeks later, on July 31, the fifth act established Customs districts and ports of entry, provided for the appointment of Customs officers, and outlined methods for the collection of duties and the apprehension of smugglers. On September 2, 1789, Congress passed "An Act to Establish the Treasury Department." Nine days later Alexander Hamilton became the first Secretary of the Treasury.

Customs had come a long way since the foggy morning when Hamilton took the oath of office. It had, indeed, come a long way since its frustrations of the decade between 1960 and 1970. During calendar year 1971, the bureau seized 1,308.95 pounds of illicit heroin, more than had been confiscated in the entire preceding ten years. That 1,308.95 pounds, seized in 568 separate operations, was enough to produce 95,680,000 doses, which at an average price per dose of $6 meant a loss to the economy of the heroin hoodlums of a whopping $574,000,000. Then, in calendar year 1972, dangerous drug seizures rose 69 percent—from 7,420 in 1971 to 18,107.

Federal narcotics authorities also announced that a record monthly average of 71 pounds of heroin had been seized in raids from Miami to Montreal during the twelve months of the fiscal year that ended the previous July. The seizures were worth a total of $13,100,000 at the addict's level, and represented a 900 percent increase in the amount of pure heroin confiscated in the Miami-Montreal corridor during fiscal 1971.

Meanwhile, President Nixon had created a new $2,500,000 National Narcotics Intelligence Office designed to serve as a clearinghouse to help law enforcement agencies fight the nation's war on drugs. At the same time, Nixon asked Congress to approve $135,-200,000 in supplemental funds to help finance the antinarcotics drive. The President noted that 90 percent of the funds would go toward drug addict treatment and rehabilitation.

Named to head the new intelligence office was William C. Sullivan, a thirty-year veteran of service with the FBI. Sullivan's espionage arm was directed to "analyze and disseminate intelligence on drug traffickers collected by existing organizations such as the Bureau of Customs and the Bureau of Narcotics and Dangerous Drugs."

Pondering these developments, especially the impressive increase in heroin seizures along the vital eastern seaboard, Customs Commissioner Mike Acree was constrained to utter a characteristically cautious comment. Said Acree: "I think we just might be approaching the point where we can start hurting some of those creeps. We're going to make it hard for the professionals. Then if the amateurs get into the business, we've got a better chance of catching them. What we're trying to do is not just catch the traffickers and put them in prison, but to save our children from becoming drug addicts."

# 4

# European Run

Newspapers in New York, Montreal, London, Paris, Brussels and Vienna gave the story page-one treatment: Twenty-three men had been indicted by a New York grand jury on charges of smuggling 1,500 pounds of heroin into the United States during the previous two years after an international investigation which included months of surveillance in countries on both sides of the Atlantic.

The indictments, returned on January 4, 1972, but kept sealed until January 16 to give authorities in the United States and abroad time to round up the suspects, named twenty Frenchmen, an Austrian national arrested in France, and two residents of the Bronx. They included André Labay, owner of a clothing factory in Port-au-Prince, Haiti, and one of the backers of the film *The Second Sigh*, André Lajoux, a Paris racehorse owner and "sportsman," and Louis Cirillo of the Bronx, alleged to be the major New York buyer of heroin.

At the time, no mention was made of Jean Joseph Tonarelli of France or Giuseppe Giacomazzo of Astoria, Long Island, an omission which the international underworld might have considered unfair. For big scores in the war against illicit drug traffickers come hard and are fashioned piecemeal, and it almost surely would have taken longer to come up with the New Year's roundup had there been no Tonarelli and no Giacomazzo to provide unwitting assistance to the international lawmen. Or, as Customs Commissioner Myles Ambrose remarked at the time, "If you work very hard and are very, very lucky, every arrest you make will lead to another."

Indeed, the Tonarelli and Giacomazzo cases in themselves were classic examples of the Ambrose Doctrine. Neither of these men would have come to the attention of the law as early in the game as they did had it not been for the arrest of Edmond Taillet, a thirty-eight-year-old Parisian, on a charge of slipping 93½ kilos of heroin into New York City on or about April 21, 1971. Taillet was arrested with his alleged receiver on April 29, and an investigation of Taillet's background, added to some information that Taillet let slip, eventually put Customs on Tonarelli's tail.

Through the investigation following Taillet's arrest in New York, operatives under the assistant special agent in charge, Al Seeley, were able to trace the heroin back to Barcelona, where it was concealed in a 1969 Citroën sedan loaded on a Spanish ship the previous March. The ship arrived in Veracruz or Tampico, Mexico, on March 17, and the car with its cargo of heroin was off-loaded. Two French couples who were passengers on the ship claimed the Citroën and on April 4 crossed the border into the United States at Laredo, Texas.

The car and its passengers arrived in New York sometime during the first week of April, and a French male known only as Fernand, accompanied by an unidentified French woman, checked into the Abbey Victoria Hotel after leaving the Citroën in a nearby parking lot. The second French couple apparently disappeared. Taillet arrived in New York at about the same time and checked into the City Squire Motor Inn. Five days later, Taillet met Fernand, who gave him the parking ticket for the Citroën. In turn, Taillet two days later handed over the ticket to an individual named Tony, later identified by Customs as the receiver, Antonio Segura, twenty-seven, of the Bronx.

Two more days passed, and on April 14 Taillet again met with Tony, and Tony returned the parking ticket, which Taillet gave back to Fernand the next day. Sometime during the next several days, Fernand sold the Citroën to an unidentified customer. On the same day, a French woman was about to board a Swissair flight to Geneva when she saw Customs security officers checking passengers and suddenly took sick. She took a later flight to Geneva the same day, carrying—as Customs learned later—a suitcase containing $100,000 in bills as part payment for the heroin. A French police source later would identify the woman as one Marcelle Asfez of Marseilles, whose passport showed she had entered the United States at Laredo on April 4.

Taillet and Fernand bought two suitcases to hold $380,000, which was a second installment on the down payment for 93½ kilos; the remainder of the total price of $981,750 was to be paid by May 15. On April 19, while Taillet and Fernand were building false bottoms in the suitcases, a guest in a nearby room complained to the management. Four days later, Taillet moved to the Abbey Victoria Hotel. That same day, Fernand flew to Geneva via Air France with $380,-

000 concealed in the suitcases. After tailing Taillet for several days, during which they saw him meet again with Tony and followed the two to an address on East 89th Street, Customs Agents Bill Mc-Mullan and Mickey Tobin nabbed Taillet outside the Abbey Victoria. Tony was picked up a few hours later.

Taillet knew the source of the heroin only as "Lule," whose name would come up in later stages of the investigation. A check showed that Taillet had put in an overseas phone call to the Bar Caesar in Marseilles and made contact with "Lule." Meanwhile, Customs men discovered in Taillet's hotel room papers dealing with the various financial details of his trade. From those papers, it was learned that the 93½ kilos of heroin smuggled into New York constituted the first of three loads scheduled for delivery to Tony in a twelve-month period. Taillet's take was $5,000 per load. On Taillet's person, agents found a slip of paper identifying his various fellow conspirators by code names.

From Taillet, Customs investigators learned about only one car, the Citroën driven by Fernand & Co. from Mexico to New York. Eventually, they traced the Citroën to a used car lot in New York and found traces of heroin in its various interior parts. But they had traced the car's route from Spain to New York and identified the steamship line used to transport the car across the Atlantic. From there, they went on to dig deeper and concluded that the smugglers were using the "lower" or last ports of exit from Europe—that is to say, the Caribbean and various other "Spanish" ports.

All this information was organized and relayed through the Customs intelligence network to the suspected areas, including Puerto Rico. Orders were dispatched to check closely the manifests of all ships of certain named Spanish lines and to look especially for French cars accompanied by French or Italian nationals. In due time, Tonarelli and his mistress disembarked in San Juan from a Spanish ship for a sight-seeing tour.

Jean Joseph Tonarelli, thirty-seven, was an electrician who earned $325 a month working for the city of Manosque, France, near the Italian border. His modest life-style extended, no doubt necessarily, to his romantic tastes; his mistress of seventeen years was a $250-a-month charwoman named Andrée Josette Gayraud, age thirty-six. ("A charwoman, yes," said one of Andrée's friends, "but, one must understand, a person of a certain standing. Andrée was of those who put money in the bank.")

As he pictured himself, Tonarelli had no soaring ambitions. A glass of wine in the evening, the simple gaiety of the local dance hall, the company of Andrée—these little things brought him contentment. Then at a dance one night in January, 1971, Tonarelli was approached by a stranger, a man with a proposition. The man refused to identify himself, but over a glass of wine he told Tonarelli he could earn $12,000 "if you will take something to the United States."

Tonarelli laughed. "It is that you make the joke on me," he told the stranger. But the stranger persisted, and as Tonarelli said later, "*Enfin*, I listened." That was Tonarelli's first mistake.

The stranger gave Tonarelli $50 worth of French francs. In return, he asked Tonarelli for an extra set of keys to Tonarelli's Peugeot 404. "In this way," explained the anonymous one, "I can communicate with you. I will leave notes in the trunk of your car, which you will read and then, but absolutely, destroy them."

One day in April, Tonarelli found an envelope containing a sum of money and a note in the trunk of his Peugeot. The note instructed him to sell the Peugeot and buy a Citroën ID-19. Tonarelli sold his Peugeot and bought the Citroën from a local dealer. He would later claim he still had no idea what the "something" was that he was to carry to the United States.

He found out a few days later when, under instructions contained in another note, he drove to a point on a lonely road a few miles from Manosque and met another stranger. (For law enforcement audiences, Tonarelli was never able to provide descriptions of the associates in his new life.) The second stranger arrived with a load of heroin, packed in a number of plastic bags, which he placed in the Citroën. The two then were joined by three other strangers, who drove off in the Citroën, leaving Tonarelli and the first stranger lolling in a field to await their return.

The wait was a long one—almost three hours. During that time, the first stranger informed Tonarelli he would be taking an ocean voyage and that his ultimate destination was New York City; therefore he should arrange for a month's leave of absence from his job. When Tonarelli asked for details, he was told that he would find all his instructions in the trunk of the Citroën when it was returned to him.

"But where do I go in New York?" asked Tonarelli.

"Someplace," he was told. "A certain person will contact you at a motel en route to New York. He will tell you where to stay in New York. Another person will contact you at the hotel there, where you will find reservations in your name. That is all you need to know now. You understand, these things are well organized to protect everyone."

When the Citroën returned, there was no sign of the bags of heroin. "They have been hidden quite safely," the first stranger told Tonarelli. "One could never find them. It is not necessary for you to know where they have been concealed. When you return to Manosque, go to a place where you may safely remove your papers of instruction from the trunk."

Tonarelli drove back to Manosque in the Citroën and sought out his superior. He explained that he had to go to America to receive an inheritance. His superior congratulated him and, with much back slapping, agreed to the month's leave of absence. "But of course, you must tell Andrée," his boss said. He winked, man-to-manlike. "The little one will be pleased."

At midnight, Tonarelli opened the Citroën's trunk and found a sheaf of papers containing his instructions. He was to drive the Citroën to Barcelona, Spain, and there book passage for himself— and Andrée if he wished—and the Citroën on the steamship *Satrustegui*, due to sail for Veracruz, Mexico, on May 5. The next day, Tonarelli presented himself to Andrée and invited her to accompany him on a vacation trip to the New World. He explained that Andrée naturally would have to withdraw some of her life savings to help defray the cost of the holiday; Jean Joseph Tonarelli was a man of obsessive frugality. Delighted, Andrée agreed to go along and to contribute $300 toward the expenses.

The *Satrustegui* did not sail until May 10, but Tonarelli and Andrée were content. The steamship company put them up at the Hotel Oriente in Barcelona, a hotel of the third class, but comfortable. From the hotel, Andrée on May 9 put through a dutiful telephone call to her mother in Marseilles.

Tonarelli's strangers had thought of everything. They provided him with a sketch of the pier facilities at Barcelona; a Rand McNally travel atlas showing the routes marked in red pencil which Tonarelli was to follow in driving the Citroën from Laredo, Texas, to New York City; a note giving the names of cities and mileage between each on the route from Laredo to New York; and a road map of metropolitan New York showing the route to be followed upon arrival in Manhattan. The detailed spelling out of the couple's route to New York—in French—must have offered them considerable comfort, since neither spoke a syllable of English. They were spared the knowledge that even American tourists are frequently confused by their own highway markers.

Wise from the results of the Taillet-Tony investigation, Customs officials had decided on a policy of inspecting every car entering the United States from Europe. Tonarelli knew nothing of this when he and Andrée disembarked from the *Satrustegui* for sight-seeing upon the vessel's arrival at San Juan, Puerto Rico, early in the morning on May 29, 1971.

About nine o'clock that morning, Special Agents Jorge Marcano and Octavio Piñol boarded the vessel, docked at Pier 15. Among other police duties, they checked the ship's manifests and learned that Tonarelli and Andrée were traveling from Spain to Veracruz and that they had aboard the ship a Citroën consigned to themselves at the Mexican port. Marcano and Piñol, assisted by an automobile body repairman named Ramón Nazario, searched the Citroën and found eighteen plastic bags of heroin secreted in a specially built compartment between the gasoline tank and the floor under the rear seat. Another fifty-six plastic bags of heroin were found in false compartments beneath the trunk floor. Before their search was completed, the agents had unearthed 201 pounds of pure heroin worth more than $22,000,000 on the street.

Meanwhile, Tonarelli and Andrée had returned to the ship, where they were arrested by Marcano and Piñol and Resident Special Agent Jesús Martínez. Tonarelli insisted that Andrée was innocent of any wrongdoing. "She knows nothing," he told the agents. "She is merely my woman." Andrée agreed. Because she had been Tonarelli's mistress for seventeen years, she said she had not questioned him about the trip to America, or about where he got the money for the voyage or his new car. She also claimed she was unaware that Tonarelli had intended to take her to New York. "I was accompanying my lover on holiday to Veracruz," said Andrée. "He wanted me with him."

Although the Citroën, after the initial search, consisted largely of disassembled pieces of automobile, Agents Marcano and Piñol were unsatisfied with their seizures. They suspected there was more where the seventy-four bags of heroin had come from. They were right. When they took all the pieces apart, with the help of assorted mechanics and welding experts, they found an additional 46½ pounds of horse hidden in secret compartments welded to the frame in such a manner that they appeared to be part of the body structure. By the time this second search was complete the Citroën had yielded 247½ pounds of pure heroin, the biggest seizure in Customs' history.

Faced with the overwhelming evidence against him, Tonarelli eventually pleaded guilty to smuggling charges, and on January 28, 1972, he was hit by the book. Noting that the defendant did nothing to help identify his higher-ups, a federal court judge in New York sentenced Tonarelli to thirty years in an American penitentiary and tacked on a mandatory six years of probation.

Apparently convinced that Andrée Josette Gayraud was a woman easily fooled, the court had dismissed all charges against her a few months earlier.

Despite Tonarelli's inability—real or calculated—to remember what any of his "strangers" looked like, and his determination to cast himself in the role of a deaf-and-dumb errand boy, Customs managed to dig up some leads to the organization that had sponsored Tonarelli's abortive trip. Working with French officials and with certain unofficial sources in the United States who had to remain anonymous for obvious reasons of personal security, the investigating agents, led by New York's special agent in charge, John W. Fallon, came up with a few interesting names, most of them furnished by Special Agent Lucido, working in various sections of the country.

The names were of individuals of scant redeeming social virtue whose movements in Europe and North America formed a series of suspicious coincidences. They were names, as the saying goes, "known to the police"—Antoine Grisoni, Joe Signoli, Richard Berdin, André Labay and Louis Cirillo—and their owners had been in certain places at certain times. This suggested strongly that these individuals might have more than a passing knowledge of the smuggling conspiracy which had employed Tonarelli's meager competence.

In any case, as the investigation proceeded, it became reasonably clear that the conspirators were locked into a *modus operandi* employing the transatlantic shipment of private cars loaded down with heroin. Because an average automobile could conceal a lot of horse —in the case of Tonarelli's Citroën a whopping $30,000,000 in street value—the organization could afford an occasional loss by seizure, and tough luck for the courier. Besides, the odds were heavily weighted against the possibility of Customs' mustering the manpower and time to search *every* motor vehicle entering the United States by ship. In Las Vegas, that possibility would be a bet for suckers.

But unknown to the organization, Customs did have a promising gimmick at hand. The Customs Commissioner, Myles Ambrose, had devised a top-priority operation by which *all* cars arriving by sea from ports in France, Italy and Spain during certain periods would be searched from radiator to tailpipe. Until the order was given at the last possible moment, only Ambrose, Investigations Chief Harold Smith and a few others knew when such searches would take place. The odds against a leak were short enough to satisfy the professional standards of even Jimmy the Greek, that celebrity among bookmakers.

Thus the day came—September 22, 1971—when the search-all-cars order was in effect. And on that day there arrived at Pier 90 on New York's North River the SS *Raffaelo*, out of Genoa. Aboard the *Raffaelo* was Giuseppe Giacomazzo, thirty-five, of Astoria, New York, a native of Sicily. Giacomazzo was traveling with a woman named Mrs. Corinne Giaquinto, also of New York, and was the owner of a 1970 Ford Galaxie station wagon secured in the hold.

As Giacomazzo and Mrs. Giaquinto were standing in line for clearance by customs, agents of the investigative Customs Agency Service and the Bureau of Narcotics and Dangerous Drugs were engaged in tight surveillance of a man who had registered the night before at the Abbey Victoria Hotel in Manhattan as Gilbert Kemmoun. The man had arrived in New York from Montreal, where Canadian authorities were cooperating with U.S. lawmen. Thus when the man deplaned at Kennedy International Airport, Customs had no difficulty recognizing his passport picture as that of Richard Berdin, whose name was on the official list of suspects in the overall smuggling picture.

It was a coincidence that strengthened Customs' determination to go over all motor vehicles aboard the *Raffaelo*, including the Galaxie owned by Giacomazzo. Berdin did not travel internationally except on business. The search by Customs Patrol Officers Michael Fahy, Daniel Cicone and Frank Martino revealed that some big business was involved; the officers unearthed 169 half-kilo plastic bags of heroin in the Ford's rear window wells, the rear seat backrest, and under the back seat.

Mrs. Giaquinto, having been informed of her constitutional rights, gave agents a statement covering her holiday in Europe with Giacomazzo, beginning on August 24, 1971, and was permitted to go her way. Giacomazzo was arrested and taken to Customs headquarters in New York, where he sang an obliging tune. He told his interrogators that his brother-in-law, one Lorenzo D'Aloisio, also of Astoria, had agreed to pay him $15,000 to smuggle counterfeit money into the United States, concealed in the Ford. Giacomazzo subsequently had sailed with Mrs. Giaquinto to Italy, where on September 7 he had driven the car to Turin and turned it over to "some men" for loading while he and Mrs. Giaquinto went sight-seeing.

After all but one half-kilo bag had been filled with milk sugar, the contraband was replaced in its various hiding places in the Ford, and a small army of Customs and BNDD agents launched Giacomazzo on a "controlled delivery"—meaning a delivery surreptitiously supervised by the law. There followed one of those maddening charades which had become practically a daily routine for Customs operatives in the dope-smuggling field.

Followed by an assortment of official cars, Giacomazzo first drove to his home in Astoria, parked the Ford and went inside. It was now 6:45 P.M., and Richard Berdin already had had a busy day. From the Abbey Victoria Hotel he had strolled up and down several streets, finally meeting with a man identified at the time only as one "Michel." Berdin and Michel hailed a cab that just happened to be driven by Customs Special Agent Lewis Culver and asked directions to Astoria Boulevard. There, they dismissed the cab and walked around awhile, chatting, before they separated; Berdin took another cab back to his hotel and Michel went his own way, both discreetly tailed.

Meanwhile, back at the Giacomazzo residence, agents got their first look at an individual later identified as Giacomazzo's brother-in-law, Lorenzo D'Aloisio. Suddenly, D'Aloisio appeared on the corner of 28th Avenue and 33d Street, stopped to peer into Giacomazzo's Ford, then walked on, twice strolling around the block before proceeding to his own home on 34th Street, Astoria.

There is no room among dope traffickers for the creep who does not, instinctively, move cautiously and evasively. For a time, everybody involved in the Giacomazzo-Berdin caper was gold-star material in this respect. The furtive, jumpy, frightened maneuverings of the characters in the silent drama of the streets won the grudging admiration even of some of Customs' more impatient operatives. None seemed willing to trust himself to make the move that would effect delivery of the heroin.

After D'Aloisio's departure, Giacomazzo left his home and drove the Ford north on 33d Street. At a traffic light, a Customs car pulled alongside and Giacomazzo was asked: "Where you going, buster?" by Agent Mario Sessa.

"Lorenzo called," said Giacomazzo. "He said I should drive around the block and that he would be watching." Indeed, Lorenzo was doing just that from a street corner.

There followed a tour of that section of Long Island that would have driven a bus driver up the wall. Giacomazzo pulled up to a parking space on Astoria Boulevard, got out and walked to the next corner, where he met and talked with D'Aloisio for about five minutes. D'Aloisio went home. Giacomazzo resumed his aimless driving; while passing one of the Customs cars, he yelled out: "Be careful, be careful; one of your cars is following me too close. My brother-in-law is watching."

Giacomazzo parked the Ford again and had another street corner chat with D'Aloisio. Then he walked back home, followed by a man with a bandaged hand. He left again at about 9:30 P.M. and shortly was deep in conversation with the driver of a Pontiac Grand Prix. Back in his Ford, he followed the Grand Prix to a shopping center, where the two cars were parked a few vehicles apart. The two drivers conversed. Giacomazzo walked off; picked up by a couple of Customs tails, he said the driver of the car was one Frank Rappa and that Rappa had told him to return home on foot. Rappa spent some time in a Chinese restaurant, then walked back to his residence. About midnight, a man walked into the parking lot, took a look at Giacomazzo's Ford, then got into the Grand Prix and drove to Rappa's home, where he parked the car and went inside. He left about five minutes later, drove the Prix around a few blocks, and returned to Rappa's place.

The man with the bandaged hand parked a 1971 Buick Electra on 25th Drive and walked around the parking lot where the Ford was stashed, keeping a virtually continuous eye on the lot. He next was seen at about 1:30 A.M exiting the Grand Prix. He reclaimed his Buick and drove away, as his tails cursed.

Meanwhile, Washington prepared to give the tails an airborne assist. Headquarters had a new helicopter for use on the eastern seaboard which had been put into service only three weeks before. Senior Special Agent Joe Price was in charge of all the bureau's aircraft, and he had been training a New York agent to pilot the chopper so that it could be used in the New York–New Jersey area. Commissioner Ambrose decided the helicopter was needed in the Giacomazzo chase and so informed Senior Special Agent Irv Weinstein.

Weinstein barged into Price's office at 10:30 on the morning of Friday, September 24, and told Price: "Get that bloody chopper up to New York an hour ago!"

Since the pilot trainee was still learning landings, Price took the assignment himself. The flight from Dulles to New York's Wall Street heliport took two and a half hours, and Price then had to fly to Floyd Bennett Field, on Long Island, to refuel. While Price was at Bennett, a New York Port Authority helicopter flew in Special Agent Rick Dos Santos to join Price as observer. Dos Santos knew the Long Island neighborhood and he had been working on the Giacomazzo case.

"We're gonna make history, pal," Price told Dos Santos. "This will be the first time ever Customs will be using a chopper on a New York case. With a buck, that'll get us a drink in any New York bar."

It was 3:15 when Price and Dos Santos took off, and as the latter turned on the radio, he heard home base telling them: "Get Mother Goose airborne; the subject is moving." Everybody, in fact, was moving. The night before, Giacomazzo had phoned a Customs agent and said D'Aloisio had ordered him to move the Ford station wagon to another location. He did so, parking the car in the lot of the Central Motor Inn. Just after noon that next day, Giacomazzo picked up the wagon again, drove it to the parking lot of the Belaire Diner, and went into the diner. D'Aloisio and Rappa were seen walking past the diner an hour later. D'Aloisio subsequently went into the diner and Rappa drove off in a Buick. D'Aloisio and Giacomazzo left the diner separately about twenty minutes later, Giacomazzo climbing into the Ford and driving off, and D'Aloisio departing on foot—both followed by their tails. The Ford was also tailed by Rappa in the Buick.

When the chopper joined the chase, the Ford had just been parked on a street about a mile and a half from La Guardia Airport. The radio told the helicopter pilots that Giacomazzo was heading for the Long Island Expressway, to be followed by three unmarked Customs cars. By this time it was late Friday afternoon and vehicle traffic was practically bumper-to-cussing-bumper.

The chopper headed out the expressway, flying at about 400 feet so Dos Santos could pick the Ford out in the traffic; he had to read the license plates with binoculars. At that altitude, the planes landing at La Guardia were passing right under the helicopter and the planes taking off from Kennedy International Airport were roaring over-head. But the Federal Aviation Administration's radar people at both La Guardia and Kennedy were cooperating with the Price-Dos Santos team to keep them out of trouble. "We had priority handling up there," Dos Santos reported later. "It wasn't really dangerous; it just seemed so."

It took Dos Santos fifteen minutes to spot the Ford wagon in the heavy traffic. Then Price climbed to 800 feet and the chopper joined in the pursuit. According to "information received," Giacomazzo was scheduled to leave the expressway at a certain exit ramp and then make a right turn into a side street. As the Ford approached the ramp, Agent Charley Simmons in the first following car overtook it by a few car lengths, went off the ramp and then made a right turn, anticipating the imminent arrival of both Giacomazzo in the Ford and Rappa in the Buick.

But neither the wagon nor the Buick followed the game plan. Both left the expressway, but then pulled up on the side of the exit ramp, where Giacomazzo and Rappa exchanged a few words through their car windows. Both then continued down the ramp and drove across a so-called preferential road onto an entrance ramp and back up into the heavy traffic of the expressway. By this time the nearest agents' car on the expressway was two exits behind the Ford and Buick, and passing was an impossibility.

Aboard the chopper, the radio sounded like a debate in the Tower of Babel. Voices from everywhere all wanted to talk at once. The agents on the expressway wanted to know what they should do now, and home base demanded to know everybody's position and whether the Ford was still in sight. Dos Santos kept repeating: "Mother Goose has not, REPEAT NOT, lost the suspect."

Giacomazzo in the wagon and Rappa in the Buick traveled only about a quarter of a mile after reentering the expressway before pulling off into a crowded rest area. Dos Santos told the radio of the latest development. From the chopper, he and Price watched as Giacomazzo drove almost to the end of the rest area, then reversed and backed into the narrow grass space between the parked cars and a fence. Thus the Ford wagon was hidden from the view of any agent driving along the expressway, and so, less than a minute later, was Rappa in the Buick, who repeated Giacomazzo's maneuver.

But the chopper was there, hovering less than 1,000 feet up, to guide the agents' cars to the suspects. Price and Dos Santos watched as Rappa strolled to a telephone booth and made a brief call; later it was learned he had told the person at the other end of the line: "I'm in Long Island. I'm leaving now."

After a brief discussion of strategy by radio, the lawmen decided the time had come to end the charade. Obviously, Rappa and D'Aloisio by their movements had provided sufficient evidence that they had monkey business with the heroin courier, Giacomazzo. Besides, there was the ever-present danger that they might still evade their tails in the swarming chaos of the expressway.

So the agents pounced, almost at the very moment Rappa climbed into the Ford wagon carrying the altered contraband. Rappa was arrested as he started to drive away. Lorenzo D'Aloisio was picked up on an Astoria street at seven o'clock that evening, and Giacomazzo joined him in jail.

The previous day, September 23, Berdin had met again with the mysterious Michel for another stroll about the precincts of drab Astoria. With D'Aloisio and Rappa in the pen, Customs decided there was no point in permitting Berdin to remain at large. He was picked up on September 26.

Under Customs' supervision, Berdin joined the singers. He put in a scheduled call to one Roger Preiss in Paris; Berdin described Preiss as his contact with the "big American buyer." Preiss was told that all was well and that he should depart forthwith for New York to make delivery of the heroin. The "big American buyer" was identified by Berdin as Louis Cirillo of somewhere in the Bronx. Preiss was to deliver the heroin to Cirillo's chief lieutenant, a Bronx neighbor named John Astuto, also known as Salvatore Rizzo.

Meanwhile, Berdin had tipped off his new friends, the Customs agents, to a deal he had pending in which André Labay, the Haitian industrialist and sometime financial angel for movies, was to carry about 233 pounds of heroin loaded in a number of expensive suitcases through United States Customs at Kennedy International Airport. Labay, said Berdin, would have the significant assistance of an airport employee, who would walk him through the inspection area.

At this point, a snag developed. Berdin had told Preiss to meet him at his (Berdin's) hotel so that transfer of the heroin could be negotiated. Preiss arrived in New York three days later. But even as Customs tails watched his every move, he was arrested outside Berdin's hotel by agents of the Bureau of Narcotics and Dangerous Drugs. BNDD naturally took jurisdiction at that point. So when Preiss identified Cirillo's photograph as a picture of the American heroin buyer, BNDD agents immediately arrested Cirillo in Miami. But all efforts to locate Astuto were fruitless.

Such things, of course, happen in a field of law enforcement where secrecy within an agency is paramount. BNDD was running its own investigation of the smuggling rings, and it was doing its job as it saw that job. However, Customs officials were hardly pleased by the next development. They had been rubbing their hands at the prospect of nabbing Labay on his "walk-through" at Kennedy Airport with those suitcases packed with heroin.

No soap. Labay never reached New York. He was arrested by French and BNDD agents in France, and the load of heroin was confiscated. At that point, BNDD Chief John Ingersoll, a dope fighter of high competence, would not have been voted Customs' Man of the Year. But BNDD had an explanation: Labay had come to the agency's office in Paris and offered to cooperate in "setting up" future heroin loads to the United States if they would let him get through with the first load—apparently because Labay was in dire need of big money. There were conflicting stories about what happened, but somebody—French or American, or possibly authorities on both sides—nixed the deal.

Customs still had Berdin talking, probably under the influence of an airline stewardess, an American girl, who was anxious that her beau purge himself. He reported that most of the 1,500 pounds of heroin smuggled into the United States during a two-year period had been concealed in secret compartments of six different cars, shipped in by sea. Customs men spent the next three months checking on Berdin's story, poring over bills of lading, hotel records and immigration forms. They found Berdin had leveled with them. In two cases, in fact, the automobiles were found—one a classic Bentley on a movie set in Los Angeles, and the second, a Mercedes-Benz, on a used car lot. The cars were dismantled and secret compartments with heroin traces were uncovered.

The indictments of January 4, 1972, naming Cirillo, Berdin, Preiss, Astuto and nineteen suspects in France, were sealed to give French authorities time to round up those named. But the French, after picking up nearly all the suspects, announced the roundup to the press. At that point, a rather discomfited Attorney General John Mitchell had the indictments unsealed and issued his own press release on the investigation.

During the period from December, 1971, to September, 1972, the government disposed of the assorted smugglers whose arrests had contributed to the slew of international indictments. Antonio Segura, the Bronx operator named as the receiver of the 93½ kilos of heroin shipped to New York in April, 1971, by the Parisian Edmond Taillet, drew eighteen years on each of two criminal counts, to be served concurrently. Taillet, who talked, was permitted to cop a plea of failing to pay tax on the heroin shipment and got three years in the pen. In the cases of Giuseppe Giacomazzo and conspirators, the sentences were more severe. Giacomazzo drew ten years, a sentence lightened as a reward for his cooperation with the state. But Lorenzo D'Aloisio, the "controller," got twenty years, and Frank Rappa, the moneyman and penultimate receiver, drew two fifteen-year sentences, to be served concurrently.

By that time, however, all five had dropped back into relative obscurity, upstaged by the wholesale roundup of VIP's involved on one level or another in the transatlantic organized crime brotherhood known as the Mafia.

# 5

# The Mafia's Man

They said about Louis Cirillo, a bulky, forty-eight-year-old self-styled bagel baker from the Bronx, that he had once paid $3,000,000 in cash for a load of heroin smuggled in from Marseilles. Whether or not the story was apocryphal, Cirillo was indeed the big fish among the twenty-three assorted international suspects indicted in January, 1972, for sneaking nearly $250,000,000 worth of horse into the United States.

Customs had every reason to believe that Louis Cirillo, from his modest Bronx home, its front yard overflowing with flowers, master-minded the Mafia's $800,000,000-a-year narcotics racket. That is to say, Cirillo was the Cosa Nostra's front man, a general manager who operated more or less in the open while leaders of the Bonanno, Tramunti, Genovese and Colombo families who owned the business in New York remained in their accustomed background. Simply put, there was no other source in the United States with the resources to provide Cirillo with the vast sums of cash he regularly disbursed for those thousands of plastic bags of heroin he ordered from salesmen in Europe and South America. The Mafia was the racket's bank, and its lower-echelon hoodlums formed a police force to control distribution and keep Cirillo and his henchmen in line.

For a "bagel baker," Cirillo had been around some. As early as the fall of 1967, he had been arrested on charges of smuggling cocaine into New York along with four other alleged members of an international ring. But it was not until after his arrest in Miami on October 12, 1971, that his importance as the Mafia's No. 1 drug-trafficking executive became known.

Then, after months of digging by Customs men headed by case agent Anthony Bocchichio of New York, and from interrogation of informants singing to save their own skin, it was learned that during 1970 and 1971 Louis Cirillo personally had paid out more than

69

$12,000,000 in cash for heroin with a street value of $293,000,000. Acting for his Mafia bosses, Cirillo had indisputably become the biggest illicit dope buyer of all time. "Don't worry about the money," Cirillo once reportedly told a smuggling chieftain in Paris. "The people behind me have got more dough than United States Steel."

Cirillo himself was pretty well heeled. Although he lived quietly with his wife, Antoinette, on the first floor of the house in the respectable middle-income Throgs Neck section of the Bronx— frugally renting the second floor to his daughter and son-in-law— Bocchichio's months-long probe revealed that he enjoyed a luxurious second life in Miami. There, he had rented an apartment under another name, making a $440 deposit and paying $238 a month rent. Bocchichio and his colleagues were not persuaded that Cirillo could manage this on the $200 a week he said he earned turning out bagels.

There was, as usual, a girl—a second wife, who shared the Miami apartment with Cirillo. She was an attractive fortyish brunette who reportedly had a Greek husband somewhere. Along with Cirillo's first lieutenant and bagman, John Astuto, she disappeared after Cirillo's arrest, and it was Customs' nasty conclusion that Cirillo—described by Bocchichio as "a man of congenital violence"—had arranged for the liquidation of these two possible witnesses against him.

At any rate, Cirillo was tabbed as a big spender—although he never went near a bank—by both Customs and agents of the cooperating Bureau of Narcotics and Dangerous Drugs. Apparently, not all of his big spending was on high living; among other morsels of information dug up during the Customs investigation was that money provided by Cirillo was financing the construction of a seagoing ship with a false keel in a Canadian port.

Following the indictment of "The 23," Senior Special Agent Doug McCombs of Customs' Washington headquarters was able to limn a sketch revealing the involvement of three international narcotics-trafficking syndicates and their *modus operandi*. In each case, Louis Cirillo was on the receiving end; he had a standing agreement to buy all the heroin the three syndicates could ship into the United States.

As drawn by McCombs' brush, the syndicate chieftains were revealed as Joe Signoli and Antoine Grisoni, operating out of Paris and Marseilles, and an Italian gang with headquarters in Lyon. Boss of the Italian syndicate appeared to be the mysterious "Lule," mentioned by Edmond Taillet when he was arrested for smuggling in New York back in April, 1971. André Labay, the French industrialist and part-time film producer, and Richard Berdin, nabbed in the Giacomazzo bust, were "transport men" for Signoli; that is to say, they arranged for couriers to bring the drugs into the United States and for deliveries to Cirillo's contact man.

Sometime early in 1971, the dark and handsome thirty-two-year-old Berdin, a skilled womanizer, decided to strike out on his own in pursuit of a faster buck. He knew Cirillo could handle more heroin than Signoli's syndicate was delivering, and he saw himself as the man who could satisfy Cirillo's needs through the Grisoni group. French laboratories were turning out plenty of horse; Berdin figured that what was needed was another delivery service—headed, of course, by Richard Berdin, hustler, ladies' man and onetime convicted holdup man.

So Berdin put his proposition to Signoli. There were no hard feelings. Signoli readily agreed to let Berdin sell to Cirillo, in return for a percentage of Berdin's take.

Berdin then approached Grisoni, who agreed to supply him with all the heroin he could afford in the future. However, Grisoni told Berdin that if he wanted a quick delivery, he should contact the Italian "company" in Lyon.

"They've got a load in transit now in an automobile," Grisoni told Berdin. "I think you can get in on it, or for a piece of it." Grisoni of course was referring to the load in Giacomazzo's car due to be shipped to the United States aboard the *Raffaelo*. Apparently the Lyon group could use a little more financing.

Berdin traveled to Lyon with Grisoni and André Lajoux, a Frenchman who owned a stable of racehorses and associated with the right kind of wrong people. At a meeting in a Lyon bistro, an agreement was reached for the sale of the multikilo shipment which by then already had been loaded aboard the *Raffaelo*. Later, Berdin was introduced to a "Michel," who was to be his contact in the United States. Berdin suggested selling part of the shipment to a buyer whose name had been furnished to him by a man Berdin called Count Jacques Soderini de Collalto.

"Perhaps," said Grisoni. "You might perhaps sell about fifteen kilos to Count Soderini's man, but you understand most of it must go to Louis Cirillo because Cirillo is our buyer—Joe Signoli's and mine."

Berdin's next step was to sign up a contact man in the United States to deliver the load of heroin. Berdin was not about to fill that role himself in his new status as an executive. So he contacted Roger

Preiss, who had been operating on the fringes of narcotics trafficking in a variety of assignments. Signoli introduced Preiss to Cirillo in Paris, and Cirillo okayed him. Deliveries, Cirillo told Preiss, should be made only to John Astuto.

Matters settled to his satisfaction with Signoli and Cirillo, Berdin arranged to take delivery of the Giacomazzo load for the Italians in New York. He flew to Montreal and then to New York to put himself in the chain of delivery. Berdin would control the delivery to Preiss, who would pass it on to Astuto. Then, in reverse order, Berdin would pick up the purchase price for the heroin, in cash. Unfortunately for Berdin's dreams of fortune, Customs learned he was in Montreal and then that he had arrived in New York. Scratch Richard Berdin. It was of course Berdin's arrest that triggered the indictment of "The 23."

Through Berdin and from products of their independent investigations, Bocchichio and other Customs agents were able to connect all the individuals named in the indictment with the smuggling conspiracy. The evidence turned up, as reflected in the Criminal Case Report, was a textbook in smuggling operations.

There was the Alfa Romeo car shipped into New York with 70 kilos of heroin concealed in its innards in the summer of 1970. The heroin was unloaded by Berdin, Labay and Raymond Moulin and stashed in suitcases, which Berdin delivered to Joe Signoli and Guido Randel at a Brooklyn apartment Randel shared with a girlfriend. Signoli verified the purity of the heroin and on the following day paid Berdin $70,000; Berdin kept $10,000 and turned over the balance to Labay.

Signoli later arrived in the United States from Paris to set up Andrea Andreani as a replacement for Randel as contact with Louis Cirillo. In August, 1970, 72 kilos of heroin were smuggled into the United States in a Mercedes-Benz by Jean Claude De Meester aboard another passenger liner. At about this time, Berdin and an unidentified woman each carried $200,000 in cash from New York to Brussels, concealing the currency in the false bottoms of Samsonite suitcases.

The smugglers almost invariably used Samsonite traveling bags because they discovered early on that the lining was not riveted in, but simply glued to the inside of the suitcase. The lining was removed by submerging the suitcase in hot water. Stacks of hundred-dollar bills were wrapped in brown paper and taped and glued to the Samsonite interior of the bag, then the lining was glued back into place to conceal the loot. Bills smaller than the hundred-dollar denomination were considered too bulky to be used. One courier complained when he was dispatched to Europe with three suitcases packed with fifty-dollar bills; he said the cache left too little room for his clothing. Berdin estimated that one Samsonite two-suiter had a capacity for $500,000 in hundred-dollar bills under the lining.

Francis Vanverberghe entered the picture in late November, 1970, when he joined Signoli and Alexandre Salles in assigning Berdin to control a heroin shipment from Labay shipped into Montreal in an old Cadillac. De Meester rode shotgun with the Cadillac on the trans-atlantic voyage, but was searched by Canadian customs authorities when he debarked and in a panic returned to Paris. Signoli ordered De Meester to go back to Montreal to drive the Cadillac across the border into the United States. This time, De Meester got the job done, crossing the border in the Cadillac at High Springs, Vermont.

Meanwhile, Berdin and Andreani drove to Farmingdale, Long Island, to a garage where the Cadillac was to be unloaded. The garage was provided by Louis Cirillo, then known to Berdin only as Louie. After the heroin was unloaded, Berdin abandoned the Cadillac in Harlem.

Enter Felix Rosso and the two unidentified seamen. On December 18, 1970, Berdin, Andreani and Rosso proceeded to Fort Lauderdale, Florida, to accept delivery of 100 kilos of heroin from the seamen. The sailors delivered the heroin in three sea bags in a parking lot in Fort Lauderdale, and it was transferred to a car rented by Andreani. While Andreani was at the wheel during an aimless drive about the city, Berdin and Rosso were in the back seat transferring the heroin from the sea bags to Samsonite suitcases. Berdin and the two seamen each got $50,000 as their share of the take.

Enter Jacques Bec. It was he who met Signoli and Berdin in the bar of the Metropole Hotel in New York in February, 1971, to inform them that a load of heroin concealed in still another car was on the high seas aboard a vessel bound for Montreal. Enter Michel Mastantuono, who was working with Bec on details involved in the shipment of the car from Canada to the United States. Berdin took control of the car from Mastantuono and Bec in front of the Holiday Inn in New York on February 17. Then Berdin, accompanied by Mastantuono and Bec, drove the car to a prearranged meeting with Signoli and a representative of the big American buyer, "Louie." Bec and Mastantuono each were paid $50,000 for their services in that operation.

Thus the American side of the law's case against "The 23," perhaps best summed up by the hardworking and indefatigable Special Agent Anthony Bocchichio: "We were able to show that all these guys were in the right places at the right times, either doing the wrong things or communicating with one another about doing them."

To the surprise of every law enforcement official even remotely aware of the heroin problem in the country, Louis Cirillo was released by Federal Court Judge Edward Weinfeld of New York on $250,000 bail bond and $500,000 personal recognizance on March 22, 1972, a little less than a month before he was to go on trial. Twenty days later, he was arrested by agents of the Federal Bureau of Narcotics and Dangerous Drugs on charges of plotting to murder the chief witness against him in the smuggling case.

An indictment handed down by a federal grand jury deposed that Cirillo conspired with five other men to blow up a building on Staten Island where the witness, Roger Preiss, was believed to be held in protective custody. It was, of course, the same Roger Preiss who had been Richard Berdin's contact with Cirillo's go-between, and Cirillo's arrest brought the public revelation that Preiss had turned state's evidence.

Cirillo, nabbed as he drove along the West Side Highway near 96th Street in Manhattan, was held on bail of $1,000,000 by Federal Judge Charles Brieant, Jr. Two of the other alleged conspirators in the murder plot were arrested at the same time—James "Jimmy Feets" Panebianco and Carmine Pepe, both of New York. Panebianco had a record of two convictions on narcotics charges and several assault arrests dating back to 1945. Meanwhile, Assistant United States Attorney Walter Phillips told the court that Cirillo's son, Louis, Jr., and one Joseph Bux were named as co-conspirators in the case.

This latest development stole the spotlight from the smuggling charges against Cirillo when he went on trail on April 17. Speaking softly and in a voice that frequently trembled, the Frenchman Preiss testified that after his arrest he kept mum about details of Cirillo's role in the smuggling conspiracy because he was afraid Cirillo would have him killed.

"If you speak, you go to jail and die," Preiss said a friend told him. The friend, identified by Preiss as a fellow smuggler, described Cirillo as a man with "big connections" with narcotics agents in Miami and police in New York, who would find out through those contacts if Preiss was talking. Therefore, Preiss testified, he had clammed up about three meetings he had had with Cirillo when he went before a federal grand jury the previous fall. Preiss said he was obsessed with fear of "this dangerous man."

But Preiss in turn was upstaged by Joseph Bux, a convicted bank robber, who testified three days later that Cirillo recruited him for a fee of $5,000 to kill Preiss. Bux, another soft-spoken witness, said plans were made for the hit during a meeting between him and Cirillo in a bail bondsman's office in New York sometime around the end of March. The two also discussed a scheme to effect Cirillo's escape from jail, Bux said.

"He showed me a picture of Preiss," Bux testified. "He said he was the government witness against him. He said he wanted to get rid of the government witness." The $5,000, Bux said, was handed to him by Cirillo's son, and later he added that he was told Preiss was being held under guard at a deserted Army barracks on Staten Island. The escape plans discussed, according to Bux, involved deploying several cars and trucks to block off federal agents while other confederates were forcing their way into the jail and releasing Cirillo, and the use of an apartment in Brooklyn as a temporary hideout for the fugitive.

Preiss testified under tight security measures that included frisking of both spectators and the press. In his first appearance on the witness stand, he testified in detail about the *modus operandi* of the international heroin-smuggling ring and Cirillo's connection with the organization.

When United States Attorney Whitney North Seymour, Jr., asked Preiss to identify the American drug buyer, Preiss looked Cirillo in the eye, pointed a finger at the defendant—owlish in horn-rimmed glasses—and declared in a heavy French accent: "This man!" Cirillo was impassive, glancing at Preiss absentmindedly, as though out of the curiosity of an innocent bystander.

Among other things, Preiss testified about the "big red car" loaded with heroin that had been driven across the border from Canada and swore that the illicit cargo ultimately was delivered to Louis Cirillo. Once the car arrived in New York, Preiss testified, the smuggling gang met outside St. Patrick's Cathedral on fashionable Fifth Avenue to map strategy. Then the car was driven across the George Washington Bridge and parked in the garage of a luxurious home in Fort Lee, New Jersey, he said.

Gesturing with his hands, Preiss told the jury of nine women and three men how he and four others had removed the door handles, paneling and seats from the car, following closely a diagram pin-pointing the hidden heroin. He remarked that John Astuto, Cirillo's right-hand man, fetched "soda, coffee and drinks" to refresh the men as they worked at the three-hour job of dismantling the car. At one point, he said, one of the plastic bags of heroin ripped open and some of the contents spilled onto the floor of the car and the garage.

"There's enough there on the floor to kill a regiment in the Air Force," one of them remarked.

Cirillo, said Preiss, paid for the haul with $300,000 in crisp new hundred-dollar bills. He testified that the money was concealed inside the lining of a brown suitcase by Joseph Signoli, boss of one of the French smuggling syndicates. Cirillo, according to Preiss, had arrived at the garage at about 12:30 A.M. to tell the men dismantling the car: "Everything's okay. No problems." Undoubtedly, Cirillo was treated with respect by the others in the garage; Preiss had recalled earlier that Signoli had warned him Cirillo was "a very dangerous man," and that if he ever mentioned Cirillo's name to a policeman, "YOU will not live long enough to speak again."

The jury deliberated for only an hour and fifteen minutes before returning a guilty verdict on two counts charging conspiracy and possession of narcotics. Although Cirillo faced a maximum sentence of sixty years in prison because of two prior drug convictions, the balding, heavyset defendant sat emotionless, as he had throughout the seven-day trial.

Then, while Cirillo sat in a jail cell under heavy guard awaiting sentencing, federal agents added a fascinating footnote to the case of this self-styled humble bagel baker. A task force from the Bureau of Narcotics and Dangerous Drugs descended upon Cirillo's common-place castle in the Bronx and, working by the light of electric torches, dug up $978,100 in cash in the backyard and another $100,000 concealed behind the wood paneling of his basement rumpus room.

Frank V. Monastero, regional director of the BNDD, surveyed the piles of currency and concluded that Louis Cirillo was the "most substantial narcotics trafficker the bureau has ever found." He might have added, as a Customs Bureau official did, that the BNDD was lucky it got there before the Mafia did.

The money dug up in the yard was found buried in a narrow stretch of turf between a gazebo and the garage which was covered by a pile of rotting wooden planks. It was wrapped in five large packages of clear plastic, each containing nearly $200,000 in tens, twenties, fifties and one hundreds, and packed in a large black plastic sack. The money found in the rumpus room was contained in a steel box, wedged into a compartment behind the paneling in back of the basement shower.

Reporters scurried about trying to interview Cirillo's neighbors, who predictably sought refuge in anonymity. An elderly Italian man glared at the Cirillo house. "I don't want to know them," he told a New York *Daily News* reporter. A young woman who knew Cirillo's daughters, Marie and Joanne, described them as "quiet—they were brought up strict." Then, "Don't quote me. I don't want to wind up in the East River."

Denounced by Judge W. Edward Weinfeld as a man whose "criminal conduct has brought untold misery to thousands of men, women and children," Louis Cirillo was sentenced on May 25, 1972, to twenty-five years in prison on charges of conspiracy to smuggle heroin. Before reading the sentence in a federal courtroom in New York City, Judge Weinfeld said Cirillo was responsible for importing one-sixth of the ten tons of heroin consumed by addicts each year in the United States. United States Attorney Seymour described Cirillo as "the most important heroin distributor ever tried and convicted in the Southern District of New York." Seymour noted that a 1967 narcotics indictment against Cirillo in Brooklyn had been dismissed when a woman who was the government's chief witness disappeared and was believed to have been murdered.

Cirillo beat the rap on charges that he conspired to "obstruct" justice by allegedly scheming to murder Roger Preiss, one of the state's leading "canaries." A jury of six women and six men freed Cirillo after three and a half hours of deliberation. Also acquitted were James "Jimmy Feets" Panebianco, Carmine Pepe, a Manhattan bail bondsman, and Dennis Wedra. Key witness for the prosecution at the trial was Joseph Bux, who claimed he was hired for $5,000 to hit Preiss.

A few months later, Preiss and Richard Berdin, both of whom had been arrested in the Giacomazzo case which led to the Cirillo prosecution, each drew three years in the pen. That was fair enough; without the information furnished by Preiss and Berdin, Customs agents would have had a harder time fingering Cirillo.

Earlier, a Boston federal court had added a footnote to the Cirillo case. Jean Claude Kella and Laurent Fiocconi, both French nationals, were sentenced to a total of twenty-five years each on three narcotics counts. It was Kella and Fiocconi, of course, who had "sold" Louis Cirillo to the French syndicate for a lifetime pension of $500 for every kilo of heroin Cirillo bought from the syndicate.

# 6

# A Fix of Paella

It started out as a housekeeping chore. A short time after TWA Flight 709 arrived at Washington's Dulles International Airport from London on the evening of July 26, 1968, a cleaning man named Daniel Roland, helping to tidy up the plane for continuing flights to St. Louis, Denver and San Francisco, found a quantity of white powder wrapped in a woman's stocking in the used towel disposal bin in the men's lavatory.

A Customs field test showed the stocking contained about a pound of pure heroin.

By the time Customs completed its investigation, eight months later, authorities in New York, Switzerland, France, Spain and Italy had smashed an illicit racket supplying an estimated $100,000,000 worth of heroin a year to American addicts.

"The Paella Story" is a story of lawmen who were dissatisfied with minor successes, who were determined to make the big score. And because they pursued every lead and banked every name for future reference, the case would eventually provide them with a launching pad for the successful investigation of a heroin-smuggling ring operating from another part of the world.

No such expectation piqued Agent George Festa as he went about his routine. First, he substituted Epsom salts for some of the heroin in the stocking and returned it to the used towel compartment. He made a personal, professional search of the lavatory and discovered more contraband—six plastic packages of heroin. These were replaced by packages of Epsom salts and returned to their hiding place. Then Festa boarded the plane for its flight to St. Louis. His quarry was worth the chase; on the street the seven pounds of heroin would sell for more than $700,000.

Festa took a seat near the lavatory, and each time a passenger used the hot comfort station he checked to make sure the contraband was still there. But it was not until the plane, after its St. Louis stop, proceeded on to Denver that Festa fingered his man. The man, later identified as one Willie Wouters, entered the lavatory carrying a small airlines bag. After Wouters had returned to his seat, Festa made another trip to the lavatory and discovered the seven packages of Epsom salts—and a gram or two of heroin—had been removed.

At Denver, Festa was met by Agent Harold King and an agent of the Justice Department's Bureau of Narcotics and Dangerous Drugs, James Petit, and together they kept Wouters under surveillance. After strolling about the airport, Wouters deposited his airlines bag in a public locker. Then he went for another walk, while Festa kept watch on the locker and King and Petit trailed Wouters. Three long and tedious hours later, Wouters returned to the locker and removed the bag. Then he bought a ticket on United Airlines Flight 178 to New York. So did Festa, King and Petit.

Flight 178 arrived at Kennedy International Airport in New York shortly after six o'clock in the morning on July 27. Waiting for Wouters and his tails were Customs Agents Edward T. Coyne and Irwin Weinstein, Customs Port Investigator John Flynn, and Narcotics Agent Mortimer Benjamin. Wouters was arrested as he was about to step into a taxicab and taken to the Customs office at the terminal.

Now the lawmen started to cash in on some string saved during Customs' continuing investigation of the illegal dope traffic. Agents Coyne, Weinstein and Albert Seeley had been digging into a minor case for the past several weeks and had run across Wouters' name and that of Jean Marc Montoya. They had nothing tangible on the men except that their names kept popping up as rather well known in certain circles not celebrated for rectitude. Coyne's notebook also showed that Wouters had had a drink with an unidentified party in the bar of the Belmont Plaza Hotel at Lexington Avenue and 49th Street in Manhattan.

Coyne took a shot. "You're staying at the Belmont Plaza, huh?" he informed Wouters. Wouters seemed startled, but said nothing. Weinstein telephoned the Belmont Plaza and learned that Wouters did indeed have a room there. Wouters and his escorts promptly departed the airport and proceeded to that room, Wouters still carrying the bag of heroin and Epsom salts.

In the room, the agents found two envelopes containing $44,000 in currency; Wouters admitted the money was used to pay off couriers, but then clammed up. Coyne, however, had some ideas. While

Wouters sulked and his captors ransacked the room, Coyne left to pay a visit to an informant, who shall here be known by the fictitious name George Smith, for obvious reasons.

"We picked up Wouters," Coyne told Smith. "It's only a matter of time before we get the rest of them. How about coming clean and scoring some points for yourself?"

Smith came clean. He told Coyne that Wouters, using the code name Victor, had arrived from France on June 25, 1968, and since then had been retrieving bags of heroin from TWA Flights 709 and 771 from two to four times a week. Smith described Montoya as Wouters' "chief assistant," and said Montoya was due in New York from San Francisco the next day with six kilograms of heroin for delivery to Wouters at the Belmont Plaza. Final delivery, said Smith, was made to one Jack Grosby, who then turned back the proceeds to Wouters for transfer to the "organization" in Europe.

Coyne did some quick mental arithmetic from Smith's amazingly precise figures on the average size of each delivery. They added up to roughly 114 kilos of pure heroin smuggled into the United States during July alone. Later, when all the returns were in, Coyne's arithmetic held up. The organization's take for the month was established at $943,000. And, following several adulterations, the street value of the heroin was estimated at a whopping $28,500,000.

Smith also had a "funny story" for Coyne, one which the organization could not have found even mildly amusing. He said that on July 12 a consignment of heroin arrived from Europe on a TWA flight but that because of bad weather the courier failed to arrive in St. Louis in time to meet the flight and retrieve the dope. The contraband had remained concealed on the plane for sixteen days, "traveling around the world several times." Smith said Montoya would board the plane Sunday to remove the consignment.

First, however, Customs agents tailed Montoya upon his arrival from San Francisco and watched him deliver the six packages of heroin to a contact in a restaurant in the Belmont Plaza. Later, the contact was arrested and the heroin seized, but Montoya was permitted to go free under surveillance. Customs would bide its time until Montoya retrieved the heroin from the TWA plane due to arrive the next day from London after carrying the stuff as deadhead cargo for so long.

On Sunday, Montoya was followed to Kennedy Airport, where he bought a ticket on TWA Flight 42 to San Francisco. The flight had arrived a few minutes before. Suddenly, by arrangement with Customs, the public address system announced that the flight would return to Europe, this time to Rome. Another plane would be made available for the San Francisco flight.

Montoya refused to panic. He walked calmly up to a TWA clerk and asked permission to board the aircraft. "I left my glasses aboard," he told the clerk. "They are very expensive."

Obligingly, the clerk accompanied Montoya into the empty plane. While the clerk looked under the seats, Montoya excused himself and, holding his tummy, disappeared into the lavatory. Emerging a few minutes later, Montoya was arrested. Agents found three half-kilo packages of heroin strapped to his body under his jacket.

In the next few days, several other TWA planes were searched and five more heroin caches of six kilos each were recovered. The loss to the organization was set by George Smith, the know-it-all informer, at $350,000.

Naturally, Customs got complete cooperation from TWA, whose top management was embarrassed to the point of furious exasperation that the smugglers should have picked on its planes. But the explanation was simple. At the time, TWA was the only airline flying from European points whose aircraft continued on to other American cities after landing in New York or Washington and clearing customs.

Probing the *modus operandi*, Customs people learned that couriers usually debarked upon the flight's arrival in the United States, although if the flight originated in, say, Frankfurt am Main, they sometimes dropped off in London. In either case, the courier himself was clean when he went through customs; his illicit cargo was safely stashed away in the lavatory, for retrieval by a colleague once the plane had taken off into the friendly and duty-free skies of the continental United States.

Meanwhile, Customs and Narcotics agents were rounding up other suspects: Jack Grosby, a naturalized American citizen from Argentina, who called himself an "entrepreneur"; Grosby's common-law wife, Nellie Alves, a naturalized United States citizen from Brazil; and Daniel Mitnik, a resident alien from Chile and a house painter by trade. Willie Wouters was described by French officials as a "restaurateur" and a Belgian national; Montoya as a Paris chauffeur.

But these were all small fry: couriers, middlemen, and bagmen. By now Ed Coyne and his regular partner, Agent Albert Seeley, were convinced they were onto something big; they lusted after information that would lead them to the fat cats in Europe who ran the organization. Joined by Narcotics Agent Norris Durham, they had a long chat in the United States Attorney's office in New York with Jack Grosby, tall, husky, and older-looking than his forty-three years, who was known as Jacob Grodnitzky to the New York Police Department. As the man who took delivery of the heroin, Grosby seemed a likely prospect to divulge a few more names.

Grosby did just that. This was his story, according to the official transcript:

In January, 1967, he met a man known to him as Philippe Spadaro in the Argentine Restaurant on upper Broadway to discuss the importation of Argentine horses into the United States for racing and breeding purposes. A few weeks later, Spadaro was arrested in New York on a narcotics charge, and Grosby learned that his real name was Louis Bonsignour, a Frenchman who traveled extensively in Europe and South America. Grosby engaged an attorney for Bonsignour and also befriended him in smaller ways. After several attempts, the lawyer finally got Bonsignour's bail reduced, whereupon Bonsignour fled the jurisdiction.

While Bonsignour was still in jail, Grosby had made two trips to Argentina at Bonsignour's request to try to raise money for Bonsignour's bail. He also made a side trip to Rio de Janeiro to visit Bonsignour's wife. It was there that he was reunited with Bonsignour after the latter jumped bail. Grateful for Grosby's help, Bonsignour let him in on the racket. They traveled separately to Madrid and then to Marseilles, and in both cities Grosby was introduced to several members of the organization whom he could identify only by various first names. One of these men was "Robert," the man who would recruit Willie Wouters and who later would be identified by the American Embassy in Paris as one Daniel Roger Vuille Dit Bille.

Eventually, with Bonsignour's imprimatur, Grosby was engaged by still another nameless operator to receive heroin deliveries in New York. Grosby was told that once he returned to New York he would be contacted from time to time by a man named "Billy," who would identify himself by displaying a picture postcard from Switzerland. From March, 1968, until May of the same year, "Billy" delivered numerous consignments of heroin to Grosby and his assistant, Daniel Mitnik. Then "Billy" was questioned by some nosy New York policemen and the organization forthwith replaced him with "Victor"— Willie Wouters.

Grosby could hardly have done much better financially had he had access to one of the money-printing machines at the Treasury Department's Bureau of Engraving and Printing. He sold the heroin, at first to a man he identified as Juan Fernández, and then to a contact he knew only as "Bruno," for $66,000 per six-kilogram package. He turned back to the organization $54,000, a profit per kilo of $2,000. Grosby boasted that in the previous six months he had made and deposited in a Swiss bank a total of $120,000.

The agents didn't have to take Grosby's word for this. They had already discovered two deposit slips for $60,000 each in Grosby's home at the time of his arrest. They also obtained a search warrant and found another $68,000 in cash in Grosby's safety deposit box at the First National City Bank Branch at 72d Street and Broadway.

The organization was taking a second profit off the top of sales by "Billy" and "Victor" to Grosby, and in August, 1968, this angle was the key to a Customs investigation of its financial arrangements, spearheaded by the indefatigable team of Coyne and Seeley. Prominent in this picture was a Swiss businessman and former banker named André Hirsch, who had been arrested and held in prison for several months in a bank failure case in 1962, then released because of poor health without being brought to trial.

Months of dogged digging seemed to indicate that Hirsch was the brains behind the international smuggling ring of which the Grosbys, Wouters, *et al.* had been merely the dirty workers. Hirsch and Robert Spira, both of Geneva, had formed the Metos Corporation, registered in Panama and with headquarters in Geneva, to engage in various export enterprises. Metos had an account in a Swiss bank of which a man identified by Customs only as "Monsieur D'Argent" was an official. D'Argent had a business relationship with George Gero, an official of the First Hanover Corporation, a New York investment house.

Through D'Argent, Hirsch arranged for all monies collected in New York in the Metos name to be transferred back to the Metos account in the Swiss bank via the First Hanover Corporation. This was legal enough, but the Coyne-Seeley team learned that most of the Metos money was deposited in the First Hanover by a man named "Victor" —their old pal, Willie Wouters.

Monsieur D'Argent told a Customs man who interviewed him that all he knew about the transactions was their amounts. D'Argent from time to time notified George Gero that "Victor" would appear at First Hanover on a certain day and deliver a sum of money for transfer to the Metos account in the Swiss bank. Gero then used either the foreign section of the New York bank at which First Hanover had an account or a New York currency exchange to transfer the money to the Swiss bank. Frequently, the money was detoured through several other countries in order to take advantage of the fluctuating exchange rates and thus make a tidy profit on the transfer before the deposit reached the Swiss bank.

Meanwhile, Coyne and Seeley picked up evidence that because the organization had suffered a loss of close to $500,000 as a result of Customs' crackdown that summer, its leaders had abandoned the use of commercial airliners as a means of delivering its goods into the United States. Customs agents learned that there had been a series of meetings at Hirsch's home in Geneva at which changes in operations had presumably been discussed. At least one of these meetings was graced by the presence of one Louis Brique, also known as La Brique, who was suspected of being the operating head of the syndicate. One report was that in a twelve-month period Brique had received from Hirsch $600,000 as his share of the take.

With the organization apparently about to come up with a new smuggling gimmick, Coyne and Seeley wanted to know more about the way André Hirsch and Robert Spira ran Metos. Even if they could not connect the pair with the illicit drug traffic, they might be able to uncover evidence of unlawful manipulations in the money market. They turned their attention to George Gero of First Hanover Corporation.

Gero, it seemed, had traveled abroad on August 10 for a meeting with the Swiss bank's Monsieur D'Argent, ostensibly to advise D'Argent in reorganizing the bank's operations. Gero had questioned D'Argent about the source of the money he had brought D'Argent from New York. D'Argent assured Gero that there was nothing fishy; the money came from Nigerian pounds bought in Switzerland from politicians who had smuggled them out of Nigeria. The pounds, said D'Argent, then were flown to New York and sold there for American dollars at a profit. D'Argent said he had never met "Victor," that all the arrangements were made by either Hirsch or Spira. D'Argent also claimed that Hirsch and Spira had been dealing in money transfers for years, in annual amounts of $50,000 to $100,000. Coyne and Seeley knew that such money transfers also were used by Swiss watch smugglers, who must sell at one price and invoice at another, after which their money must be delivered to them abroad.

Besides his alleged involvement in the 1962 Swiss bank failure, Hirsch was known to authorities abroad as a possible smuggler and money manipulator, but there was no hard evidence against him. Spira's reputation was described in every report reaching the Coyne-Seeley desk as "unsavory."

Monsieur D'Argent already was in what could turn out to be trouble. Two years before, he had been named by United States Attorney Robert M. Morgenthau of New York as one of six persons being sought for the service of grand jury subpoenas concerning Swiss bank manipulations and/or as associates of persons involved in racketeering and smuggling. At that time, D'Argent was believed to be a representative of the Cambio Advalorem Bank in Zurich, and Coyne and Seeley learned that he later was discharged by the bank for "questionable operations." He had bought into another bank in May, 1968, and in October of that year he had finally agreed to accept subpoena in New York.

Thus, in their efforts to fill in the outline of the heroin-smuggling syndicate with some plausible faces, Coyne and Seeley had reason to believe they were not pursuing shadows. D'Argent might be merely an overly casual banker, but Hirsch seemed to be the stuff of which big-money smuggling enterprises were made. They could bide their time, if impatiently, waiting for the organization to make its next move.

Five months later, on December 13, Coyne and Seeley learned through an informant that:

"1. Hirsch had ordered a special tin sealing machine which was delivered on 12/5/68.

"2. Hirsch and/or his associates would use this machine to open and reseal cans of Spanish foodstuffs, 16 centimeters by 6 centimeters. The food would be removed, replaced with heroin, and the cans exported to the U.S."

Seeley and Coyne then checked on importers of this type of foodstuffs and discovered a brand-new entry in the field: Panamanian Chemist and Food Products, Inc., 87-65 153d Street, Jamaica, New York. The company had imported 100 cartons of canned Spanish foodstuffs on November 19, 1968, with a value of $883.60. They asked to be alerted concerning any future shipments to this importer.

The 153d Street address in Jamaica turned out to be a private dwelling; Panamanian Chemist and Food Products had moved to another private residence at 157-24 22d Avenue, Whitestone, Queens. Agents found the address located in "an excellent residential area" and consisting of a two-story dwelling with a built-in garage. A sign on the front lawn bore the company's name. Although the "excellence" of the neighborhood was far from ideal for gumshoeing operations, a twenty-four-hour surveillance nevertheless was put on the house.

Meanwhile, Coyne and Seeley had been alerted by the American Embassy in Paris, via Washington, to be on the lookout for Christian

Hysohion, a French national, who had been issued a visa to travel to the United States. Hysohion was described as a "possible receiver of illicit drugs." A check of the files at the New York office of the Immigration and Naturalization Service located the entry form filled out by Hysohion on his arrival in New York via Geneva on September 22, 1968. Hysohion had a B-1 (businessman's) visa valid until October 10, 1968, but had applied to extend his stay in the country on October 9. The application said Hysohion was a supermarket owner who had come to America to study its marketing system and that he needed more time to complete his study.

Hysohion gave as his address the house of Charles Darge at 87-65 153d Street, Jamaica, the original location of Panamanian Chemist and Food. As expected, Hysohion now was discovered to be living, with Darge, at the company's new address.

At about this same time, a phone call from the New York Customhouse informed the team that 100 cartons of Paella Marinera (Spanish rice and shellfish) had been listed on a Customs entry and were awaiting clearance. The food was in cans measuring about 16 centimeters by 6 centimeters and had been imported by Panamanian Chemist and Food from Málaga, Spain, where the Hirsch organization was known to have "business interests."

A spectroscope examination of the shipment by Customs agents proved negative for drugs. But the finding was not unexpected. From experience, Customs people had learned that the first two or three shipments by exporters suspected of involvement in the illicit drug traffic almost always were clean in order to lull suspicion about subsequent shipments. They also learned that the canning machinery ordered by Hirsch for delivery on December 5 would not now be delivered until about December 16. The paella shipment had arrived in New York on the SS *Kalliope* on December 12.

The Hirsch crowd was buying assorted Spanish victuals, in cans, from Ribas y Hijos S. A. in Vigo, Spain, for delivery to a Panamanian Chemist and Food representative at an unknown Spanish port, and forwarding the stuff to New York on cargo ships of the Fresco Shipping Company, a Spanish line. The forwarder's job, it was discovered later, was to open some of the cans with the dandy little machine acquired by Hirsch, substitute heroin for the paella, add a chunk of lead to give the cans the proper weight, then reseal and commingle them with the legitimate merchandise.

Agents assigned to watch the house in Whitestone, Queens, had to be replaced every two or three days because curious residents were inclined to ask embarrassing questions. Fortunately for Customs, a prolonged longshoremen's strike that shut down New York's harbor intervened. Obviously, the businessmen at Panamanian Chemist and Food would stay put to wait for the expected shipments of heroin which Coyne and Seeley now had every reason to believe were on the high seas. So it was not until early February, 1969, that a court order was obtained to monitor the company's telephone line.

The SS *Ragunda*, one of the Fresco line's ships, arrived in New York on February 20. Unloading of the vessel was delayed for two weeks because of the strike, but when it finally was unloaded, Customs agents located on the pier a shipment of 714 cases of paella for Panamanian Chemist and Food. During the dark early-morning hours, when no one but cooperating guards were about, the agents used fluoroscopic equipment to determine that many of the cases contained heroin. Later, a code painted on the cases made their job easier. One of the cases containing heroin was removed from the shipment, and four days later the remaining 713 cases were picked up by rented truck and transported to the house in Queens, with Customs men in discreet pursuit.

At the house, agents watched Christian Hysohion help the truckdriver and his partner unload the truck and stack the cases in the small garage. Two days later, at precisely 5:30 A.M. on March 9, a man who later would be identified as Edward Louis Rimbaud, a French national, knocked on the front door and was admitted by Hysohion. Both men emerged shortly thereafter, Hysohion lugging a large simulated leather bag, and stepped into a cab that had just drawn up in front of the house.

The lawmen knew where the cab was heading. One of the agents monitoring Hysohion's telephone line had heard him call the cab the moment Rimbaud arrived and tell the dispatcher he was going to Grand Central Terminal. Two carloads of agents took off in pursuit of the cab. Whether the men suspected they were being followed or were merely nervous, they forced the cabdriver to keep a heavy foot on the accelerator, and as the cab turned onto Grand Central Parkway, it was traveling at a heart-grabbing 75 miles an hour.

Their trailers had hoped Hysohion and Rimbaud would lead them to other members of the ring, perhaps even to one of its higher-ups. But now the agents were in danger of losing the two men; playing it cute had become too risky. So they joined in the race, and after more than five nerve-racking miles to near-collisions with cars carrying bleary-eyed New Yorkers to or from their jobs, they finally forced the cab to the curb and took Hysohion and Rimbaud into custody. The simulated leather bag was found to contain 62 pounds of pure heroin, with a street value of more than $6,000,000.

Three days later, the second and final shipment of paella arrived on another Fresco Lines ship and yielded 53 pounds of pure heroin, worth more than $5,000,000 on the addict level. Had the syndicate succeeded in processing the two shipments through illicit sales channels, the contraband would have provided each of New York City's estimated 50,000 heroin addicts in 1969 with at least twenty shots of the drug.

The next few months were filled with furious activity by hordes of lawmen in the United States and on the European continent, working in the labyrinth of a many-sided international conspiracy.

In America, Hysohion and Rimbaud were hit with the book; each drew twenty years in prison for smuggling narcotics and ten years for conspiracy to do so. Jean Marc Montoya, who had told the TWA clerk he'd left his glasses on a TWA flight and then retrieved a cache of heroin in the plane's lavatory, got eight years. Mitnik, the house painter, got seven years.

Willie Wouters, the first courier arrested, agreed to turn state's evidence and began a new life in which he spent several hours a day talking to a tape recorder. Jack Grosby, Wouters' receiver and sometime syndicate bagman, jumped bail and disappeared for several months. Swiss police finally picked him up in Geneva, and he was returned to the United States, where he, too, was persuaded to cooperate with Customs investigators.

In Switzerland, the banker André Hirsch drew a six-year prison sentence and a 20,000-franc fine; Louis Brique and Daniel Roger Vuille Dit Bille each got four years and were fined 20,000 francs. One Gilbert Grandi was sentenced to 15 months in the pen and fined 2,000 francs; Grandi's appeal was rejected.

Back in the United States, Nellie Alves, Jack Grosby's common-law wife, was released after questioning, and so were Charles Darge, with whom Hysohion lived at the Panamanian Chemist and Food "office," and Mayo Mastronardi, landlord of the premises. George Gero of First Hanover Corporation, who cooperated fully with the authorities, drew Customs' formal thanks for his help. Swiss police questioned the Swiss bank's Monsieur D'Argent but gave him a clean bill of health.

Meanwhile, Spanish police picked up Eugene Castaldi, whom they identified as the freight forwarder who had arranged shipments of the adulterated paella to New York. French authorities nabbed Louis Bonsignour, alias Philippe Spadaro, who had recruited Jack Grosby in Rio de Janeiro. An Italian narcotics squad took into custody Ametto Milazzo, described as a courier.

The Bureau of Customs, as represented by Agents Edward T. Coyne and Albert Seeley, was even credited with an assist by New York's United States Attorney Morgenthau, who had named Monsieur D'Argent among a select group of people he wanted to talk to about Swiss bank manipulations. When D'Argent agreed to accept service of a subpoena in New York, he told Morgenthau he had done so at the Coyne-Seeley team's request. Although D'Argent was questioned by Morgenthau, no action was taken against him and he was permitted to return to Switzerland.

Ed Coyne and Al Seeley were glad to be of assistance. After all, it was Monsieur D'Argent who had shown them André Hirsch's bank records. And those records played a big part in a ball game which, besides ending in a victory for Customs, prompted its sleuths for the first time to turn their attention to the activities of a major smuggling syndicate in South America. To the names Jack Grosby and Louis Bonsignour, alias Philippe Spadaro, Customs agents soon were able to add that of Auguste Ricord, czar of the Latin American ring.

# PAN-AMERICAN
# UNION

# 7

# El Comandante

Addressed to the Secretary of State, Washington, D.C., the "Limited Official Use" cablegram from the American Embassy in Paris was dated March 8, 1967, and marked PRIORITY. The cablegram was for transmission to the U.S. Customs Bureau, whose New York field office had inquired about the activities of Paul Chastagnier, a Paris exporter suspected of dealing in junk. It read:

"Chastagnier contacted the Centrade Company at Annecy, France, to ask about his order of oscilloscopes for the U.S. He asked to be notified as soon as the intermediary receives them. It is learned that Chastagnier has placed three orders for oscilloscopes from the Centrade Company, two this month, one for 12 oscilloscopes and one for 10 oscilloscopes, and an order next month for 25 oscilloscopes.

"It seems that Chastagnier still owes $1,775 for a previous delivery. Price quoted in U.S. dollars. Chastagnier told Centrade Company that they could 'square that account with the house at New York.'

"Seems this delivery will be made 3/13. French police and Customs want to make seizure at France, stating that due to information they now possess they will be able to arrest all suspects involved in French phase this investigation. Every effort being made by this office to allow delivery or part to reach U.S. in order to implicate receivers."

Chastagnier was a French wheeler dealer who had been convicted in the United States of counterfeiting some years before. Posing as an export agent, he had ordered from the Annecy company 500 oscilloscopes, boxlike instruments about 14 inches long by 7 inches wide and 4 inches high that electronically detect changes in electric voltage in waves on a cathode tube. The oscilloscopes were shipped in small lots of six or a dozen to Paris, where Chastagnier and his fellow conspirators removed the transformer and ripped out the wiring, then fitted the gaping innards of each instrument with a package containing one kilo of heroin.

Suspicion did not fall on Chastagnier until two shipments of the horse-carrying oscilloscopes had already arrived safely at the New York office of his New York "principal," Foreign Trade Representations, in December, 1966. There Customs agents, working with the French Sûreté, dug up evidence that Chastagnier was involved in the dope racket, as well as learning that the New York principal was so small it did business only with Chastagnier.

Thus it was deemed urgent police strategy to let Chastagnier make at least one more shipment to New York in order to lay hands not only on him but on his receiver. Customs' New York office was especially interested in learning whether the heroin was intended for wholesalers connected with the so-called Corsican Organization, which had a near-monopoly on heroin distribution in the eastern United States.

French authorities agreed to let part of the shipment through, and on March 21 a parcel containing six oscilloscopes arrived at Kennedy International Airport on Air France Flight 015. Prudently, the parcel was accompanied by Émile Angeles, National Commissioner Principal of the Sûreté. It was addressed, as usual, to Foreign Trade Representations, Export Managers, 90 West Street, New York, N.Y.

Customs agent Adam J. Olszewski directed removal of the package from the plane to a private Customs office in the International Arrivals Building. There, agents unscrewed the sides, tops and bottoms of the devices and found in each of them two plastic bags whose white powdery contents tested positive for heroin. Baking soda was substituted for some of the heroin, the oscilloscopes were replaced in the package, the package sealed, and then forwarded to the Air France cargo terminal to await instructions from the consignee for delivery.

The next day, Customs was informed that the Sûreté was about to announce to the press the seizure of six kilograms of heroin from "the Chastagnier group" in Paris. So Agent Olszewski phoned Air France and asked that the package be released forthwith to Airport Clearance Service at Kennedy Airport, the customhouse broker used by Foreign Trade Representations for previous deliveries. Delivery was made early that afternoon to the West Street address.

FTR's export manager, George Varsa, took delivery and signed for the oscilloscopes while Customs agents under Olszewski lurked in an office across the hall. While the lawmen waited for the ultimate receiver to arrive or for Varsa to make a move, a man left the FTR office and stepped into an elevator to descend to the street.

Olszewski did some quick thinking. He decided the man could be carrying some of the heroin concealed on his person, for enough time had passed since the delivery to dismantle some of the oscilloscopes. He radioed to agents in the street to follow the man but to make no move to arrest him unless or until he met someone they suspected was a contact. Two agents accordingly tailed the man on foot from West Street to the vicinity of Trinity Church near Wall Street and Broadway—a distance of about a mile. Then the suspect suddenly broke into a run, and there was a chase of more than a half mile before the agents collared him as he was about to enter a subway station. They frisked him but found no heroin.

Meanwhile, Varsa received a telephone call from a French newspaper correspondent who asked him what he knew about the arrest a few hours earlier of Paul Chastagnier at Orly Airport in Paris. Chastagnier, Varsa was told, was caught with six oscilloscopes packed with six kilos of heroin, which he was about to ship to New York by airfreight.

Varsa hung up on his caller, grabbed his coat and hat, and fled via a back door leading to the staircase. He was taken into custody in an alleyway by Customs agents who were part of a stakeout surrounding the building.

Having been collared in his attempt to escape, Varsa had some swift second thoughts about life, especially his own. Within a few hours he had agreed to "cooperate"—a term the authors of all law enforcement documents prefer to the more positive "squeal" in order to spare the feelings of the world's George Varsas. And indeed, Varsa "cooperated" so well that he was soon released on $5,000 bond and was still free more than five years later, in the spring of 1972. Meanwhile, he had told some important things about the activities of assorted individuals suspected by narcotics lawmen of being involved in the big-time dope trade. The oscilloscope case had not been an important bust for Customs. But Varsa's talking made it important.

As the agents went about their pursuit and investigation of other assorted leads and suspects, they made another informative arrest. They nabbed a Frenchman from Argentina with a familiar name— Louis Bonsignour, alias Philippe Spadaro. Bonsignour was indicted as an accomplice in the oscilloscope case in May, 1967, and promptly jumped bail of $50,000, but not until Customs had unearthed some interesting information about Bonsignour's blood lines.

Specifically, the agents learned that Bonsignour was a nephew of El Comandante, *nom de guerre* of the general manager of Grupo Francés, the Corsican syndicate which operated the dope-smuggling racket in South America. For the first time, the sobriquet El Commandante, employed by a professional rascal named Auguste Joseph Ricord, was entered into the bureau's official reports on its investigation of what at that time was known as the Chilean Conspiracy. It was also noted that Jack Grosby, alias Jacob Grodnitzky, engaged a lawyer for Bonsignour and helped him raise bail. A year later Grosby was involved in the notorious conspiracy, reaching into the staid atmosphere of a Swiss bank, to smuggle heroin into the United States in cans of Spanish seafood.

But for the moment, the pinpointing of the name Auguste Ricord as a man with wide dope-smuggling interests, reaching from Europe to South America and up into the United States, overshadowed all other developments.

Auguste Joseph Ricord obviously was well cast for the role as Rascal No. 1. Born in Marseilles, he was only sixteen years old when he was convicted in 1927 of theft and extortion. He went on to become a pimp, always avoiding prosecution for that trade, but meanwhile picking up convictions for carrying prohibited weapons and "assault and insults." In the latter case, an Interpol report noted that he was "released on orders of the legal authorities of the Federal Republic of Germany" in Paris. That went without saying: Ricord at the time was serving the Nazi occupiers as informant and general dirty-work man.

Shortly before the liberation of Paris, Ricord fled to Italy and subsequently took refuge in Argentina. He operated several restaurants in Buenos Aires but derived most of his income from the white slave traffic. He was an habitué of the French Union of Veterans, which Interpol described as a "refuge for international criminals." Meanwhile, in 1951, he was sentenced to twenty years' hard labor and ten years' local banishment, in absentia, by the Court of Assize of Burc-et-Loire for aggravated theft. He was arrested by Argentine police in 1957 for corruption and illegal association, but took refuge in Uruguay. In October, 1958, he was in Caracas, Venezuela, operating a prostitution syndicate from a cabaret, Le Domino. One of his collaborators in the drug racket was said by Interpol to be Christian David, "wanted for the murder of Commissaire Principal Gallibert in

Paris." In short, it was inevitable that Ricord should come to the attention of authorities trying to stem the flood of illicit drugs into the United States. He was almost too bad to be true.

But although Ricord's activities were watched more or less closely by lawmen in Argentina, Chile and Paraguay—the three countries in which he was most frequently seen—he managed to keep his nose clean. Meanwhile, almost every smuggling case developed by U.S. Customs seemed to bear the unmistakable hallmark of El Comandante's shrewd and tightly knit operation.

The operations of the Ricord syndicate during the period from December, 1969, to March, 1970, were reflected in a report to Commissioner of Customs Myles J. Ambrose by Senior Special Agent Albert Seeley. The report estimated that 203 kilograms of heroin and cocaine had been smuggled into the United States through South America in that three-month period and that various law enforcement agencies had seized only 37 kilograms of this lot.

"Extensive investigation," said the report, "indicates that the members of this international smuggling organization are well-entrenched in their narcotic trafficking" in South America, Mexico and Europe. "They are unique in that they seem to have gained access to a steady source of supply of both cocaine from South America and pure heroin from Europe [which] they are able to dispatch . . . directly into the U.S. from Argentina or Chile. In addition, Mexico City is being utilized as a base to and from Europe."

One of the shipments thus dispatched directly into the United States was carried in by a "mule," or courier, named Arsenio Augusto Araya Murchio, thirty-one, a Chilean national living in Argentina. Customs records depose that "the exposure of this international narcotic trafficking" began with Araya's arrest on December 8, 1969, at the International Arrivals Building of Kennedy International Airport in New York.

In the course of their grinding, day-to-day routine of observing arriving passengers at the airport, Special Agents E. Meade Feild and Donald L. Willey had noted casually that some of the passengers' carry-on luggage included jugs of South American wine. This was not unusual; most international travelers bring in alcoholic potables. But most of the jug carriers were Latin Americans, who might have been expected to invest in whiskey and other liquors which were more expensive in New York than in duty-free airport shops.

Accordingly, when Araya approached the Customs examination

belt, Feild and Willey found themselves wondering about the two big wicker-covered bottles of wine protruding from one of Araya's two pieces of luggage—a zippered satchel. When Inspector Emile Dolce completed his examination of Araya's identification documents, Feild and Willey asked Araya to accompany them into a nearby conference room.

"You got anything else to declare to Customs?" asked Feild.

"No, nothing," replied Araya. "I have only clothing and wine."

Willey was examining Araya's passport. "I see you entered the United States last November thirteenth and returned to Argentina on November twenty-sixth," he told Araya. "How come you're back again—two weeks later?"

Araya's reply may have reflected a world's record for errand running. "Both times I come to buy medicine for my wife, who is sick in Argentina," he said. "Tomorrow I go back to Argentina."

The agents decided to have a look at the wine jugs. Feild used a wire probe to penetrate the cork and discovered that the probe struck an obstacle after going only about three inches deep, although the jug was twelve inches high. He cut away the wicker covering and found a seam in the jug about three-quarters of the way from its bottom. Then he inserted a knife into the seam, pried it open and found what he was looking for—what a field test showed was three kilograms of heroin secreted below a glass separator. The other jug revealed another three-kilogram cache, concealed in the same fashion. The smugglers had cut the jugs in two, painted the inside of the lower, larger section with wine-colored paint, stashed the heroin in that section, and then sealed the glass separator into place and molded the jug together again to accommodate a small quantity of wine in the upper section.

Araya's story was a familiar cliché protesting innocence. He said the two wine jugs had been given him by a man he knew, but not by name, and that this anonymous one had written the name of a hotel on his airline ticket and told Araya "someone" would call at the hotel to relieve him of the jugs. "I know nothing of drugs," Araya insisted. "I know only about wine."

Escorted to the Customs office at 201 Varick Street in Manhattan, Araya was given a chance to prove his innocence and good faith. Senior Special Agent Seeley, after assuring Araya of his rights in both English and, through an interpreter, in Spanish, persuaded him to cooperate with the law. Seeley accompanied Araya to the Carriage House Hotel on East 38th Street to await the arrival of the receiver.

It was no deal; the receiver never showed up. Obviously, he had been on hand at the airport, as was customary in smuggling attempts, and had seen Feild and Willey stop Araya and lead him away. He probably also had stuck around long enough to see Araya being escorted out of the terminal, under arrest. This surmise was bolstered by a report from an undercover agent, who said he had seen one Pedro Fernández strolling about the terminal at about the time Araya was taken into custody. Customs knew Fernández had done some business with Louis Bonsignour, nephew of Auguste Ricord, but lacked the admissible evidence to prove it in court.

At any rate, Fernández' presence at the airport was a touch too timely to be dismissed as mere coincidence. Seeley, Willey and Feild were convinced Araya was a Ricord mule. They pursued their investigation, including chats with sometime informers, on this assumption, while Araya was shipped off to jail and eventually, on April 10, 1970, sentenced to a fifteen-year prison term for illegal possession of heroin.

For Customs, it was a long haul from the day in March, 1967, when the State Department received that cablegram from the Paris Embassy on Paul Chastagnier's oscilloscope shipments. Ricord still went about his assorted business enterprises, including operation of the restaurant Paris-Niza on the outskirts of Asunción, the capital city of Paraguay, and although he traveled a good deal to various South American cities, his errands remained clouded in mystery. He was never seen publicly with any individual known unfavorably to any law enforcement agency in either South America or the United States, although some of his associates were not people whom a fastidious man would invite to his home.

As a police official in Chile put it: "But what would you? If the American police were to arrest every businessman who plays with bad companions you would have to build many new prisons."

Possibly. But Auguste Ricord was not to be compared with the American businessman who might while away a few hours with a feminine ball of fluff or dally with the boys at an all-night crap game sponsored by men with criminal records. Customs people were convinced Ricord was the kingpin of the biggest South American narcotics-smuggling ring, and they kept digging in the hope that they could establish a pattern of names, places, dates and various to-ings and fro-ings that would put him where they wanted him.

In New York, Special Agent E. Meade Feild would hear the name Miguel Leal Galindo in the course of the questioning of a suspect by a colleague, and would recall an informant's remark that he had once worked on a Chilean merchant ship with "Mike Galindo." In Miami, Assistant Special Agent in Charge Stan Schachter had been saving the name Yolanda Sarmiento for several months; Yolanda reportedly was doing a lot of traveling between Santiago and Panama City. In Washington, Senior Special Agent Doug McCombs, modishly dressed and tonsured, was having suspicious thoughts about another inveterate traveler, a soldier-of-fortune airplane pilot named César Bianchi, who operated out of Argentina. The people to whom these names belonged all were strongly presumed to be hirelings of Auguste Ricord, but although the outlines of a pattern were emerging, Customs could do nothing about those people until they surfaced.

Nevertheless, under constant prodding from Commissioner Ambrose, Customs men continued to uncover bits and pieces about the South American Conspiracy, and among these bits and pieces was a big chunk provided by a police squad's four arrests in New York City on April 15, 1970. Those arrested, on charges of possession of 100 kilos of heroin seized in Apartment 4F at 210 West 19th Street, Manhattan, indisputably were members of the syndicate operated by Auguste Ricord.

They were: Yolanda Sarmiento, an Argentinian, identified as ring leader of the operation; and three Spanish nationals, Emilio Díaz-Gonzales, Yolanda's lover; Juan Redondo-Pedrazas; and Juan Aparicio-Mulas.

Their arrests, put together with evidence extracted from informants and investigations throughout the United States and in certain South American cities, revealed Ricord, the former Nazi collaborator, as an organizational genius.

This was the picture, as painted brush mark by brush mark by the Customs investigation:

As a protégé of Ricord, Yolanda Sarmiento set up shop as a dope smuggler in Santiago, Chile, in about 1967, taking in Díaz as a junior partner and common-law husband. The team made shipments of heroin and/or cocaine in lots of 150–200 kilograms every thirty or forty days with the connivance of certain crew members of an airline in Panama. Also involved was a Panamanian exporting firm with an affiliate doing business at a prestigious Fifth Avenue address in Manhattan. The New York receiver was a Spaniard who operated a bar and grill on West 23d Street.

About two years later Yolanda Sarmiento met Pedrazas in a radio and television shop in Colón, Panama, and recruited him as her "moneyman." That is to say, Pedrazas' job was to collect all proceeds from narcotics deliveries in New York and then change the smaller bills into currency of larger denominations for transmission to Yolanda through various banks and currency exchanges.

Pedrazas opened checking account No. 10477443 on April, 1969, at the main office of the First National City Bank at 399 Park Avenue, New York. As a reference, he gave the bank the name of a beauty parlor, Basil and Anita, located on West 23d Street, because the proprietors were friends of Yolanda. Carmen Ramos of the beauty parlor was the lessee of record of the West 19th Street apartment where the 100 kilos of heroin were seized. Pedrazas deposited the one- and five-dollar bills from narcotics sales in his checking account, then a few days later withdrew large amounts of cash in bills of higher denominations, which he turned over to Yolanda and Díaz.

From time to time, Yolanda and Díaz entrusted large sums of money—all running to six figures—to Pedrazas, for delivery to a Frenchman named "Marcel" in Europe. Customs agents were able to pinpoint two such deliveries, both of them amounting to $200,000, to "Marcel." The first delivery was made in Marseilles sometime in 1969. Pedrazas, with the cash in his trouser and coat pockets, flew from New York to Buenos Aires, thence to Madrid and finally to Marseilles, via Majorca. The second delivery was made in 1970, in Madrid; that time Pedrazas flew direct to his rendezvous with "Marcel."

Shortly, "Marcel" was identified as the Sarmiento-Díaz team's principal source of heroin. The horse was smuggled into various South American ports, where delivery was taken by assorted agents of Ricord's Grupo Francés. From South America, it was flown into Panama's Free Zone by the Panamanian airline and then delivered to Miami and New York receivers by courier. The airline, it was learned, was doing a good business smuggling electronic equipment, including radios and television sets, into Santiago, Chile.

More digging enabled Customs agents to identify the go-between in the Sarmiento-Díaz team's dealings with the receiver as a blond American male of about forty-five, but that was all they knew about him. However, with the help of New York police, they did manage to learn that Yolanda had furnished this man with a key to the West 19th Street apartment and that deliveries and payments apparently were made there. Depending on the state of the market, Yolanda and Díaz collected $10,000 to $12,000 per kilo for their heroin and

$9,000 a kilo for cocaine. Pedrazas got between two and three thousand dollars per deal, plus expenses for his extensive travels.

The Sarmiento-Díaz-Pedrazas relationship was cozy. Because the three spent most of their time in Argentina, traveling to New York or Miami only when a delivery was to be made, they mostly lived and worked as a family.

When the 100 kilos of heroin arrived at the West 19th Street address in New York, for example, Yolanda and Díaz met Pedrazas in Miami and they headed for New York by car. In New York, Yolanda bought some groceries, and they recrossed the Hudson River into New Jersey, where they drove to a motel. Mother Yolanda registered for herself, her lover and Pedrazas, and then—after Yolanda and Díaz installed themselves in one room and Pedrazas in another—the squat, portly Yolanda cooked dinner. They were drinking coffee when the New York police busted in and performed a wholesale frisking. The three were arrested when the cops found the key to the West 19th Street apartment in Yolanda's purse; the other man, Aparicio, was picked up later.

Back in South America, U.S. agents learned that Díaz' first common-law wife, who had set up housekeeping with him in Madrid when she was just past her twelfth birthday, took a dim view of her former mate's love life with Yolanda. They persuaded authorities in Buenos Aires, where Visitación Soria de Díaz lived with her mother-in-law and two sons, to invite the lady in for a gossip session.

The señora talked freely, her tones bitter with the fury of a woman scorned. She and Díaz, she said, had moved from Madrid to Buenos Aires with their two boys in 1958. Three years later, Díaz went to Chile on business and remained there for five years, living in a common-law union with Yolanda Sarmiento. When Visitación descended upon the couple in their Santiago apartment, she discovered that they were engaged in the dope-smuggling racket, and flounced back to Buenos Aires.

There, a few days later, Díaz rejoined her and promised to love and cherish her forever if she took him back. There was a reconciliation, and Señor and Señora Díaz spent the next few years traveling in Chile and Panama with various accomplices of Díaz *père*, including a couple of pickpockets who had turned to dope trafficking. The two broke up again a few years later, but not until Visitación had learned something that Customs headquarters in Washington found of more than ordinary interest.

Díaz, according to Visitación, had mentioned to her that he and

Yolanda were partners in a lucrative enterprise headed by a man he first referred to as El Tío (the uncle) or Oscar. One night, however, Díaz had a few too many drinks and let drop the name Ricord. Questioned by Visitación, Díaz would only say that Ricord was a man of great importance and that Visitación should be proud that her two sons had been sired by a father who had business associations with an individual of such great power and wealth.

Possibly, Visitación did nourish a secret pride in her man's lofty status. But as a woman who had talked perhaps too much to the cops, she must have suffered mixed feelings over the next development in the law's case against Sarmiento, Díaz, *et al.*

Yolanda was released on $100,000 bond. Forthwith, Yolanda jumped bail, returning to Argentina on an aircraft of the Panamanian airline, some of whose crew members had been mentioned in official reports on the smuggling mob. Díaz was left in his cell in the Federal House of Detention to await trial, but escaped several months later.

The virtually anonymous Aparicio, who seems to have been an all-around handyman for the gang, was deported to Spain by the U.S. Immigration and Naturalization Service even as Customs was gathering evidence charging him with using false documents to enter the country. Pedrazas was another package of goods. He was indicted on four smuggling counts, but the charges were dismissed, and Customs had to be satisfied with sending him up for illegally entering the country—a painless slap on the wrist.

On the whole, however, the people at Commissioner Myles Ambrose's shop added the case up to a plus for their side. Their investigation, nourished by intelligence obtained after the arrests of the Sarmiento-Díaz gang, had led them to Auguste Ricord's trail, and they had discovered a new and major heroin-smuggling route, opened up from the previously casual south while they had been watching Europe. Knowing this, they believed they could do something about it—perhaps even arrange to put Mr. Big in jail.

# 8
# The Big Bust

As Washington headquarters expected, business picked up in what Senior Special Agent Bill Knierim called the Rat-Catching Department as a result of the information put together on the South American Conspiracy after the arrests in April, 1970, of the Sarmiento-Díaz group. Beginning in June of that year, arrests and dope seizures tripled in number and size, and to Customs' intelligence agents, now familiar with the Auguste Ricord organization, almost every case bore the Ricord hallmark and thus added to Customs' knowledge of the operation.

Some of the cases merited special attention because they were developed as the direct result of investigations based on the contents of intelligence files. All suggested that Customs could be coming closer to a showdown at law with the elusive Ricord.

There was the arrest on June 12 at New York's Kennedy International Airport of a twenty-four-year-old Chilean male who wore a woman's black girdle with pockets found to contain five packages of cocaine totaling almost 10 pounds. In Santiago, the man was identified as a known "associate" of one of Ricord's controllers. On June 20 Customs men nabbed two more Chileans disembarking from a Chilean cargo ship in Baltimore with 4½ pounds of cocaine. On July 1, the same agents picked up a man and two women, all Chileans, at Friendship International Airport in Baltimore and seized a blue and white airline bag containing 3 kilograms of cocaine. The agents also confiscated the key to a safe-deposit box at the First National City Bank in New York in which they found $60,000 in cash. Serial numbers showed that some of this money had passed through the Ricord organization. On August 8, a Brazilian was arrested at Kennedy Airport with a kilo of cocaine contained in the woman's girdle he wore, and on August 30 Customs people nabbed an Argentine courier with 2 kilos of cocaine. The names of both men were on a "lookout list" furnished by Argentine authorities engaged in an investigation of Ricord's activities. Thirteen pounds of cocaine were seized on a Chilean ship in Baltimore, and six days later Customs picked up three seamen whose names also appeared on the Argentine list. Obviously, Ricord's operation was big business.

By this time Customs agents in Miami and New York had some bigger names to tuck away in the Ricord file. From their own investigations and from information pried out of an assortment of South American lawmen and informants, they were able to sketch an outline of Ricord's table of organization.

Accurately, as it later developed, the table named one Enio Aníbal Varela-Segovia and one Juan de Dios Rodríguez, also known as Aaron Muravnik, as Ricord's top lieutenants in Paraguay. Felix Becker, who had spent most of his thirty-seven years dealing in contraband, was fingered as the contact between Varela-Segovia and Rodríguez and lower-level couriers, and as a sometime Ricord bagman. One report was that Becker made periodic trips from Paraguay to New York to pick up proceeds from heroin deliveries and to carry the money back to Ricord in Asunción. In any case, all three men had been seen in Ricord's company in various places in Asunción, including the international airport, where Ricord seemed to spend a great deal of his time.

Day by day, as the digging proceeded, more information flowed into Customs' secret intelligence hoard. But what the bureau needed was the one big case that would crack the Ricord conspiracy wide open, and in October, 1970, the exhausting and time-consuming labors of its sleuths produced that break. It was triggered by the arrest of a thirty-four-year-old bandit pilot from Paraguay, César Bianchi.

Customs had established to its own satisfaction that the Grupo Francés had taken over a ready-made means of smuggling French heroin into the United States. This was the well-organized fleet of light planes operated by daredevil Latin soldiers of fortune which fast-buck South American merchants had been using for more than twenty years to smuggle American whiskey, radio and television sets, cigarettes and clothing into the continent south of the border. Grupo Francés ambassadors asked the obvious question: "Why fly the planes to the United States empty?" And money talked; there was immeasurably more profit in smuggling heroin north than in smuggling TV sets south.

Accordingly, by 1970 the *contrabandistas* had been absorbed into the Ricord organization. On schedules as rigid as those of commercial airlines, the light planes were operating out of bush airfields in Paraguay and other Latin American states, and even from private airstrips on the ranches of rich and powerful landowners.

With this intelligence at hand, Customs launched a concentrated effort in the Miami area and in the waters of the near Caribbean, using its new fleet of fast boats and planes. Some good hits were made, confirming the bureau's intelligence reports. Then the Rat Catchers got an assist out of the blue.

On October 2, a cablegram from the State Department to the American Embassy in Panama advised that the Federal Bureau of Investigation office in Miami had received an anonymous letter dated September 23. The letter reported that an airplane of Argentine registration LV-HOW or LV-HDW "brought cocaine from Chile to Miami about three weeks ago."

State's cablegram went on: "Follow-up by Customs indicates aircraft Argentine registration LV-HDW arrived Miami September 2. Crew consists of César Bianchi, Dayai Bianchi. Plane owned by Renato Balestra. Bianchi's address given as 369 N. E. 61st Street, Miami, Florida. Aircraft is white Cessna 210 single-engine high-wing. Has wide yellow stripes along fuselage with two black stripes bordering the yellow stripe. On September 28, 1970, LV-HDW left Miami for Panama via Kingston, Jamaica, carrying television sets, clothing, etc. Crew consisted of César Bianchi, Dayai Bianchi and Renato Balestra. Customs believes return of LV-HDW with contraband is imminent. Extensive BNDD-Customs surveillance will be attempted if information can be developed regarding the anticipated time of return and place of entry."

The letter to the FBI was a maze of names, dates, aircraft identifications and airfields to be "watched." It urged the FBI to "check OPA-Locka," an airfield in southern Florida, and Tocumen Airport in Panama, and mentioned the name of Joaquín Him, "working for aeronational civil or tower comptroller at Tocumen Airport." (Him, of course, was arrested in the Canal Zone in a major diplomatic incident.) The letter added: "Check at Belmar Hotel or Motel in Miami Beach the name of two Argentinian fellows." It also referred to one "Big Ed, connected with the Cosa Nostra which lives somewhere in New Jersey in a Holiday Inn."

To Customs, everything seemed to add up to a conclusion that the gang mentioned in the anonymous letter was something special. The names of its members and the description of their furious activities suggested to the Rat Catchers that if they could put the arm on someone like, say, César Bianchi, they would find the means of cracking down on the Grupo Francés. On September 28, Customs had established a twenty-four-hour surveillance of a number of airfields in Florida, looking for twenty-one suspect aircraft. Now the agents concentrated their watch on LV-HDW, the Cessna piloted by César Mendice Bianchi.

The Cessna 210, piloted this time by Balestra, touched down at the General Aircraft Center (GAC) at Miami International Airport with Bianchi as its only passenger on October 18. After parking the plane and clearing customs, they took a cab to Bianchi's former apartment, where they picked up a 1970 Ford Maverick which they drove to the Town Motel. Meanwhile, agents kept the plane under close surveillance.

Next day, the pair rented a second car and drove separately to North Perry Airport in Miramar, where they left the Maverick and immediately drove back to the General Aircraft Center at the international airport. Confident that they could prevent the plane from leaving the country, the agents permitted Bianchi and Balestra to take off; two Customs planes trailed the Cessna to the North Perry Airport. There, the pair got into the car they had left at the airport earlier and drove back to the GAC, where they returned the rented car.

"That's when we knew they knew we were on them," an agent recalled later.

The plane was safe on the ground; nothing had been removed from it but clothing and other personal effects. But then the agents lost Bianchi and Balestra, due, as a Customs report put it, "to the many evasive turns by Bianchi" as the pair sped off into the Miami highway maze.

As reinforcements took up the hunt for the pair, other agents searched the plane; they had delayed their search because they wanted to catch Bianchi and Balestra unloading contraband. After three hours of poking about, they found three suitcases secreted in a compartment near the plane's tail. In the suitcases were 93 pounds of 98 percent pure heroin, worth more than $9,000,000 on the street.

The next morning, agents checked a bank where they had learned Bianchi had an account. The check showed Bianchi had withdrawn $26,000 in cash only a half hour before. While the agents were in the bank, other agents finally had picked up Bianchi's trail and followed him closely to the Pan American Airways ticket counter at the airport, where they watched him buy a one-way ticket to Asunción. He was arrested on the spot and taken to the Customs office at the airport, where he was dutifully informed of his rights and where he quickly agreed to cooperate. He sent a squad of agents to the Georgian Hotel in Miami Beach, where Balestra was picked up. Balestra also agreed to cooperate.

Bianchi, a former racing driver, was cool and articulate. He took the agents with him on the roundabout route he had taken since he left Miami on September 28—a dizzy recital that almost lost his audience.

From Miami, he and Balestra had flown to Kingston, thence to Panama, to Guayaquil, Ecuador, to Lima, and to Antofagasta, Chile. From Antofagasta the pair flew to Asunción, took off again two days later, and eventually landed on a dirt road just north of General Paz, Argentina. There, the narcotics were loaded on the plane by a person unknown to either men. Then they flew back to Asunción and thence to Arica, Chile, and back to a large cattle ranch in Paraguay. This was on October 9. Balestra stayed two nights at the ranch. Bianchi was picked up by a Cessna 182 air taxi carrying a passenger named Enio Varela and returned to Asunción. Bianchi, Varela, and a man Bianchi described as Varela's bodyguard returned by car to the ranch on October 11, and stayed the night. The next morning, Varela and his bodyguard drove off in a car, and Bianchi took off in another air taxi for a "conference" at an unknown location with some people he didn't know. Bianchi returned to the ranch on October 14, and he and Balestra flew to Arica that day, then to Lima on October 15, to Guayaquil on October 16, and then to Panama, to Kingston, and, finally, to Miami on October 18.

"It seems to me," Harold Smith said later, "that the creeps were getting a little nervous."

At the time, however, Uncle Sam's men—Special Agents K. J. Wagner, R. J. Hopkins, Bob Perez—wanted Bianchi and Balestra to get down to cases; they were interested in members of the gang reachable on U.S. soil. Obligingly, Bianchi started talking in specifics. His receiver was Felix Becker at the Four Ambassadors Hotel.

With Customs men stage-managing the show, Bianchi phoned Becker, and Becker shortly arrived at the Georgian Hotel and picked up Bianchi. The two drove off, under careful surveillance, for a business conference. During the drive, Becker told Bianchi to meet him in New York for the delivery and instructed him to stay at one of a list of hotels.

Both the Bianchi-Balestra team and Becker checked out of their hotels the next morning to fly to New York. Bianchi and Balestra were in the casual custody of their new Customs friends on one flight. Becker, by now joined by a man later identified as Juan de Dios Rodríguez, also known as Aaron Muravnik, took a later flight, unobtrusively accompanied by two other agents. The Becker plane was met by agents of the New York office, who took over the job of tailing Becker and Rodríguez. With their Customs companions, Bianchi and Balestra checked into the Saint Regis Hotel; Becker and Rodríguez went to the Sheraton Motor Inn—in a cab driven by Special Agent Mario Sessa, incognito.

Now the Customs men started getting some action for their pains. About twenty minutes after registering at the Sheraton, Becker and Rodríguez took a cab to the New York Hilton, where they tried in vain to reach one Pierre Gahou, registered in Room 3456, a onetime steward aboard French ocean liners. Leaving the hotel, they met Gahou at the corner of Sixth Avenue and 53d Street, and the three went through the formalistic ritual practiced by their kind everywhere in the world. After many evasive expeditions, Gahou finally made contact with a tall, dark, husky, Latin-looking man, later identified as Nicholas Giannattasio of Buenos Aires.

For four more days, Gahou, Becker and Rodríguez walked around New York, going in and out of hotels, restaurants and bars, behaving generally like tourists. They even spent ten minutes in Madison Square Garden in an off moment during their eating and drinking rounds. Their only departure from their routine came on the afternoon of October 26, when Becker and Rodríguez emerged from the Sheraton Motor Inn, Becker carrying a large package. They went to an address at 106 West 32d Street and a half hour later emerged; this time Becker was carrying a different package and Rodríguez also had a parcel. They proceeded to the Mar Export Company at 10 West 30th Street and subsequently left that address, each carrying a still different, smaller package.

"These guys were driving us nuts," said Special Agent Frank De Santis. "All those goddamn packages. But we had to let them run us ragged because we wanted a big score."

De Santis and his pals hadn't much longer to wait. Shortly after noon on October 27, Becker and Rodríguez left the Sheraton Motor Inn accompanied by an unidentified man. As the agents took up the trail again, the man's description was phoned to Bianchi at the St. Regis. "That's Varela," said Bianchi. "Now things will happen."

It was the same Enio Varela who had picked up Bianchi on the Paraguayan cattle ranch in an air taxi on October 11. Customs investigators already had identified him as a prosperous and influential cigarette merchant of Asunción—full name Enio Aníbal Varela-Segovia.

Again, the suspects took up their wanderings—to the Market Diner, back to the Sheraton Motor Inn, to the Americana Hotel at 54th Street and Seventh Avenue, back once more to the Sheraton Motor Inn. Then Becker took the plunge; he walked over to the St. Regis and went up to Bianchi's room, well bugged by agents in adjoining quarters. Other agents followed Becker and Bianchi as they took a half hour's walk. When they separated, Bianchi returned to his room and his own personal Customs men, while Becker took evasive action, dropping in at the Hotel Shoreham and then the Gotham Hotel before proceeding to the Hilton. From the Hilton, Becker emerged thirty minutes later with Gahou.

Now the chase began in earnest. Becker and Bianchi had arranged for delivery of the heroin during their stroll. The contraband was in the trunk of a car rented by Bianchi, a Ford Torino, parked in a garage near the St. Regis. Most of the contraband by now consisted of milk sugar; some genuine heroin had been left in the suitcases in line with the official procedure required to make a case.

Agents tailing the various suspects could feel the tension mounting as their subjects embarked on their final round of evasive action. It was the stuff of which implausible late-night television movies are made, but most of the agents involved had been through this tortuous routine many times.

With Varela back at the Americana Hotel, in Room 724, Becker and Gahou walked from the Hilton to 55th Street and Fifth Avenue, where they entered a coffee shop on the south side of 55th Street. Fifteen minutes later, Gahou left that coffee shop and strolled into another coffee shop on the north side of the street. Shortly, Gahou and Becker emerged from their respective coffee shops to walk separately to the block on Fifth Avenue between 53d and 54th streets, where they met and conversed briefly before separating again.

Becker then proceeded to the St. Regis for another chat with Bianchi. The delivery, he told Bianchi—and the listening Customs agents—was on. But he told Bianchi to be patient. Then he departed, took a cab, and proceeded to 54th Street and Fifth Avenue, where he was joined by Gahou; they both returned to the Sheraton Motor Inn at about 6 P.M.

Meanwhile, Rodríguez and Varela also were on the move. They

left the Americana Hotel about 3 P.M. and took a cab to a business address at 30 Church Street, downtown. Varela remained in the lobby of the building while Rodríguez paid a visit. Thirty minutes later, both men took a cab to that citadel of tourism, Radio City Music Hall, where they spent ten minutes. Outside, they were joined by Becker, and the three had a brief chat before Becker and Varela proceeded separately to the St. Regis and Bianchi's room. They remained there for about ten minutes, discussing the mechanics of the delivery, and then left to make their way to the Hilton.

Becker shortly returned to the St. Regis and paid still another visit to Bianchi, this time loitering for a half hour. Then Becker and Bianchi went downstairs and out front where, a few minutes later, an attendant drove up with Bianchi's Torino—and the contraband.

Bianchi opened the trunk and Becker peeked in with elaborate casualness. Then Bianchi closed the trunk and the two took off, driving in the general direction of the Sheraton Motor Inn, with Bianchi at the wheel. A conspirator to the end, the cooperating Bianchi made what the Customs report called "several visible evasive maneuvers which lasted approximately 15 minutes and which took place entirely in the proximity of 43d Street and Eighth to Eleventh Avenues." Their pursuers finally put an end to the fun and games by stopping the Torino at Eighth Avenue and 45th Street and taking Bianchi and Becker into custody.

Varela and Rodríguez were arrested that same evening as they took their ease in Room 724 of the Americana Hotel. Gahou was nabbed while sitting in the lobby of the Hilton Hotel, reading a copy of *Playboy* magazine. But it was not until three months later, in January, 1972, that the Feds tracked down and arrested the mysterious tall, dark Latin, Nicholas Giannattasio.

Customs and the cooperating Bureau of Narcotics and Dangerous Drugs had finally bagged the whole American end of Auguste Ricord's network. Varela probably was the most important of the lot, as the man who had organized the smuggling operation. Giannattasio was the receiver, or wholesaler, who was buying the heroin. Gahou had been dispatched to the United States by Ricord to collect the money due the syndicate. Bianchi and Rodríguez-Muravnik were the vital junior partners, charged with transportation and arrangements.

But although all those arrested could be traced to the Ricord organization, either by their own words or by the U.S. agents' many-sided investigation which followed the New York hit, it was Felix Becker who provided the most damning information on the former Nazi collaborator. Becker, a Ricord go-between in the Bianchi case charged with overseeing the delivery to Giannattasio and keeping tabs on his colleagues, submitted an affidavit describing how he picked up a $100,000 payment for a heroin shipment at the Waldorf Astoria Hotel in early October, 1970, and flew the payment to Ricord in Paraguay.

Eventually, all charges against Renato Balestra were dismissed because of lack of evidence and because Bianchi backed up Balestra's protests that he was an innocent traveler who had been gulled by his friends into going along, as it were, for the ride. That was small loss to Customs in its case against the Ricord conspiracy. Suddenly, however, two big ones got away.

About 6:30 A.M. on Sunday, January 24, 1971, seven prisoners awaiting trial in the Federal House of Detention in New York escaped from their cells and disappeared into the morning gloom. One of them was Varela and another was Rodríguez-Muravnik. They had joined forces with Yolanda Sarmiento's lover and lieutenant, Emilio Díaz-Gonzales, in Díaz' second breakout attempt. After somehow gaining access to a third-floor cell, they had sawed through three bars, then cut their way into a ventilating shaft with tin shears and jumped to the roof of an abandoned warehouse adjoining the jail, finally descending to the street by a rope improvised from bed sheets.

Obviously, the prisoners had had help from both inside and outside the jail; there were reports from South American informants that Yolanda Sarmiento had arranged to smuggle $5,000 in small bills in to her fellow conspirators. However the business was managed, Varela, Díaz and Rodríguez-Muravnik took with them Guillermo Hernández, who had been nabbed at Kennedy International Airport the previous August after his arrival from Buenos Aires with a kilo of cocaine secreted in his woman's girdle. A month later, all four were reported seen in Asunción, Paraguay—Ricord's headquarters city.

Meanwhile, however, Customs not only had identified Ricord as the czar of the South American Conspiracy, but had put together evidence and agents' testimony solid enough to get him indicted by a federal grand jury in New York. In March, 1971, therefore, the United States asked the Paraguayan government to put the czar under arrest. Although the so-called Bianchi Bust had been spread over the pages of newspapers around the world, Ricord apparently could not believe he was in any danger from the law. Perhaps he kept counting all the good friends he had in high places in official Paraguay.

In any event, Ricord was still fussing with papers at his desk in his Asunción restaurant, the Paris-Niza, when Paraguayan police arrived to take him into custody. As the cops poured into Paris-Niza, the sixty-one-year-old smuggling king slipped out a back door, jumped into his own Torino, and sped toward the nearby border of Argentina. He almost made it, too; he was nabbed three hours later in a launch in which he was preparing to cross the Pilcomayo River into Argentine safety.

Washington had efficiently provided an Air Force jet to fly the prisoner to the States, either by extradition or by "informal removal" —that is to say, removal outside diplomatic channels. But although Paraguay's strong man President Alfredo Stroessner had become, literally, his nation's law and had always enjoyed a close and friendly relationship with the United States, his personal bureaucracy, refused to move that fast.

Ricord was tossed into jail, but Paraguayan officials mildly reminded Washington that Paraguay had no law on any of its books banning the use or sale of drugs. They did say that they found not inconsistent new laws and treaties, enacted to stamp out narcotics worldwide, which made it possible for the United States to request extradition of Ricord even though he had never set foot on American soil. Paraguay, they added, would do everything possible to be of service to its good friend to the north in a manner touching on "very grave crimes."

Indeed, the Paraguayan Solicitor General, in effect representing the United States under the treaty, handed down a favorable opinion when Washington's extradition request was presented by Ambassador Ray Ylitalo. But the Court of Original Jurisdiction in Asunción turned down the request, and the case went into appeals procedures.

U.S. officials seemed confident even as the Ricord case dragged on into July, 1971. One Customs interoffice memo reported that "State Department has advised that the extradition of Ricord from Paraguay looks very favorable. The time frame probably will be in 1-2 weeks, probably closer to two weeks. State suggests that arrangements be made for a military aircraft to bring Ricord out to avoid stopovers in other jurisdictions. Also, having an aircraft on standby, ready to go as soon as we get the word that the papers are to be signed, will enable us to pull Ricord out as soon as the papers are signed. This will avoid Ricord's defense having enough time to file appeals."

Meanwhile, the courts had disposed of a couple of the men nabbed in the Bianchi Bust. Ricord's bagman, Gahou, and the receiver, Giannattasio, each were sentenced to seven years in a federal penitentiary for their part in the vicious frolic. For several months, Bianchi and Becker languished more or less happily in detention as possible government witnesses against Ricord. Becker cooperated and told all he knew about the conspiracy; he was rewarded with a relatively mild five-year sentence under which he was eligible for parole in twelve months' time. But Bianchi balked at turning stool pigeon and was remanded to trial with Ricord.

A clutch of Customs agents were honored with special recognition for their work on the complicated case. Senior Special Agent Bill Knierim won a Superior Work Performance Award of $500, and Wallace D. Shanley, assistant director of the Field Liaison Branch, and Senior Special Agent Larry Kane received $300 awards. In addition, Group Special Service awards were handed out to Agents Albert W. Seeley, Paul Boulad, Robert Nunnery, Robert Van Etten, Philip Zisk, Victor Cabrera, Hector Santiago, William McMullan and Michael Tobin.

Paul Boulad's name was mentioned with something close to reverence by Pierre Gahou when he entered a plea of guilty. The judge asked Gahou if he understood the possible consequences of the crime he had admitted. Yes, Gahou replied, he understood very well. Then he added: "My conscience tells me to believe in two people—my mother and Customs Special Agent Paul Boulad."

Meanwhile, Auguste Ricord was installed in a comfortable, well-furnished cell in a private wing of the Asunción prison and had all his meals catered by his own restaurant. And after ten months in this cozy apartment, Ricord was happy to learn that a Paraguayan court had set bail for him at a relatively beneficent $317,460.

Most United States government officials familiar with Paraguayan politics expected that the short, balding, sixty-one-year-old Corsican would make bail easily and then disappear. Ricord's influence in the top levels of the Paraguayan government had always been vast, and there were stories that certain military types wanted Ricord to get lost. But, almost incredibly, Ricord could not dig up the bail money, although even conservative figures put his wealth well into seven figures and he boasted that his interests in seven other restaurants in South America netted him $180,000 a year. By this time President Nixon himself was putting diplomatic pressure on President Stroessner, and that strong man apparently concluded it was in his own best interest to keep Ricord behind bars while he considered the case.

There followed a seventeen-month diplomatic tug-of-war. At one point, a report surfaced that a deal had been made with Paraguayan officials which would permit American agents to kidnap Ricord and fly him to the United States, but nothing came of it. Meanwhile, the Nixon administration's patience grew short and the White House applied the screws to Stroessner. Military aid to Paraguay was halted "for study," and over a period of weeks the strong man found that more than $5,000,000 worth of lines of credit had dried up. Washington warned that it might use its power to reduce funds from international lending organizations.

Finally, President Nixon dispatched a personal emissary to Paraguay—Nelson Gross, senior adviser to the Secretary of State and Coordinator for International Narcotics Affairs. Gross's assignment, in his own words, was "to tell Stroessner in unequivocal terms that the extradition of Ricord was a matter of prime importance." That was in August, 1972. Stroessner got the message. Ricord's extradition to the United States was approved on September 1, and that same day the Corsican big wheel was flown to New York aboard a chartered American jetliner, attended by ten security agents, a doctor and two nurses. Arraigned in Manhattan federal court, Ricord showed off his new muttonchop whiskers and was all smiles for reporters—until bail was set at a whopping $1,500,000.

Nelson Gross was jubilant. After paying tribute to Customs' dogged four-year investigation which led to Ricord's indictment, he described the prisoner as "probably the highest-placed narcotics trafficker ever indicted. From what the experts say, he's among the top 10 or so in the world on a loose board of directors."

Events of the following few weeks supported Gross's appraisal of Ricord's importance. Lawmen of seven Latin American and European nations launched a campaign against men suspected of involvement in Ricord's operations. One of these men was killed in France in a running gun battle, and seven others were hauled off to assorted European and South American jails. With Ricord in custody, the lawmen's theory was that his accomplices might be willing to talk to save their own skins—or at least win lighter sentences.

Sure enough, Uncle Sam's sleuths gathered enough intelligence to come up with another wholesale batch of indictments on November 18, 1972. In a cooperative effort, the Customs Bureau, the Bureau of Narcotics and Dangerous Drugs, and the Brooklyn Strike Force

Against Organized Crime pooled their resources and evidence to secure two sets of indictments naming twenty suspects, including the reputed leaders of two international heroin-smuggling rings. All those indicted were identified as having worked with or for Auguste Ricord and other smuggling chieftains in a loosely knit international cartel. They were charged with conspiring to smuggle more than 1,100 pounds of heroin, valued at $250,000,000, into the United States between January, 1968, and April, 1971.

The big names in the indictments were those of Christian David, a forty-one-year-old Frenchman living in São Paulo, Brazil, and Michel Nicoli, forty-two, also a French national with several addresses in Brazil. David and Nicoli were flown from Brazil at the request of the Justice Department and held in New York in record bail of $2,500,000 each. In the billion-dollar underworld of illicit drug trafficking, both men were said to rank on the same executive level as Ricord.

French police had been looking for David for six years for the slaying of a police commissioner on February 2, 1966. Meanwhile, David had been sentenced to death in absentia. His criminal record included a whopping twenty-one convictions, and lawmen charged that he had been personally responsible for the smuggling of 103 kilograms of heroin into the United States. The indictment noted that Nicoli was wanted in France for armed robbery, for which he had been sentenced to a twenty-year prison term. He was arrested on a narcotics charge in Brooklyn in March, 1968, under the name Abraham E. Goldman, also known as Miguel Dos Santos, and jumped $50,000 bail.

It took David only two weeks to decide between a probable lifetime in American prisons and the French guillotine. On December 1, he pleaded guilty in a New York federal courtroom to a charge of receiving, concealing and transporting 66 pounds of heroin in June, 1969, and was sentenced to twenty years in the pen, without parole, and socked with a $20,000 fine. David's court-appointed lawyer, Stephen Lowrey, told the court, "Frankly, we are trying to avoid his extradition and execution." Because David faced four additional counts of narcotics trafficking carrying prison terms of up to eighty years in jail, he was virtually assured of never having to return to France for his date with the Big Knife.

The next day, a report from the Nassau County Jail suggested that David had not exactly gone straight. César Bianchi, the thirty-four-year-old Paraguayan pilot arrested for allegedly flying Auguste Ricord's heroin into Florida, charged that David had threatened his life if he testified against Ricord. Two days later, the alleged threat was used by the prosecution successfully to oppose a delay in Ricord's trial.

Although Customs was dutifully impressed with the David and Nicoli arrests, it had a more personal interest in other suspects among the six Frenchmen, four Americans, three Swiss, two Argentines, two Italians and three John Does named in the indictments. Nine of the men were old pals from the "The Paella Story" (Chapter 6) in which a European syndicate had attempted to smuggle heroin into the United States in cans of Spanish seafood. They included Willie Wouters, whose arrest as a courier in July, 1968, eventually led to the breaking of the case, Louis Bonsignour, Luis Stepenberg, Jack Grosby, Daniel Mitnik, Christian Hysohion, André Hirsch, Louis Brique and Daniel Roger Vuille Dit Bille.

Hirsch, a Swiss banker, Louis Brique, alleged operating head of the paella caper, and Vuille Dit Bille, who recruited Willy Wouters, were listed in the new indictments as fugitives, although all had been convicted and sentenced to prison terms. Bonsignour had jumped bail. Stepenberg, Grosby, Wouters, Mitnik and Hysohion were named in the indictments only as co-conspirators rather than defendants because they had cooperated with Customs by telling what they knew about assorted smuggling operations. Stepenberg died in his jail cell after having been convicted on fifteen counts of narcotics violations. Hysohion had drawn a thirty-year prison term in the paella case and Mitnik seven years before they decided to talk. But Grosby and Wouters had cooperated from the very beginning and thus were still "awaiting trial" when the indictments of November, 1972, were announced.

Accordingly, while emphasizing the cooperative nature of the operation which led to the new indictments, Customs officials could take considerable personal satisfaction in the knowledge that the arrests in the paella case played an important part in the eventual breakup of the David-Nicoli rings. That, after all, is what the care and feeding of "cooperating witnesses" is all about—the gathering of information that will lead to the big-time operators. In Customs' New York and Miami offices, men like Al Seeley and Stan Schachter had spent four long years tying bits of string together as their quiet contribution to another big bust.

Auguste Joseph Ricord, a grandfather figure with white muttonchop whiskers, was brought to trial on December 5, 1972, in Federal District Court in Manhattan. The specific charge against him was conspiracy to smuggle 94 pounds of heroin into the United States in October, 1970, but federal officials claimed that Ricord was responsible for arranging the delivery into the country of as much as 15 tons of heroin during the previous five years. Tight security was imposed on the courtroom as Ricord, held in bail of $1,500,000, faced a jury of seven men and five women and District Judge John M. Cannella. Everyone entering the chamber was scanned by United States marshals with portable metal detectors that emitted squeals in the presence of the tiniest piece of metal, and the short, almost elflike Ricord was guarded by two marshals.

After disposing of Renato Balestra, the twenty-six-year-old copilot who was arrested during the big 1970 bust, the prosecution quickly got the show on the road. Balestra, who had been held only as a corroborating witness, testified that his "boss," Pilot César Bianchi, had told him the suitcases concealed in their plane on the flight to the United States contained only "uranium sand," and he was forthwith dismissed and permitted to go free. Then a parade of other witnesses took the stand under the stage-managing of Walter M. Phillips, Jr., an assistant United States Attorney, to put thousands of damning words into the record.

Bianchi, who had cooperated in a controlled delivery of the 94 pounds of heroin in New York and then turned mute for several months while Washington was pressuring Paraguay to extradite Ricord, had another change of mind once Ricord was flown to the United States, and agreed to testify against the Corsican who had worked for the Nazi Gestapo in occupied France before fleeing to South America. Bianchi's testimony was long and convoluted, tracing as it did his many stops en route to the United States, but its essence was matter-of-fact: He had received three suitcases containing the heroin shipment from Ricord at the latter's motel-restaurant in Asunción.

Felix Becker repeated the story he had put into affidavit form for his Customs captors—that he had picked up the $100,000 proceeds of a 15-kilo heroin sale in New York, carried it to Asunción and had seen the box containing the money handed to Ricord. Becker also identified Enio Aníbal Varela-Segovia and Rodríguez-Muravnik as Ricord's top lieutenants, and said he saw Varela count the $100,000 at the Asunción airport before handing it to Ricord.

Pierre Gahou, who seemed pleased to announce he had once been a waiter on ocean liners, testified that he had been recruited by Ricord personally to assist in the heroin delivery in October, 1970. Gahou said his contact was a "Mr. Nick"—Nicholas Giannattasio, the receiver, by then serving seven years in a federal pen—and that he had passed a suitcase containing 10 kilos of heroin to "Mr. Nick," whom he knew only as a former professional soccer player. The next day, Gahou said, "Mr. Nick" handed him an Iberia Airlines flight bag containing $107,000 at 22d Street and Broadway.

There was Salvador Victor Ibarrola, who arrested Ricord as the narcotics overlord was attempting to cross over into Argentina in a motor launch. Ibarrola testified that when he went to Ricord's restaurant with a picture of the suspect, he was directed to the office "by a man wearing a wig, or a beret." When he told the girl at the desk, later identified as Ricord's niece, thirty-four-year-old Helene Bonsignour, that he was looking for Ricord, she fainted.

"There was no one left to cooperate with me so I called the chief of police for instructions," Ibarrola said. "Then I became suspicious. I thought perhaps the first man who helped me was the man I was seeking." Ibarrola was right. When he caught up with Ricord, the smuggling kingpin was wigless.

Ricord took the stand in his own defense. Through an interpreter, he spent most of his day in the box discussing his bank accounts in various countries. He pictured himself as a sickly man, interested only in his motel and restaurant business in South America, but he stumbled frequently and he was forced to retract or modify eight statements when confronted with documents or the testimony of witnesses. Ricord testified in both French and Spanish, depending mostly on the latter language when his testimony was contradicted. But although he had told Judge Cannella he didn't understand English, on several occasions he answered questions put to him in English before they were translated.

Ricord's case went to the all-white jury on December 15, and it took the jurors only two hours and twenty minutes to find him guilty on the single conspiracy count. Judge Cannella ordered Ricord continued in custody in $1,500,000 bail, pending pronouncement of sentence.

Finally, on January 29, 1973, the United States Bureau of Customs closed the file on its five-year pursuit of the little Corsican restaurateur who began his career as a small-time pimp in Marseilles, worked for the Nazis' Gestapo in France during World War II, and became one of the world's most-wanted narcotics traffickers. Ricord was sentenced to a maximum twenty years in prison, fined $20,000, and ordered to pay the costs of prosecution from his estimated fortune of more than $2,000,000.

In thus imposing the harshest possible penalty on the plump little dope mastermind, Judge Cannella took note that Ricord was a VIP in the narcotics trade. "This is a sale of a very large quantity of heroin," said Cannella of the charge that Ricord's syndicate had smuggled at least a ton of pure heroin a year into the United States. "The end product in suffering and mortality from this quantity would probably equal the recent figures given for the war in Vietnam."

The sometime intrepid pilot Bianchi, who also was looking at twenty years in the pokey before he finally decided to play ball with the law, got off easy. On February 16, 1973, Bianchi was allowed to plead guilty to a charge of importing narcotics without paying duty and drew a token five years in the pen.

# 9
# Pigeon Peas and Picture Frames

In both the paella and the Ricord-Bianchi cases, certain individuals who Customs operatives had reason to believe were involved in drug trafficking and who conceivably could lead lawmen to other bigger traffickers were under virtually twenty-four-hour-a-day surveillance for as long as a year. The burden of such surveillance falls heavily on Customs' Intelligence Division, although it is a joint venture, with its parent Customs Agency Service, also frequently in donning the varied disguises of undercover men in order to melt into the neighborhoods where their espionage activities take them.

While engaged in these activities, the undercover man seldom, if ever, goes near a Customs office; there have been several instances in which undercover agents didn't venture within a few blocks of their offices for a year or more. The undercover man dresses and looks the part of a street loiterer, a truck driver, a messenger, a TV repairman, a furniture mover, a window washer. One week he will be a hippie type with long hair and beard, the next a "straight," dressed as an insurance company adjuster. He plays whatever role will make his presence in a certain building or a certain neighborhood appear normal to those who live or work in that building or neighborhood. Frequently, he is forced to move out of his own home so as not to arouse the curiosity of his family or neighbors. Most often, he works out of a Customs office in another city so he can set up housekeeping and a life-style suitable to his role.

In some cases, the undercover man doesn't even know, at first, the identity of the man or woman he is shadowing. He is watching merely a face and figure with a certain walk, perhaps, or the nervous habit of massaging his jaw, or adjusting his eyeglasses. The name he finds on a mailbox often is an alias; then either the agent or more likely his colleagues at their desks must go elsewhere, asking cautious questions, to establish the individual's true identity. There have been instances when an undercover man has been able to find a latent fingerprint that has led to his subject's identification. But at the beginning and often for long weeks—even after the subject's identity has been established—the undercover man knows only that the person he is watching could be someone Customs would find interesting.

An undercover man reports daily, by telephone, to his superiors. A typical twenty-four-hour report by a surveillance team was one concerning the day's activities of a man who later turned informant and helped the government find the path leading to men who in turn led the investigators to two of the principals in the Ricord-Bianchi Bust:

"Subject left apartment at 175 East —— Street at 9:04 A.M., carrying an umbrella and a package about seven inches by twelve inches wrapped in brown paper. Took cab to office building at —— Wall Street. Emerged two hours later carrying just umbrella, walked north three blocks, then took cab to apartment building at 220 West —— Street. Entered apartment number 654; door opened by woman, medium height, black hair, wearing kimono. Subject remained in apartment until 5 P.M. when he emerged and walked to bar on lower level of Rockefeller Center. Subject drank three Dubonnets on-the-rocks, then went to table and ate dinner.

"As subject was drinking coffee he was joined by a white male, Spanish-looking, about five feet nine inches tall, 155 pounds, narrow black mustache, black hair, small scar about two inches long on his left cheek just under eye. Subject and companion conversed for about 15 minutes, then both left restaurant, walked two blocks to a parked 1968 Lincoln Continental, maroon coupe model bearing license tag number ——, New Jersey. Both entered car and drove to subject's apartment building where car was parked and both entered building and went up in elevator to subject's apartment. Companion exited after two hours and twenty-two minutes and drove to Americana Hotel, where he delivered car to doorman and entered hotel and took elevator to Room 543. Both subject and companion remained in their respective apartment and hotel room rest of the night."

Within a few hours, the owner of the car had been identified as the driver. Police records showed the man had been arrested eighteen months earlier as an alleged accomplice in a heroin delivery from Miami but that charges had been dismissed for lack of evidence. But the surveillance, plus some hard reasoning by Intelligence analysts in the Washington office, had provided Customs with information linking both men to associations with known members of the Ricord syndicate.

The Intelligence Division also of course works closely with Interpol, the international information-liaison organization, and with Customs agents stationed at United States embassies. Its operatives keep up to date such bread-and-butter data as cargo handlers and aircraft repair shops that might be involved in the narcotics traffic; cargo and other airlines that have figured in narcotics investigations here and abroad; travel agencies which have issued tickets to known narcotics carriers entering the United States from abroad; and ships used by narcotics couriers apprehended in all previous cases.

All these activities in the espionage field were upgraded in 1969 when the tireless and indefatigable Myles Ambrose reorganized the Intelligence Division as one of the first steps in his three-year regime. The division also got a new director, a friendly, swarthy veteran of undercover work bearing the melodious name Andrew Agathangelou. A soft-spoken and courtly operator, Agathangelou set two goals for his unit: 1. To collect all the information available in the United States about possible narcotics smugglers. 2. To convert this information into usable intelligence.

Shortly, five Sector Intelligence Units were established in New York, Miami, Houston, Chicago, and San Pedro, California. Their functions were to collect, receive, abstract, analyze and enter into the CADPIN computer every scrap of information available in the regions they served. Sector chiefs were also charged with establishing lookouts and so-called suspense files on possible conspiracies and establishing liaison with their counterparts in other law enforcement agencies to assure mutual cooperation.

As in the military, the Intelligence Division's operations are divided into strategic, operational and tactical. In the first category, special agents are expected to prepare studies on the diversion of overseas opium crops to dope traffickers, appraise the quality of local and foreign police (Are they cooperative? Are they honest?), become familiar with the political situations in U.S. cities and in foreign countries, and collect arrest and seizure statistics as a basis for establishing patterns for the illicit flow of narcotics into the United States. In the operational branch, agents poke around in assorted neighborhoods seeking information on individuals who might be involved in the dope racket because they spend too much money, associate with unsavory companions, or are seen in the wrong joints. The tactical people work on specific cases, to wrap them up in a package admissible in a courtroom.

This information is then analyzed by experts in Washington headquarters, whose function is to do the horse-sense thinking necessary to grade the information. It is these analysts, having years of familiarity with the regions assigned to them, who decide whether, say, a particular name is important enough to insert in a suspect's file. If it is learned that a suspect has been calling fifteen telephone numbers with regularity, fourteen of the numbers may be listed to innocent people; the fifteenth will be listed to the alias of a known principal in a smuggling ring. In law enforcement, the first step in establishing a conspiracy is to prove that two persons communicated with each other.

Probably best known to laymen is Intelligence's function of seeking out people who might become informants and then convincing them it is in their interest to inform. Although Customs spends more than $2,000,000 a year buying information, most informants offer their merchandise for personal reasons. Thus Intelligence undercover men look for the individual with a grudge against a suspected dope ring member. They do a booming business with husbands whose wives are playing around with big-spending pushers and wives whose husbands have deserted them for women involved with men named in "suspense files." The work can be dangerous because it calls for a great deal of loitering in high-risk neighborhoods and the asking of ticklish questions. But as Agathangelou once put it, "A reliable informant is worth his weight in heroin."

Intelligence operatives from time to time are dispatched to foreign countries to make or renew acquaintance with their law enforcement counterparts, to case the situation in a given country, or merely to do some general sleuthing with foreign agents. It was just such a piece of keeping-in-touch routine that led in January, 1971, to the exposure of a conspiracy to smuggle 56.73 pounds of heroin, with a street value of more than $6,000,000, into the United States through Puerto Rico. The heroin was concealed in a shipment of pigeon peas (the brown, edible seed of the *Cajanus indicus* plant) from Santo Domingo, capital of the Dominican Republic.

About a year earlier, Customs had become interested in the various international goings-and-comings of Andrés Alfonso Rodríguez-Méndez, a forty-four-year-old Dominican, who did some speculating in food crops and also operated as a part-time shipping agent for various Dominican exporters. Rodríguez-Méndez had made several trips to the United States, most of them to Puerto Rico, during the previous eighteen months. A Customs Intelligence operative was dispatched incognito to Santo Domingo, where he nosed around and discovered that Rodríguez-Méndez' known income was not of a size to support his frequent travels.

Thus, in July, 1970, a Customs undercover man was watching when Rodríguez-Méndez arrived in New York and a couple of days later rendezvoused with a man known as Ángel Camacho-Rivera at the Liborio Restaurant on the upper West Side. Official eavesdroppers fluent in Spanish heard Rodríguez-Méndez urge Camacho-Rivera to "visit" him in Santo Domingo at any time and tell him that he would be happy to put him up in his home. Customs officialdom decided that it should keep an eye on both Rodríguez-Méndez and Camacho-Rivera on the chance that the former's obsession with travel made him a prime smuggling suspect.

About six months later, on January 5, 1971, Camacho-Rivera arrived in Santo Domingo and registered at the Hotel Comercial; two days later he moved to the more luxurious Jaragua Hotel. During his twelve-day stay in Santo Domingo, Camacho-Rivera did considerable palling around with Rodríguez-Méndez, accompanying his host to numerous restaurants and nightclubs—and also to the warehouse of the Productos Agronoquimicos Ramón Mella-Mateo. At the warehouse, Camacho-Rivera helped Rodríguez-Méndez remove the back seat of his car and replaced it with thirty cartons of pigeon peas. He also watched while another fifty-three cartons containing green peppers were loaded into a truck by some warehouse workers.

There was nothing illegal about this, of course. After all, Rodríguez-Méndez was a buyer and seller of food crops. But in New York, Customs undercover men had learned there was some dispute about Camacho-Rivera's identity. There were those in Spanish Harlem and various other neighborhoods in upper Manhattan who said they knew Camacho-Rivera as a Dominican, although he claimed United States citizenship. None, however, could provide another name for him.

In any case, the lawmen wanted to know more about both men, and in particular they wanted to find out something about the destination of the cargo of pigeon peas and green peppers loaded at the warehouse on the night of January 17. They had not long to wait. The pigeon peas and green peppers were loaded aboard an Aerovias Quisqueyana Airlines flight at the Santo Domingo airport the next morning. Rodríguez-Méndez boarded the plane as a passenger bound for San Juan. Camacho-Rivera remained behind in Santo Domingo.

The flight arrived at San Juan International Airport at about 11:15 A.M. the same day and was welcomed by—among others— Humberto Colom, Customs port investigator (later a Customs inspector), and Pedro Rivera-Disdier, a Customs patrol officer. They watched quietly as cargo handlers began unloading the pigeon peas and green peppers. By what officialdom was prepared to explain as a coincidence, one of the handlers noticed a plastic bag inside a carton of pigeon peas which had been damaged in transit and was leaking a white powder.

By that time Colom and Rivera-Disdier had been joined by Customs Inspector Jack Shepard-Umpierre. No one seemed surprised when the cargo handler reported the damaged plastic package among the pigeon peas. And no one seemed surprised when a field test of the white powder showed it was heroin of a fairly good quality. A telephone call was put through to Special Agent Jorge Marcano at the U.S. customshouse, and Marcano ordered that the unloading of the cargo be halted until he could get to the airport. When he arrived, Marcano had the rest of the cargo off-loaded and taken to the cargo office at the airport for intensive examination. The examiners found fifty-two more hermetically sealed plastic bags of heroin concealed in the pigeon pea shipment.

The cargo manifest filed with Customs by the airline showed that the cargo of fifty-three cartons of green peppers and thirty cartons of pigeon peas was consigned collect to one Miguel Ángel Solla-Santiago of Santurce, Puerto Rico. Meanwhile, Rodríguez-Méndez had disembarked and disappeared.

Whether Rodríguez-Méndez attempted to warn Solla-Santiago was unknown. In any event, the consignee arrived at the airport within the hour, accompanied by the airline's airport manager. Solla-Santiago was whisked off to the Customs office for questioning after being informed routinely of his rights to remain silent and to find himself a lawyer.

But Solla-Santiago was willing to talk without counsel's advice; he was all innocence. He told Marcano and other agents that Rodríguez-Méndez had phoned him from Santo Domingo two nights before and arrangements had been made for Rodríguez-Méndez to ship him the green peppers and pigeon peas; Rodríguez-Méndez was to retain ten cartons of the pigeon peas after the shipment arrived in San Juan. Solla-Santiago said he had picked up a truck that morning at Puerto

Rico Transport, Incorporated, in Santurce and then had driven to the airport to accept delivery. Upon his arrival, the airport manager had told him there was a problem with his merchandise and it would have to be ironed out with Customs. Goodness gracious, said Solla-Santiago, he planned to truck the peas and peppers direct to the public marketplace in Río Piedras; he didn't know anything about any old heroin.

Nevertheless, Solla-Santiago was placed under arrest on a smuggling charge. Then he telephoned his wife and discovered that Rodríguez-Méndez, "the scoundrel," had dropped in at the Solla-Santiago home a short time before and had left a handbag there.

An hour later, Customs agents learned that Rodríguez-Méndez had not attempted to warn Solla-Santiago for the simple reason he had no idea Customs had moved in on the shipment. Rodríguez-Méndez made this plain when he arrived at the airline office to inquire about his cargo while Customs Patrol Investigator Pedro Alberio was talking to the manager. Rodríguez-Méndez' reappearance was a tribute to the quiet manner in which the matter had been handled.

Alberio escorted Rodríguez-Méndez to the Customs office, where Marcano officially took him into custody and gave him the constitutional rights spiel. Like Solla-Santiago, however, Rodríguez-Méndez was eager to reveal his purity of conscience. He told his interrogators the whole shipment was consigned to Solla-Santiago, that he had no intention of retaining ten cartons of the pigeon peas (presumably those containing the sacks of heroin). His story was that he had no idea who transported the peas and peppers from the warehouse to the airport in Santo Domingo and that he had never laid eyes on the pigeon peas until they were already aboard the plane in Santo Domingo. Vehemently and indignantly, he denied any knowledge of the cache of heroin.

But Special Agent Marcano figured he had enough on both Rodríguez-Méndez and Solla-Santiago to stand up in court. True, the physical delivery had not been made to Solla-Santiago by Rodríguez-Méndez, but Rodríguez-Méndez was the shipper of record and Solla-Santiago the consignee of record, and both had tried to go about the business of seeing that the cargo reached the consignee. And when Rodríguez-Méndez was searched, agents found the original cargo airwaybill No. 2345-0307 covering the shipment.

Furthermore, Marcano and Special Agent Carlos Rivera-Gierbolini flew to Santo Domingo several days later and did some suc-

cessful checking on Rodríguez-Méndez. Accompanied by a Dominican police official, they visited Rodríguez-Méndez' home and found
several plastic bags similar to those used to package the seized heroin; pigeon peas also were found scattered about the yard. And two
workers at the Mella-Mateo warehouse gave sworn statements that
they had seen Rodríguez-Méndez and another man load twelve cartons of pigeon peas in the back of his car.

At about the same time, Dominican police found and took into
custody the mysterious man known to some acquaintances, but not
to all, as Ángel Camacho-Rivera. Three employees of the warehouse
identified Camacho-Rivera as the man who had accompanied
Rodríguez-Méndez when the pigeon peas and green peppers were
loaded in Rodríguez-Méndez' car and the truck. One of the employees said twelve cartons in the pigeon pea shipment had been brought
to the warehouse by Rodríguez-Méndez and stored in the freezer
until the truck arrived to carry the shipment to the plane. To the
suspicious agents, this testimony shrieked that Rodríguez-Méndez
had hidden the heroin in those twelve bags before including them in
the cargo consigned to Solla-Santiago.

Earlier suspicions that Rodríguez-Méndez was deep in the smuggling racket were heightened by perusal of various airline flight records. They showed that food shipments had been dispatched by
Rodríguez-Méndez to Solla-Santiago on two previous occasions. The
first, consisting of 15 cartons of pigeon peas, arrived in San Juan on
December 11, 1970, and the second, consisting of 30 cartons of
pigeon peas and 59 cartons of green peppers, arrived in San Juan on
January 11.

Camacho-Rivera admitted nothing except that he knew Rodríguez-
Méndez and had accompanied him to the Mella-Mateo warehouse on
the night of January 17. Camacho-Rivera was released by Dominican authorities after posting $30,000 bond and took off for parts
unknown; he was nowhere to be found when his trial was called on
March 5, 1971. By this time Customs investigators had learned
through a check of his fingerprints that he had borrowed the name
Camacho-Rivera from an acquaintance living in an upper West Side
neighborhood in New York. The real Ángel Camacho-Rivera knew
the phony one, but not by name; he thought a picture of the fugitive
resembled that of a dope pusher he used to see in his neighborhood.

Subsequently, however, the machinery of law enforcement ground
out the information that the Camacho-Rivera of the pigeon peas case
was a Cuban national named Ángel López-González, who had served

a one-year prison term on a grand larceny charge in New York and then had disappeared into the criminal woodwork. Somewhere along the line, he had found a genius in the art of forgery; his passport and other documents identifying him as Camacho-Rivera were superb pieces of craftsmanship.

Eventually, Alfonso Rodríguez-Méndez was convicted of the smuggling caper and sentenced to twenty long years in a federal pen. Miguel Ángel Solla-Santiago was a different package of goods. After nine continuances granted to the defense, he went to trial in September, 1972, and after three weeks of testimony the judge declared a mistrial when the prosecution charged Solla-Santiago had tried to intimidate a woman member of the jury. Subsequently, there were more continuances, and in the late spring of 1973 Solla-Santiago's case still hadn't been settled in a courtroom.

In "The Case of the Hopped-Up Pigeon Peas," considerable credit for the bust went to those Customs personnel who operate officially as intelligence agents; they work out of the division designated by the bureau's table of organization as involved in a form of nonpolitical espionage. But in a sense everybody who works for Customs is an intelligence operative, starting with the polite and seemingly perfunctory inspector who checks the travelers' luggage at airports, piers and other official points of entry into the country. Customs' *raison d'être* is to play the role of Nosy Parker, whether it is making sure the proper duty is paid on legitimate imports, ranging from watches to milling machines, or defending against the smuggler with a pound of heroin strapped to his paunch.

Thus, when a Customs import specialist named John Flinn took a look at an airfreight shipment at Kennedy International Airport in New York on October 6, 1971, his primary objective was a routine one. He was interested simply in discovering whether the shipment was as described in its manifest—original oil paintings with wooden frames.

The manifest seemed to be in order; Flinn found four oil paintings framed in wood. But then, because Flinn had learned the value of a second look, he examined the frames with more than routine care. On one of them he noticed a white powdery substance which could be an innocent something but which also might be the traces left by an illicit cargo. In any event, he notified his supervisor, Jorge Santucci, and Santucci made a field test for heroin. The test was positive; someone had found still another way to try to sneak dope into the United States.

At first glance, that someone seemed to be one Juan Beretta of Buenos Aires, described on the manifest as the individual who had shipped the oil paintings. If so, Beretta had thought big. When Special Agents Hector Santiago and Robert Nunnery took the frames apart, they discovered 76 bags of heroin and 30 bags of cocaine secreted in hollow compartments affixed to the four picture frames. The bags contained 38.6 pounds of heroin and 19.7 pounds of cocaine with a street value of $21,500,000.

The oil paintings were consigned to Juan Carlos Iribarne, care of Rodolfo Ruiz, 206 East 75th Street, New York. Naturally, Customs wanted to have a little chat with Ruiz, so the picture frames were reassembled, with one-ounce sample bags of heroin in their secret compartments, and repacked in their original crates. Then the shipment was trucked to United States Customs Public Stores Building No. 80 for delivery to the consignee. Next day, the paintings were released to an employee of Luigi Serra, Incorporated, a customs brokerage firm, and loaded into a delivery truck for their ride to East 75th Street, furtively escorted by a carload of Customs agents.

Upon arriving at the 75th Street address, the driver parked the truck and went to Ruiz' apartment. Shortly, Ruiz emerged with the driver and examined the crate containing the pictures with what seemed to the watching agents to be inordinate care. As one Customs man put it, "He acts like he's afraid there's a bomb in the thing."

Eventually, Ruiz returned to his apartment and came out a few minutes later with an assortment of tools, with which he proceeded to open the crate. Then he removed the paintings, and he and the truck driver carried them into his apartment.

The agents followed normal procedure, hanging around outside for the receiver to make his move or for Ruiz to give some signal that the horse had been delivered. Unknown to the watchers, however, the building was under surveillance by another interested party. A man later identified as one Alfredo Mazza of Buenos Aires was loitering across the street, apparently waiting for a cab, when Ruiz left his apartment again about five minutes after accepting delivery of the pictures.

"Don't stop!" yelled Mazza to Ruiz. "Don't look at me. The police are following you. Run!"

Ruiz and Mazza took off in opposite directions. Mazza, who had had time to plot his getaway, disappeared into the late-afternoon throngs on Third Avenue, but Special Agents Frank De Santis and Bill McMullan grabbed Ruiz as he was jumping into a taxicab.

The law was luckier than it might have expected. Although Mazza, who was either the receiver or the receiver's representative, had escaped, Ruiz was an excellent catch. After listening to the usual statement of his constitutional rights, he folded and agreed to tell his interrogators all he knew. Among other things, his singing would connect the picture-frame smugglers with the Latin-American ring masterminded by the notorious Auguste Ricord. But first there was a farrago of nonsense unworthy of professional smugglers.

Ruiz revealed that a second receiver he knew as José Orso was scheduled to pick up the paintings at his apartment, and he agreed to await Orso's coming in Customs' company. Meanwhile, the agents got a search warrant and seized the four paintings and their valuable frames.

At about seven o'clock that evening, Ruiz double-crossed his custodians. Alfredo Mazza called to ask Ruiz, "What is happening there?" and before the agents could stop him, Ruiz yelled in Spanish, "I have been arrested by the police!" Incredibly, Mazza did not hang up forthwith. He first told Ruiz, "Don't worry."

Mazza called again an hour later. He asked Ruiz if he had the paintings, and Ruiz told him, "Yes, I'm waiting for Orso to come and pick them up." (The agents had had a little talk with Ruiz.) Mazza, whose knowledge of American police methods must have consisted solely of the handling of traffic jams, told Ruiz that Orso had gone to Washington, "but I'm trying to get $2,000 to pick up the paintings and pay you off." He said he'd call Ruiz back, and he did—a half hour later—to report he was unable to get the money to pay Ruiz and that Ruiz should hold the paintings in his apartment until he could raise the $2,000.

"It's no use," Ruiz told his captors. "He knows I'm arrested. He's just trying to find out what's going on."

So the surveillance was called off and Ruiz was taken before a United States magistrate, who set bail at $200,000 on heroin smuggling charges. It was after his arraignment that Ruiz did his most important talking. He identified José Orso as Juan Carlos Franco-Lorenzo, a Uruguayan living in Argentina, and implicated still a fourth man in the conspiracy—Alfonso J. Aspilche, an Argentine who Ruiz said owned and operated the Tabogo Money Exchange in Buenos Aires. Ruiz claimed the gang had smuggled five loads of cocaine and heroin into the United States in picture frames and said the proceeds of these operations were transmitted to the South American organization through the Tabogo Exchange.

Pursuing leads furnished by Ruiz and dug up by independent sleuthing in informed circles, Customs people subsequently were able to prove to their own satisfaction that remnants of the Ricord syndicate had been taken over by others since Ricord's arrest and incarceration in Paraguay several months earlier. Their expert guess was that the busting of Ricord had damaged the syndicate severely at the higher levels, and that lack of discipline at the top probably was responsible for the amateurish behavior of that compulsive telephone user, Alfredo Mazza.

Meanwhile, Mazza's unpredictable partner, Rodolfo Ruiz, finally was haled into court for sentencing on May 12, 1972, eight months after his arrest. He drew eight years in a federal penitentiary.

# 10

# Diplomatic Stew

Cases like that of the heroin-carrying picture frames have caused United States Customs inspectors everywhere to adopt an amiably sardonic attitude toward their more glamorous colleagues in the investigative Customs Agency Service. The mostly anonymous inspectors, many of them now women, like to joke that the sleuths are "the first line of defense against junk—after us." In point of fact, this is true because the overwhelming majority of dope smugglers try to sneak their stuff into the United States through the legal channels provided by the Customs inspection routine. If the inspector misses the contraband in a suitcase or picture frame, the agent has no case. But in the past decade Customs inspectors have become more than just people in uniform who paw through a traveler's personal effects with infuriating care. They have been trained in their own investigative procedures. They have learned to recognize the smuggler's "profile," to be suspicious of numerous visa and entry stamps showing extensive travel, and to take a second look at an individual whose passport bears the seal of a country with a casual, if not corrupt, attitude toward smuggling. Among other characteristics, the average inspector tends to view with leery eye the wayfarer with diplomatic credentials. He has learned that some members of this elegant tribe are wily practitioners of the old shell game and that it is unwise to take them on faith. Thus the interest shown in a young Latin American who arrived in the United States on a summer evening in 1971.

As any poker expert can testify, a successful bluff depends to a large extent on an accurate appraisal of the other players' intelligence. Raphael Richard González, twenty-four, son of the Panamanian Ambassador to Nationalist China, was handsome and personable, but he was not very bright. It had never occurred to him, apparently, that United States Customs inspectors knew a thing or two about the international regulations applying to diplomatic passports.

When Richard arrived at New York's Kennedy International Airport from Panama shortly after 7 P.M. on July 8, 1971, he was carrying a diplomatic passport that showed he was a member of the ambassador's family. The passport bore a B-2 visa issued at the United States Embassy in Panama for multiple entries into the United States until August 31, 1974. With a casual elegance befitting his position, Richard presented the passport to Customs Inspector Joseph Ania, who greeted him with the courteous respect due an envoy's son.

But if Ania was courtly, he also had the instinctive suspicion of his breed. He wondered about that multiple-entry visa and about Richard's luggage, which consisted of four large Samsonite suitcases and an attaché case.

"What's in your bags, sir?" Ania asked Richard.

"Summer clothing," replied Richard, abstractly.

Ania hefted one of the large suitcases. It seemed unusually heavy for a bag containing "summer clothing." He also noted that when he turned the suitcase from one end to the other, the contents shifted.

Customs, in the person of Inspector Joseph Ania, had good reason to be interested in travelers entering the United States from Panama. During the preceding eighteen months, the little "republic" operated by the strong man General Omar Torrijos had become one of the principal conduits for illicit dope trafficking aimed at the American market. One estimate was that as much as one-twelfth of the heroin used by American addicts passed through Panama, which meant that approximately 20,000 drug users in the United States got their daily supply by this route.

Moreover, the Panama Canal Zone was an American military base, and law enforcement people were concerned over the statistic which revealed that one-third of the prison population in the Zone was incarcerated on drug charges. Diplomatically, too, there was the danger that the narcotics traffic could complicate months-old negotiations on a new treaty arrangement that would recognize Panamanian sovereignty over the 500-square-mile Zone but keep the defense and operation of the canal under American control.

There was also gossip, some of which found its way into print in American newspapers, that cronies of General Torrijos and officials of his regime were involved in the heroin trafficking and were stashing huge profits in Swiss bank vaults. Thus Richard's diplomatic passport made him suspect rather than giving him the privileged respectability such a document commonly bestows on its holder. Customs had no desire to meddle in foreign policy, but the bureau willy-nilly had an official, obligatory curiosity about the baggage of potential smugglers.

"Would you mind opening your bags?" Ania asked Richard.

Richard politely demurred. Waving his passport languidly, he told Ania, "I have diplomatic immunity."

"I'm afraid not," replied Ania. "Your passport shows that neither your father nor you is accredited to the United States, only that your father is accredited to Taiwan. Immunity is granted only by the country to which a diplomat is accredited."

There was a brief legal discussion. Then Richard informed Ania that, anyway, he was in transit to Madrid and therefore his luggage was subject to examination only when it reached its final destination. If that was true, Ania retorted, why was Richard's luggage not in the custody of Braniff Airlines for transshipment to Spain? Richard was unable to account for this. "It's the airline's fault," he said. At any rate, Richard was not about to stand still for an examination there and then of his luggage.

Inspector Ania went through channels. He notified Supervisory Inspector Leonard Simon of the impasse, and Simon escorted Richard to a small conference room for a little chat. Richard steadfastly refused to open his bags. He now explained that, anyway, he had lost the keys to the luggage. Thereupon, Simon dispatched an aide on an errand. The aide was back in a few minutes with a set of duplicate keys obtained from a large Customs collection at the airport.

Simon opened all four suitcases and the attaché case. None contained clothing or toilet articles. They did yield 140 plastic bags of white powder. A simple field test of the powder revealed a positive finding for heroin.

Special Agent John Giery was summoned, and he placed Richard under arrest for violation of the federal narcotics laws. After Richard had been informed of his rights under the Constitution, Agent Giery offered the young man some fatherly advice. Richard thought things over, then agreed to cooperate.

He told his interrogators that he had traveled from Panama with Nicolás Polanco, "a kind of bodyguard." Polanco, said Richard, had already cleared Customs and had observed his arrest from the "Fishbowl" area of the observation deck in the International Arrivals Building. Both Richard and Polanco had been instructed to contact the heroin shipper, an uncle of Richard's named Guillermo Alfonso González López, upon their arrival in New York. Richard gave Agent Giery González' telephone number in Panama—645-357.

An alert was placed with the New York Telephone Company to put a hold on any calls to the Panama number. Meanwhile, according to Richard's instructions, the agents checked the young man into Room 897 of the McAlpin Hotel at 34th Street and Broadway.

At about 10 P.M., Customs got a call from the telephone company. Agents forthwith descended on a public telephone booth at 42d Street and Eighth Avenue. There they arrested Polanco while he was waiting to get through to González. An agent hung up the phone for Polanco. Customs hoped to have its own little chat with González later, an eventuality Polanco's warning call would have thwarted.

Thus when agents escorted Richard to his room at the McAlpin about midnight, they were delighted to hear the telephone ringing. Richard had his instructions. When the caller turned out, as hoped, to be González, he told his uncle, "Everything is okay."

The agents heard González ask Richard why he was so late checking into the hotel.

"I got lost," Richard told him. He also informed his uncle that Polanco, by then incarcerated in a cell in the Federal House of Detention, was "downstairs getting a sandwich."

"Okay," González told Richard. "I'm leaving on a Lan-Chile flight arriving at ten o'clock this morning at Kennedy. Stay in your room and wait for me."

As the official Customs report put it: "Arrangements were made in New York for the expected arrival of Guillermo González." Some arrangements. A call was put through to the Customs office in Miami, and instructions were given to the agent in charge there to put a man on the plane González would be taking to New York. Thanks to Richard, the Miami office could be provided with a description of the youth's uncle—Panamanian, five feet, five inches tall, slim build, about 135 pounds, mustache, black hair, white complexion, forty-two to forty-six years of age.

Then Richard talked some more. He told his interrogators he had made five previous flights from Panama to the United States with heroin in his luggage—four in the fall of 1970 and one in January, 1971. On all these flights, Richard said, González accompanied him as "bodyguard."

González arrived at Kennedy Airport at 11:30 A.M. via Miami. Unknown to González, it was a couple of Customs agents who escorted him to a taxicab operated by Special Agent Mario Sessa. González told Sessa to take him to the McAlpin Hotel. En route, the Panamanian informed Sessa that he had a friend in the Hotel Edison and asked if Sessa knew the Edison address. Sessa gave him the address. González thanked him and remarked that he must remember to call his friend that night.

Upon his arrival at the McAlpin, González went directly to Room 897, where he greeted Richard and made some small talk. Then, with Customs men eavesdropping, González told his nephew to place a call to the Hotel Edison. When the call was put through, González took the phone and was connected with an Óscar San Martín in Room 834. González and San Martín arranged to meet in the bar of the Edison within the hour. When González hung up, he was arrested by agents who had been sequestered in an adjoining room.

Like Richard, González was willing to talk. He explained that his arrangement with San Martín for delivery of the heroin required him to place the four suitcases and attaché case in the locked trunk of a rented car, then leave the car in a public parking lot and deliver the parking ticket to San Martín. Ten minutes later, agents had rented a car and stashed Richard's luggage in the trunk. Under surveillance, González drove to a parking lot at 1250 Broadway where he left the car, then set off to deliver the parking ticket to San Martín.

With Customs men still dogging his footsteps, González dutifully arrived at the Hotel Edison, where he met San Martín and turned over the ticket. With González and his guardian agents standing by, San Martín placed a phone call from the hotel lobby. González then departed with his agents, while other Customs men remained to keep an eye on San Martín. Within a few minutes, a man later identified as Américo Altamirano arrived at the Edison and had a brief conversation with San Martín, after which San Martín returned to his hotel room under surveillance.

Agents followed Altamirano to a building at 310 West 47th Street. He left the building several minutes later, accompanied by a man later identified as his brother, César. The brothers walked around in aimless fashion for more than twenty minutes before arriving at the lot where the rented car was parked. There they separated, with César proceeding to the parking lot office while Américo strolled about in the immediate neighborhood.

César presented the parking ticket to a uniformed attendant named Duane Lane, whose full-time job was special agent of the Bureau of Customs. Lane drove the rented car from its space and delivered it to his customer. Then, as César attempted to climb into the car, he was arrested. When César refused to talk, his brother, Américo, was arrested on a nearby street. At about the same time, agents arrested San Martín at the Hotel Edison.

It was a little after 4 P.M. on July 9, 1971. It had taken Customs less than twenty-four hours to round up all six persons involved in the smuggling attempt. Agents had seized 151 pounds of pure heroin with a street value estimated at up to $27,000,000—enough to supply the habit of every addict in New York City for almost a month.

The apprehension of Guillermo Alfonso González López also provided the Customs' Intelligence Division with some raw intelligence to be squirreled away for possible use on another day, in another case with diplomatic ramifications. On González' person were found various papers and an address book, which, in Customs' carefully calculated—and absolutely necessary—double-talk, "indicated" that González had had "associations with" some big names in Latin-American governmental and diplomatic circles, including at least one head of state, at least two ambassadors, assorted Cabinet ministers, and a couple of high-ranking military officers.

As one Customs official put it: "All these names make fascinating reading, but we couldn't lay a glove on their owners even if we had admissible evidence. They're a problem for their own countries unless they get in trouble on American soil and even then we probably couldn't hold them. In the meantime, we're not in the business of toppling foreign governments no matter what kind of creeps they have running their stores."

Besides, Customs at the time was preoccupied with its part in the final disposition of the case of Raphael Richard, *et al.* As receiver of the heroin, Óscar San Martín drew the stiffest penalty—a twelve-year prison sentence on each of three indictment counts, to run concurrently. González, the operation manager, got seven years in the pen, and Richard three and a half years after both pleaded *nolo contendere*. Américo and César Altamirano each got two years, but charges against Richard's bodyguard, Nicolás Polanco, were dismissed by the United States Attorney's office after he had served almost six months in jail awaiting trial.

Meanwhile, however, Congress had become inquisitive about the drug situation in Panama, and in March, 1972, Customs' intelligence on official Panamanian involvement in heroin trafficking became a matter of public record. The vehicle of this exposé was a draft report by the unlikely Panama Canal subcommittee of the House Merchant Marine and Fisheries Committee headed by Representative John M. Murphy, Democrat, of New York.

The connection lay in the fact that the subcommittee had been studying and conducting hearings on the United States position in Panama vis-à-vis the future operation of the Panama Canal and jurisdiction over the Canal Zone. Among the experts to which the subcommittee turned was Customs Commissioner Myles J. Ambrose, who arranged a briefing for the panel by a group of special agents on January 24.

In a far-ranging review, the briefing agents cited some chapter and verse on thirty major heroin seizure cases during the preceding eighteen months. The seizures ranged from 13 pounds to several hundred pounds, and five of the seizures—or one-sixth of the total—involved the Republic of Panama. According to the subcommittee's draft report, "The briefing team concluded that based on the Customs investigation" the Richard case "reached into the highest levels of Panamanian officialdom and included Moises Torrijos, the brother of General Omar Torrijos, and the Panamanian Foreign Minister, Juan Tack."

The report on the briefing also noted that Nicolás Polanco, Richard's bodyguard, was a chauffeur for Richard's uncle, Guillermo González, and that González was a longtime friend and former bodyguard of Moises Torrijos. Added the report: "The Customs agents claimed that because Richard's father was in Taiwan at the time of these transactions that he got his diplomatic passport from Moises, who had access to them as a Panamanian ambassador. Customs confirmed the Bureau of Narcotics and Dangerous Drugs' report that Juan Tack had signed the diplomatic passport."

Although the subcommittee acknowledged that narcotics trafficking was "basically an American problem run, in part, by Americans and criminals in other countries . . . as in every other part of the world, local nationals and officials succumb to the enticement of easy money and are lured into the drug traffic. This has happened in Panama."

The subcommittee was almost as rough on the State Department, which it charged "has had an historic policy of ignoring or denying the involvement in the narcotics traffic into the United States of high-ranking officials of friendly foreign governments. . . . The question is [whether] the United States is negotiating a treaty that involves a 70-year, five-billion-dollar U.S. commitment, not to mention the security of the United States and this hemisphere, with a government that condones or is actually involved in a drug-running operation into the United States."

Although it flopped, the Richard caper combined two smuggling methods—one as old as international relations and the other a product of the jet age. A proper diplomatic passport has been the perfect *laissez-passer* for the carrier of contraband since the days of ancient Canaan. Travel by commercial airline enables the dope supplier in Marseilles to promise speedy, often same-day delivery to the wholesaler in New York, Miami or Chicago, and payment within a matter of days. It has brought to the narcotics trade the rapid turnover of the supermarket.

However he travels, an accredited diplomat's person and baggage are safe from customs inspection. The same is true of the individual traveling with a head of state or a high government leader paying an official visit to a foreign country, no matter how clerkly his status. By courtesy and tradition, none of the visiting team's baggage is examined; and, of course, the diplomatic "pouch"—which might be as big as a piano box—is always inviolate. Occasionally, however, authorities are able to gather enough evidence of suspicious associations to move against even these privileged persons, in what might be called "the international interest"—for want of a handier term.

Such action was taken successfully in the sixties against two Latin-American ambassadors: Mauricio Rosal, Guatemalan Ambassador to the Netherlands and Belgium, and Salvador Pardo-Bolland, Mexican Ambassador to Bolivia. Both were caught with dirty hands in New York through a cooperative effort by Customs and the Bureau of Narcotics, then a Treasury agency.

The cases were notable because they were the first big hits against diplomatic smugglers and thus represented a show of power by American law enforcement authorities; they served notice that diplomats were not immune to suspicion and that striped-pants smugglers could discover they were living dangerously if they were careless of their associations.

In *"L'affaire Rosal,"* as it was called by the cooperating French Sûreté, the first tip came in 1960 from the Beirut office of the Narcotics agency, which reported to Washington on the smuggling activities of a Frenchman named Étienne Tarditi, who boasted of his Corsican birth. An Arab informer had told Narcotics Agent Paul Knight that a considerable amount of heroin processed in the Lebanon capital from morphine base smuggled in from Turkey had been shipped to the Tarditi organization in Paris. The courier was said to be a Latin-American diplomat named Maurice.

At Customs headquarters in Washington, a check was made of assorted records. Several tedious days later, Agent Mario Cozzi came across a report dated in the fall of 1941. It said that one Mauricio Rosal, a Guatemalan chargé d'affaires, had been investigated in the alleged smuggling of $40,000 worth of essential oils and diamonds valued at $37,000 into New York. But Customs had been unable to get its hands on enough evidence to prefer charges against Rosal and the case was closed.

Investigators learned that Rosal, now forty-seven, had climbed the ladder to the post of Guatemalan Ambassador to Belgium and the Netherlands. He was a small, portly man, balding and something of a clotheshorse; a man who affected a regal air and was known as something of a caustic wit. Agents stuck his name in their hats.

Étienne Tarditi, it was learned, was a fifty-five-year-old Parisian with a bad reputation even in the permissive French underworld—short, potbellied, with hanging jowls. He had been investigated in several narcotics deals, but he had managed to remain in the background and thus had stayed out of jail. Tarditi had been seen in Paris in the company of a TWA airline steward named Charles Bourbonnais, a ladies' man who spent more money than his salary would seem to support. In turn, Bourbonnais was found to have done some public drinking with an inelegant New York longshoreman named Nicholas Calamaris, forty-seven, a big man with big ears, a long nose and a tight face that resembled a skin-clothed skull.

A few months later, Customs had compiled a dossier on Rosal as an international gadabout. Checking airline records, agents discovered Rosal had made frequent transatlantic trips during the previous eighteen months, and that on several of these trips his traveling companion had been one Étienne Tarditi. Customs inspectors had always given Rosal the customary diplomatic treatment, passing him on without examining his luggage. They had noted one curious fact: The ambassador seemed always to leave New York with fewer pounds of luggage than he had brought into the country. Could Rosal be bringing in his own meals, in chic brown bags? Customs thought not.

Then the Sûreté informed Washington that Rosal and Tarditi had bought tickets for still another flight to New York. Tarditi would arrive at Kennedy International Airport a day before Rosal. Bourbonnais was also headed for the United States as a steward aboard a TWA flight.

If the men held to their reported *modus operandi,* Rosal would be the courier. This conclusion seemed accurate when neither Tarditi nor Bourbonnais was found to be carrying anything illicit. Customs could have given Rosal a hard time, because investigators had made inquiries at the State Department and that discreet institution had learned in a roundabout way that the Guatemalan embassy in Washington knew nothing of Rosal's trip to the United States and that, furthermore, there were no plans to accredit him to this country. But Customs and Narcotics had longer-range plans. All they wanted to do was keep track of the men for the big score.

Thus Tarditi was under constant surveillance from the moment he noted on his Customs declaration that he would be staying at the Sherry-Netherland Hotel. The word of a Tarditi is not taken by Customs as from Sinai. An agent disguised as a porter grabbed Tarditi's one bag and escorted him to a cab driven by another agent. Tarditi told the ersatz cabby to drive him to the Savoy Hilton; as the cab slowly pulled away, the agent wrote the name of the hotel on a piece of paper and casually dropped it from the window as he signaled his intention to merge into the traffic. An agent in a following car jumped out and picked up the piece of paper. An hour later, Bourbonnais was tailed to his home on Long Island.

Upon Rosal's arrival, he was given the diplomatic immunity treatment again; none of his four suitcases was opened. Then he in turn was driven to the Plaza Hotel, hard by the Savoy Hilton, by a Pan-American World Airways passenger representative, with two cars filled with agents in casual pursuit.

Rosal's neighbors in the room adjoining his at the Plaza also were federal agents.

That night after dinner Rosal strolled to the Savoy and met Tarditi in the lobby, where they embraced and repaired to a quiet corner for a chat that lasted until midnight. Rosal then returned to the Plaza. The next morning, Tarditi took a cab to an apartment building on East 78th Street, emerging a few minutes later with a parcel wrapped in brown paper. He took another cab to the Plaza, where he left the parcel with Rosal, lounging in his room, then returned to his own hotel. Meanwhile, Customs' Mario Cozzi had noticed a Ford station wagon parked at the northeast corner of Central Park South; the skull-faced man at the wheel seemed familiar. Cozzi wrote down the wagon's license number, out of habit.

By this time more than a dozen agents were dispersed in the general area in radio cars, in instant communication with Narcotics Supervisor George Gaffney and the Customs agent in charge, Carl Esposita, who sat in a parked car near the Plaza's entrance. The alert came when Rosal called for a bellman to take his bags from his room to a taxicab; Tarditi had left his room at the Savoy only a few minutes earlier and was tailed to 72nd Street and Lexington Avenue. There he was met by Bourbonnais and a man with a face like a skull.

As the lawmen had expected, Rosal's cab soon pulled up at 72d and Lexington, where he got out to join Tarditi and Bourbonnais, after telling the cabdriver to wait. The skull-headed man, Nicholas Calamaris, walked over and sat down in the driver's seat of a Ford station wagon parked nearby. Agent Cozzi took particular note.

At Rosal's order, the cabby opened the trunk of the cab, and all three men looked into it. Then, suddenly, as if seized by a second thought, Rosal told the cabby to close the trunk lid. While Bourbonnais strode to the station wagon, Rosal and Tarditi got into the cab. Calamaris and Bourbonnais drove toward Third Avenue, with the cab following.

The agents wanted to wait until the suitcases were transferred from the cab to the station wagon before making their move. But Gaffney and Esposita decided to take no chances on losing the men in the heavy Manhattan traffic. Their car sped forward and swerved in front of the cab. Other cars blocked the path of the station wagon.

Tarditi was the picture of outraged innocence. "Do you know who this man is?" he shrieked. "He is entitled to diplomatic immunity."

"Not today he isn't," snapped Cozzi.

Still protesting, the four men were hauled from the cab and station wagon. The startled cabdriver was told to open the cab's trunk. The suitcases were packed with plastic bags containing the inevitable white powder that later tested as almost pure heroin. Inside a small case which Rosal insisted was his only luggage was the parcel wrapped in brown paper which Tarditi had given him the night before. The parcel contained $26,000 in U.S. currency—Rosal's payoff. Later, another paper sack containing $41,949 was found secreted under the front seat of the station wagon—Tarditi's share.

The heroin in Rosal's luggage tipped the scales at 49.25 kilograms. But there was more to come. From information gleaned during the interrogation of Rosal and Bourbonnais, both of whom were scared into near-hysteria, agents located another 51.89 kilos of heroin, which Tarditi had cached in a trunk in a Long Island row house. At the time, it was the biggest seizure ever made in the United States, with an estimated street value of more than $22,000,000.

Rosal, the courier, and Calamaris, the receiver, were sentenced to fifteen years in a federal penitentiary. Tarditi, the smuggler, and Bourbonnais, the errand boy who had picked up Tarditi's payoff from a man in a gray suit standing on Fifth Avenue across from St. Patrick's Cathedral, each got nine years. Because all four had pleaded guilty, the court refrained from imposing the maximum sentence permitted—twenty years.

But the arrests of Rosal, Tarditi, *et al.* would have been important had their sentences been even lighter than those imposed. They led in 1967 to the apprehension of the second diplomat, Salvador Pardo-Bolland, Mexico's Ambassador to Bolivia. Following leads produced by the Rosal case, Customs and Narcotics Bureau agents picked up information in 1964 that one Gilbert Coscia, a Marseilles wheeler dealer, was widely regarded in the more sordid international circles as another general in the Paris-New York trafficking. They decided to dig deeper into Coscia's activities and opened up another line of cooperation with the French Sûreté.

Among them, the Sûreté, Customs and Narcotics undertook the gargantuan task of screening more than 1,000,000 cables between New York and Marseilles, Marseilles-Cuba and Marseilles-Beirut. The job took three maddening, frustration-filled years, but finally the lawmen saw what looked like a *modus operandi* involving a courier named Lambo.

No one could provide a clue to "Lambo's" identity, but a coincidence gave the sleuths some ideas. In the period encompassing four short trips made to the United States by Gilbert Coscia, airline records and hotel registers revealed that Ambassador Pardo-Bolland had also been in this country. In French, *l'ambassadeur* Pardo-Bolland could be shortened to "Lambo," couldn't it?

Anyway, there was enough circumstantial evidence to turn the law's attention in the Ambassador's direction. He was seen on the Riviera with Coscia and with a former Uruguayan diplomat, Juan Arizti, an old Pardo-Bolland pal. A few months later, Pardo-Bolland flew to Paris and then to New York. Arizti flew to Paris and then to Montreal. The plot did indeed seem to be thickening, especially after that Coscia-Pardo-Bolland-Arizti conference.

In Montreal, Arizti sailed safely through customs. But U.S. Customs agents and Canadian police were watching as he took a cab to Montreal Central Station and placed four of his six suitcases in two luggage lockers, then repaired to the Queen Elizabeth Hotel across the street, where he stayed for three nights. In the "international interest," Canadian police opened the lockers while Arizti was visiting with the sandman and found that the four suitcases contained 56 kilos of heroin. They substituted identical packets of milk sugar for all but two of the bags of heroin, replaced the suitcases in the lockers, and locked them up again.

Arizti checked the lockers the next day and was satisfied his contraband was safe. Two days later he reclaimed the suitcases and took the overnight train to New York, where he checked the bags in lockers at Pennyslvania Station. He then taxied to the Elysee Hotel and went up to a room occupied by Pardo-Bolland. The next morning, the two men called on one Jacques Leroux at the Americana Hotel and delivered to him the keys for the two luggage lockers at Pennsylvania Station.

That was that—or so the three men believed. Leroux, who had been identified by Customs as René Brouchon, a known French narcotics trafficker, booked a flight to Switzerland. Pardo-Bolland and Arizti bought airline tickets to Paris. The lawmen grabbed Leroux-Brouchon on a New York street as he tried unsuccessfully to drop the locker keys down a drain. Pardo-Bolland and Arizti were taken into custody at an airline office to which they had gone to try to book earlier flights out of the country. Four months later, Pardo-Bolland was sentenced to eighteen years in prison, Brouchon to fifteen years, and Arizti to ten years.

In both cases, law enforcement agencies had received the customary wholehearted cooperation from the airlines involved. But the airlines' responsibility was relatively simple; all they had to do was open their passenger arrival lists to the investigating agents and alert them to the presence of names in which the law was interested. The air carriers' job is much tougher when their own people join up with the bad guys, for pay.

Junk smugglers have found a number of ways to use airlines as a means of transport for their goods. They can bribe a member of the aircraft's crew to act as a courier or to conceal the dope on the plane for pickup by a passenger on the plane's continuing or return flight. They can hire a ground technician—sometimes a lowly cleanup man —to hide the contraband for pickup when the plane is serviced at its destination. They can buy the services of cargo handlers to steer a shipment away from Customs. And they can juggle cargo manifests on airfreight flights.

Using a member of an air crew as a courier is ideal from the syndicates' point of view. The crew member is legitimate; he must travel as part of his job and therefore he has a built-in reason for being in Paris one day and in New York the next. Even if he uses a satchelful of passports, the ordinary courier is eventually in danger of being recognized as a touch too peripatetic and thus a suspicious person. Stewards and stewardesses are the chief targets of the dope recruiters because they are the lowest paid; the syndicates seldom approach pilots, flight engineers and radio operators, most of whom are well paid and, besides, have too much to lose if caught.

One French Corsican heroin gang all but controlled Air France's routes to Chicago and Montreal in the sixties. It bought off several stewards and also the dispatcher who made up the air crew rosters and who could make sure that certain crooked stewards were on certain flights. Moreover, a supervisor at the airline's communications center in Paris was paid so much a month to permit transmission of the syndicate's messages to their bought stewards while the planes were in flight.

No authority in Customs will undertake the depressing chore of trying to estimate how much heroin or hashish or cocaine is smuggled into the United States concealed in shipments of legitimate cargo —or shipments disguised as legitimate cargo. After all, the bureau's inspectors must clear more than 2,500,000 cargo shipments a year. Usually, the dope is removed from the shipment by cargo handlers at airports or on the docks before it is picked up by the unwitting importer. Obviously, some importers make a fast buck by accepting delivery of both legitimate and dope cargo, then holding the dope for pickup by the syndicate's receiver.

Airlines, especially in Western countries, have recognized their vulnerability to infiltration by dope smugglers. Most of them switch crews to new routes every month and prohibit last-minute swapping of flights. They also have their own security teams, whose members operate internationally as intelligence agents for law enforcement agencies. That is to say, while they have no power of arrest and may not function in any way as policemen, they can arrange for the detention and interrogation of suspects.

Such tips of course are invaluable and have helped break some big cases. But for the most part, Customs relies on its old reliables—the anonymous and honest cargo handlers, airline employees and examining inspectors at every port of entry. Thus it was a Braniff Airlines worker and an inspector named Gerard Donovan, on duty at New York's Kennedy International Airport, who broke the case of the overshipped suitcase on September 29, 1971.

The suitcase, a gray Samsonite model, was addressed from Buenos Aires to Miami on Braniff Flight 974 but had been overflown to New York because it had been stowed up forward in the cargo hatch and a considerable amount of baggage was loaded on behind it. Thus the little helper in Miami who had been assigned to pull the bag off couldn't get to it, or even see it, and concluded there had been a snafu. The suitcase was sitting on the floor at the airport in New York when the Braniff man noticed it. He hefted the bag and found it heavy—much heavier than the 44 pounds listed on the airway bill. He called over Customs Inspector Gerard Donovan, who opened the suitcase and found it contained 66 pounds of pure heroin valued at $29,000,000 on the street.

After substituting milk sugar for most of the horse, Customs agents sent the suitcase back to Miami with Agent Frank De Santis. There it was delivered by agents dressed as cargo handlers to the Braniff warehouse at Miami International Airport.

Because of the size of the warehouse, roughly that of a football gridiron, Special Agent Kenny Wagner of the Miami Customs office decided the only way to watch the place was to station two agents in the rafters. Wagner maintained surveillance from the outside in a car with radio communication to the two agents perched precariously on a couple of steel beams. The agents were equipped with earphones so that Wagner's messages wouldn't be broadcast to everybody who sauntered into the building.

On the second day of a twenty-four-hour watch, a Braniff cargo handler named James Fletcher walked into the warehouse, looked at the suitcase, picked it up, moved it a few feet, and then put it down and walked off. To the watching agents, it seemed at the time that Fletcher was merely thinking in terms of petty pilferage and was casing the joint. But Fletcher returned just after midnight the next day, grabbed the suitcase, and ran outside, where he put it on the back of a Braniff truck. Then he apparently recognized a Customs agent among the loiterers in the area. At any rate, he drove the truck with the suitcase back into the warehouse and was about to replace the bag where he had picked it up when he was arrested.

Fletcher told the agents he was to be paid $1,000 for delivering the suitcase to Robert Ottavegio, another Braniff employee. According to Fletcher's instructions, he stashed the suitcase in a baggage locker at the airport, and other Customs men took up surveillance of the locker. Ottavegio arrived the next day to pick up the bag, and he, too, was taken into custody. Ottavegio also sang. Under Customs' supervision, he made two phone calls to his contact, one Donald Eugene Robertson, a third Braniff worker, during which the two arranged to meet at a shopping center in South Dade County, South Miami.

Agents in a Customs helicopter tailed Ottavegio's car as he drove to the shopping center with the heroin. Also in the car were two agents, who were dropped off about half a mile from the meeting place and joined other agents in an unmarked Customs car. At the shopping center, Ottavegio and Robertson decided to repair to a more secluded area about five miles away. They were followed to a point in Cutler Ridge by the helicopter, which radioed directions to agents following in Customs cars.

At an isolated spot, the car containing Ottavegio and Robertson pulled up, and Robertson got out, opened the trunk of the car, and took a look at the contents of the suitcase. Then he spotted the helicopter and got panicky, jumped back into the car, and drove off again. He was nabbed after going only about 200 yards down the road by a Customs car that forced him into a ditch. There, Robertson joined the choral group, announcing that his contact was one Juan José Trovato, an Argentinian who worked as a Braniff purser.

Four telephone conversations, all monitored by agents, were necessary before Trovato and Robertson agreed that the time was ripe for a delivery. The situation was complicated. Although Robertson was to hand the heroin over to Trovato, the latter was scheduled to return it after examination so that Robertson could make the final delivery to two men due to arrive from Buenos Aires.

At any rate, the penultimate delivery was to be made to Trovato at Robertson's house outside Miami. Three agents accompanied Robertson to his home, while other agents in a Customs helicopter took up an air surveillance. Shortly after noon on October 6, a brown sedan pulled into the Robertson driveway and Trovato got out and knocked on the Robertson door. He and Robertson then walked over to where Robertson's car was parked, and Robertson opened the trunk of the car and satisfied Trovato that the suitcase was in the trunk, ready for delivery. Trovato stared at the suitcase for a few minutes, then told Robertson to close the trunk. The two were about to go into the house together when Trovato was put under arrest.

With all his pals cooperating with the law, Trovato apparently felt he had no alternative but to join the club. From the McAllister Hotel in downtown Miami, Trovato put through an overseas call to one Brondoni Florencio Sepe in Buenos Aires. "Everything is all right," Trovato told Sepe, according to the Customs interpreter's instant translation. "I've seen the suitcase. Robertson, he has it."

But Sepe was prudent. "Very well," he told Trovato. "I'll call you back. Stay there." When he called back several minutes later, Sepe got Robertson's phone number from Trovato and hung up. Then, with other agents monitoring Robertson's phone, Sepe phoned Robertson and arranged for the final delivery.

Sepe and one Antonio Ricardo Pellini-Carrilli, another Argentinian, arrived in Miami aboard Air Argentina Flight 360 from Buenos Aires at about nine o'clock that night—October 6. Sepe called Trovato and again asked for Robertson's phone number. "Just to make sure," he told Trovato. But it was not until the next morning, at about ten o'clock, that Sepe called Robertson and made a date for delivery of the heroin at noon outside the McAllister Hotel. Robertson delivered the suitcase to Pellini inside the hotel, then drove off. Almost immediately, Sepe drove up to the Flagler Street entrance of the hotel. Pellini put the suitcase in the trunk of Sepe's car and they drove off. They were arrested a few minutes later.

Looking back, Customs' chief of investigations, Harold Smith, was constrained to comment on the routineness of the case. "In a sense it was easy, because everybody talked as soon as they were caught," he said. "But even so, all sorts of things could have gone wrong if those agents in Miami hadn't followed the book, hadn't stuck to routine procedure. With six suspects involved, patience and just plain disciplined, dogged police work were vital. You don't want anybody trying to pull something spectacular on a case like that. You've got to make all the right moves—and wait it out. As it is, the case was wrapped up in a little less than nine days—pretty fast work."

Pretty fast work also described the outcome in a Miami federal courtroom. Fletcher, Ottavegio, Robertson, Trovato and Pellini all entered guilty pleas: Fletcher drew eighteen months in prison: Ottavegio three years; Robertson five years' probation; Trovato five years; and Pellini eighteen months. Sepe went to trial on five counts, but halfway through the trial he pleaded guilty to three counts. The judge sentenced him to seven and a half years, plus three years of special probation, on the first count; seven and a half years, plus a $15,000 fine, on the second count; and seven and a half years on the third count.

Among other things, it was a victory for honest, put-upon airlines everywhere.

# 11

# Murder to Order

Although Customs people had their suspicions, there was no way of knowing how long the so-called Samsonite Gang of Juan José Trovato, Brondoni Florencio Sepe, *et al.* had been working their smuggling gimmick. But as Customs' Harold Smith noted, the gang was broken up in jig time once it came to the law's attention. In contrast, a respected businessman in Orlando, Florida, was able to pursue a wide variety of illicit operations for more than three years before the people of the state caught up with him.

Thirty-three-year-old Errol Bernard Resnick, slightly built and stoop-shouldered, had been alternately described in Florida newspapers as a wealthy Orlando businessman and as central Florida's major narcotics supplier. Indeed, Resnick made enough money to come close to the millionaire category. He lived with his wife and three children in a luxurious home in a high-income neighborhood in Orlando, a home equipped with a battery of spotlights protruding from under the eaves on each corner and a costly burglar alarm system. He could pay cash on the barrelhead for a $50,000 twin-engine Beechcraft Baron airplane. Resnick's problem was that various law enforcement agencies took a dim view of his many enterprises.

Resnick had moved to Orlando from Atlanta in 1962 and hired on as a draftsman at the Martin-Marietta plant. At that time he was twenty-four years old, with the looks and air of a teen-ager, and collected guns and old coins. He made his first big money by collecting Jefferson nickels in the early 1960's—buying nickels by the rolls and picking through them for those bearing the Jefferson image. When the nickels soared in value, Resnick sold them and invested in a small smelting plant along the Little Econlockhatchee River, buying his hoists, furnaces and crucibles from the Moore Foundry and Machine Company in Orlando.

His activities brought him to the attention, in 1968, of Treasury

Department agents. They snooped around until one day in March, 1969, when a pickup truck and a brown Cadillac hearse arrived at Resnick's smelting plant and later departed the plant and proceeded to Herndon Airport, where Resnick kept his DC-3 surplus plane. The agents thereupon raided the plant and arrested Resnick and three of his employees on charges of illegally reducing United States coins to their silver content, worth from 6 to 18 percent more than their face value. The quartet was convicted in January, 1970, and Resnick was sentenced to two years in prison. He appealed and was released on bond.

That gave Resnick time to launch another enterprise—the smuggling of marijuana from the Bahamas. As reconstructed by Customs officials, Resnick's conspiracy had the value of simplicity. He set up a *modus operandi* whereby one of his hirelings would engage a pilot for a business trip to the islands. There, the hireling would decide to take a holiday trip to Jamaica, where he would pay cash for a load of marijuana, to be picked up by the pilot at an isolated landing strip. The marijuana would be flown to a similar landing strip in Florida's interior for unloading. Then the pilot would fly back to a regulated airport and clear customs.

Resnick directed one Alfred W. Harrison, one of his employees, to locate a good pilot. Harrison found one through the good offices of the Embry-Riddle Aeronautical Institute in Daytona. The pilot's name was Kevin A. Phillips, a decorated combat flyer recently returned after his second tour in Vietnam.

But Harrison, in the habit of a casual age, neglected to investigate Phillips' background. He merely checked Phillips' license and hired him at $100 a day. Had he looked more deeply into Phillips' personal ambience, he undoubtedly would have discovered that the pilot had an obsessive fear and hatred of drugs. It seems one of his friends had been murdered by two thugs high on dope, and another friend, an addict, had committed suicide.

Phillips flew Harrison to Jamaica and stood silent while Harrison counted out $10,000 to a Jamaican for a cargo of marijuana—silent, but appalled and determined to sever his connection with Resnick & Co. Phillips took off, alone, for the landing strip to pick up the load, but never landed. Back at their hotel, he told Harrison that the sellers had failed to show up with the merchandise.

In Florida, Phillips contacted a Customs agent. The agent convinced him that he could strike a blow against drug trafficking if he continued to work for the Resnick ring.

Phillips was not summoned to Harrison's presence immediately. Resnick had hired a second pilot, a potbellied, genial World War II veteran named Horace Hartwig, nicknamed Twig. Hartwig signed up to fly his own Beechcraft to the Bahamas for $5,000 to pick up a passenger and some merchandise. Hartwig didn't like what he found at the Jamaican airstrip—a husky male with a gun in his belt who hoisted four heavy suitcases into the aircraft. But he figured it was too late to back out. He wrote his son later, "I didn't report it because I was afraid they would kill me."

At any rate, Hartwig flew the plane back to Florida with its cargo and gun-toting passenger. Then it was Phillips' turn again. He was ordered to report to the Daytona Airport "for a tryout." There Phillips saw Resnick for the first time and mistook him for a flunky. "I thought he was some kind of errand boy," the pilot told his Customs friends. But Resnick had just bought his Beechcraft Baron, and he wanted Phillips to fly it around so that Resnick could be sure the pilot knew how to handle the aircraft.

Phillips passed the test flight and a few days later was ordered to Jamaica in the Beechcraft. With Harrison, he picked up 600 pounds of marijuana and started back to the Bahamas. The Nassau tower approved his alternate flight plan to Florida before Phillips had had a chance to mention it. This bugged Harrison; it suggested that some people wearing badges were interested in the flight. He pulled out a .45 caliber pistol from a brown handbag and placed it near his right hand on the seat, away from Phillips.

"Okay," he told Phillips. "Let's go back to Florida. But watch it."

If Harrison had any idea of using the gun, he had to abandon it. The plane ran into strong head winds and accompanying turbulence, and Phillips had to struggle to keep the aircraft aloft when the bumping about ate up his fuel supply. One engine had quit and the fuel gauge read empty when Phillips finally sighted the lights of Stuart Airport and managed to glide into a landing—and into the arms of Customs agents and Martin County deputy sheriffs. They impounded the marijuana and took Harrison into custody on the spot; later, they arrested Resnick and two others. All were charged with conspiracy to import marijuana. All made bail.

At about this time, a comely girl named Nancy Gray, who worked for Resnick in his gun store as secretary and general helper, entered the picture. As was brought out by the lawmen later in connection with official charges, Nancy became Resnick's "communications connection"—a kind of one-woman, twenty-four-hour-a-day switch-board operator. None of Resnick's conspirators reached him without calling Nancy first. The conspirators were given a telephone code, which Resnick changed periodically. Then, when calling Nancy, the individual would use the right code words ("I have a message for Big Daddy") and leave her a name and telephone number—always that of a pay booth. Nancy then phoned Resnick, who would return the call from another phone booth.

Customs agents working on the case suspected Nancy was in-volved in Resnick's illegal gun sales as well as doing small errands in connection with his smuggling activities. Thus, while pursuing the smuggling investigation, they were able to give occasional assistance to agents of the Internal Revenue Service's Alcohol, Tobacco Tax and Firearms Division who were handling that facet of the Resnick enterprises. In turn, the IRS unit passed on bits and pieces about Resnick's smuggling operation to Customs. Meanwhile, the Secret Service was still working on Resnick's gold smuggling and his ma-nipulations in silver currency. An awesome number of federal au-thorities were interested in Errol Bernard Resnick.

But Resnick was not about to quit when he was behind. He still had the Twig and plenty of money. Twig was available ostensibly because he needed work; in fact he was afraid to turn Resnick down lest he wind up in a block of concrete. The money was available from the receipts of Resnick's gun shop, Triggermart, where customers could buy firearms in large quantities without having to answer a lot of embarrassing questions, and from Resnick's business dealings with Canadian peddlers of gold coins.

Hartwig signed up for another flight to Jamaica on March 14. But Customs by this time had the Resnick operation taped. When the plane touched down in Florida with 510 pounds of marijuana and a Resnick "bodyguard" aboard, agents were waiting to take over. The Twig agreed to sing; he seemed relieved to be getting it all over with. He would have been better off in jail, however.

On May 12, 1971, Hartwig wrote his son that he had talked to the FBI the day before, and that he had to go to a conference in Miami. "It will take some time to convict these guys, and then I can clear my name," he wrote. The Twig never made it.

On the same day he wrote his son, Hartwig had a visitor who introduced himself as Ray Burgess, an electrical contractor. Burgess said he wanted to buy a piece of Hartwig's land along Lake Harris outside Leesburg. The two left town to look over the property, and two days later Hartwig called his wife from Burgess' motel and said they were going to Clearmont to see some other property.

"I don't like that Burgess," his wife told him. "He's got soft hands. I don't believe he's a contractor." Hartwig kidded her gently about "bucking for detective."

Four and a half months later, Horace Hartwig's badly decomposed body was found buried in a Lake County, Florida, orange grove. He had been shot once in the head.

In the meantime, Kevin Phillips also had discovered the perils that dog an informant. One June night, he got a telephone call from a man who identified himself as a Federal Aviation Administration inspector. The man asked Phillips to meet him the next morning at the Daytona Airport. Phillips agreed, then phoned a Customs contact and asked him to find out whether an FAA inspector by that name had placed the call. The call was a fake.

Accordingly, Customs agents had staked out the airport when Phillips arrived for his appointment with the inspector. Answering a page by the Eastern Airlines ticket desk, he was handed a message telling him the inspector would meet him at his (Phillips') home. Phillips strode off, followed by two men who had been loitering in the airport. The men climbed into a Cadillac driven by a third man and tailed Phillips' car.

As instructed by his guardian agents, Phillips stopped at a doughnut shop, to give the agents time to catch up with the pilot's pursuers. But the two cars of agents lost the Cadillac in traffic, although one of the men in the fleeing vehicle was identified as Alfred Harrison, Phillips' companion on both Jamaica flights. Customs moved Phillips into a downstate hotel, where he remained in hiding for six long months.

Clayton Walker, an old friend of Resnick's, wasn't that lucky. He had made tapes of telephone conversations with Resnick and turned them over to the Florida Department of Law Enforcement. One night in August, Walker had a visitor who said his name was Ray Burgess. They found Walker's body, shot once in the heart and twice behind the right ear, a mile from his Orlando home.

A month before, Walker had made his last smuggling flight for Resnick—and the lawmen. Customs set up this one by arranging that Resnick meet one of its agents named Charley Martinez, a licensed pilot, who told Resnick he was looking for "any kind of work that paid big money." Resnick hired him on the spot to pilot his plane to a Bahamian airstrip to pick up a cargo of 925 pounds of marijuana.

Federal agents were on hand, concealed in the lush vegetation, when the plane collected the marijuana, and a horde of lawmen, including Customs and Narcotics Bureau agents and Florida state, county and local police, watched the plane touch down at an abandoned military airfield near New Smyrna, Florida.

Hastily, the smugglers unloaded their cargo and hid it in the brush ringing the airfield. Harrison, free on bail again, and one Leonard White settled down to guard the contraband. When a pickup truck arrived on the scene, obviously to transport the marijuana from the field, the lawmen moved in for a roundup. There was a brief fire fight before Chesly Slaughter, driver of the truck, surrendered. Harrison and White fled into a patch of nearby woods but were hunted down and taken into custody.

That little shootout led in September to a courtroom contretemps in Jacksonville, Florida, in which a federal judge ordered White and Slaughter to spend every night in jail even if they posted bonds of $100,000 each. White and Slaughter were cooperative witnesses for the state, and Charles J. Moniak, an agent of the Florida Department of Law Enforcement, had testified that "the head of the smuggling racket, Resnick," had ordered that the two defendants be executed as dangerous to his smuggling empire.

Resnick also was charged with "attempting to take care of" Alex Forrester, another cooperative witness. Slaughter said Resnick offered him $5,000 to kill Forrester. Subsequently, Resnick ordered Forrester to Orlando on an errand, but Customs agents persuaded Forrester he was flirting with sudden death and Forrester declined to run the errand. In due time, Resnick was indicted again—this time for allegedly "attempting to help two prisoners to escape Federal authority."

The law was closing in on the Resnick ring. Burgess was identified as David Mack Hicks, thirty, of Elmira, New York, wanted as a fugitive in a murder case in Atlanta. Police picked up Hicks in Bassfield, Mississippi, and in September, 1971, Mrs. Emily Hartwig paid a visit to the Orange County jail to examine the lineup. Unhesitatingly, she picked Hicks out of the lineup as the man who had been with her husband shortly before Twig disappeared the previous May.

Hicks and Resnick were indicted for the murders of Hartwig and Eugene Clayton Walker, but the two defendants were tried separately for the Walker slaying. On October 28, 1971, a jury in a Clearwater courtroom found Resnick guilty of directing Walker's murder, and Resnick was sentenced to die in the electric chair.

"Well, you can only die once," Resnick's attorney, Edward Kirkland, quoted his client as saying.

Then, in November, 1971, a Brevard County jury found Hicks innocent of the Walker killing, apparently influenced by the testimony of Nancy Gray, who told the court that another Resnick cohort, Willard Travis Brunson, had bragged to her that he had killed Walker. The state had charged that Resnick planned the murder and hired Hicks and Brunson to carry it out. Brunson was granted immunity and testified for the prosecution.

Brunson, described by Customs Agent Lowell Miller as a "punk . . . a former armed robber, a rapist . . . and just a general all-around mean bastard," had admitted on the witness stand at the Resnick trial that he lured Walker to his death at the hands of David Hicks. But at Hicks' trial, Nancy Gray told a different story.

Nancy testified that Brunson had told her he had to "pull the trigger . . . because Hicks had no guts."

But Hicks' relief at the not guilty verdict in the Walker killing lasted only four months. On March 4, 1972, he and Resnick were convicted of first-degree murder for the Hartwig killing. Because the jury recommended mercy, both were sentenced to life imprisonment, mandatory under Florida law. Predictably, Resnick showed no emotion when sentence was pronounced; he was still under a death sentence in the Walker slaying.

Another anticlimax for Resnick was his indictment along with Nancy Gray on charges of selling guns illegally to out-of-state residents and selling guns without asking for proper identification. The Internal Revenue Service also charged that Resnick cheated the government out of nearly $600,000 in income taxes in 1967 and 1968. Its claims were based on alleged income earned by Resnick from illegal importation of gold into the United States from Canada.

These were minor troubles for a criminal entrepreneur who had been quoted by the raffish Brunson as telling him before the Walker murder: "If Walker can dig up the body of that pilot [Charley Martinez] he's okay. If not, put him in the same hole [with Martinez]." Back at work for several months, Martinez was no longer in danger of winding up dead in some ditch.

Earlier, Resnick's pal, Alfred Harrison, was ordered by a judge to stop his feverish pursuit of his trade. He was sentenced to fifteen years in prison, and then to another five-year term for the shootout at the airstrip near New Smyrna.

Nancy Gray pleaded guilty to two counts of a multicount indictment handed down as a result of the Alcohol, Tobacco Tax and

Firearms Division investigation, and was sentenced to a mandatory five-year term, plus five years of probation, to be served upon completion of her prison sentence. White and Slaughter both pleaded guilty to one count of conspiracy in the airstrip shootout, with White drawing a four-year sentence and Slaughter three years.

In rounding up the Resnick gang, federal agents struck another blow against a *modus operandi* that had become a mounting problem —the use of private aircraft by dope smugglers. Yet, although Resnick's career was cut short in a swift operation that took less than a year, the problem remained. As the decade of the seventies moved onto history's center stage, more and more smuggling organizations were graduating from the relatively unsophisticated means of transportation—cars and trucks from Mexico and Canada, freighters, ocean liners, commercial airliners—to planes which could take off anywhere and land anywhere without getting involved in customs examination procedures.

Most of the smugglers were using light single- and twin-engine aircraft, sometimes equipped with special accessories enabling them to use shorter, improvised landing strips. But they were also using bigger planes—surplus DC-3's and other military transport, turbo-prop "executive" planes and even the big Lockheed Constellations, with space for 40,000 pounds of cargo. The smaller planes were perfectly suited for bringing in heroin, because a smuggler could make a fortune bringing in a few kilos a month or every few months.

The Resnick gang used a relatively new route, from the Caribbean islands direct to Florida. Law enforcement on these islands had always been more of a catch-as-catch-can affair than in the United States. Police agencies are generally understaffed and underpaid and thus targets for bribes. Besides, islands such as Jamaica are little more than interior wildernesses, fringed with coastline civilization comprising mostly vacation resorts. Police and customs agents do not operate in the interior because they cannot spare the manpower to sweep the jungles, forests and swamps.

Moreover, some of the islands are still under European rule, and thus goods from the home country pass freely onto the islands without customs inspection. Heroin from Marseilles and Amsterdam can be carried into French Guadeloupe and Martinique and Dutch Aruba and Curaçao as safely as perfumes and jewelry. From the islands, the dope is flown into Florida by private planes. The islands also are used as refueling stops for flights from Central and South America.

Customs put together a fleet of eleven airplanes and eight helicopters between 1968 and 1972, and it has had some successes in pursuing smugglers in the clouds and arresting them when they landed—as in the Resnick case. In a six-month period in 1971, for example, flying Customs agents made fifty-seven arrests and seized fourteen planes, at high cost to the smugglers concerned. But the bureau never claimed it was catching more than a small fraction of the airborne racketeers. There is just too much sky to patrol over the American coastlines and along the borders of Mexico and Canada. And, as Investigations boss Harold Smith put it: "The smuggling rings are developing their own air forces and finding plenty of pilots to fly contraband, especially among jobless returning Vietnam War veterans."

Air smuggling became big business in Mexico in the waning years of the sixties. The trafficker can buy marijuana in the Mexican interior for from $2 to $30 a kilogram brick, depending on how well he knows his way around. If he takes out the seats and otherwise strips a small private plane, he can fly 500 bricks into Texas or California, where the grass is sold to wholesalers for from $130 to $200 a brick. If the trafficker has the transportation—and many of them own fleets of cars and trucks—he can move it to Boston and get as high as $450 a brick. But even if he buys the marijuana for $30 a brick and sells it for $130, that's a profit on 500 bricks of $50,000 for one night's work. Ten ounces of heroin bought in Mexico for $3,500 can be sold in Los Angeles for $140,000.

Flying from Mexico into California or Texas or Arizona, the outlaw pilots often descend to a few hundred feet above the ground when they reach American airspace, in order to dodge searching signals from Air Force or Federal Aviation Administration radar antennas. They are playing it safer than necessary; radar is largely ineffective below 9,000 feet and at some points it is useless below 18,000 feet.

Pilots who cross the international frontier are required to file an official flight plan with the FAA or the foreign government, depending on where the flight originates. Most pilots ignore this regulation. But some merely take off and land on the route indicated in their plan, dropping the drugs to confederates on the ground, or land briefly in an isolated spot, unload the contraband, and then land at a regulated airport according to their flight plan.

Then there are the free-booting pilots, descendants of the first Queen Elizabeth's more unscrupulous ship captains who moonlighted as pirates. Lured by big paydays, these pilots take advantage of their positions as hired hands of, say, an oil millionaire or a huge corporation to do a little dope smuggling on the side. They gamble on the odds that Customs inspectors will have neither the time nor the inclination to conduct thoroughgoing searches of aircraft owned or operated by respectable citizens or companies. The dope is hidden aboard the plane in Mexico, Panama or a Caribbean country and left there while the pilot sails through customs. Later, the contraband is picked up by the pilot or a confederate from the parked plane.

Take the case of Hovsep Caramian, Pedro Saralegui, *et al.* Among other things, it showed that a man can't know too much about the pilot of his private airplane.

In the spring of 1971, a well-to-do Argentinian named Juan Felipe Germana was part owner of a Lockheed Lodestar (LV-JNH), which he used for charter flights from Buenos Aires to Miami. His pilot was a personable forty-three-year-old fellow Argentinian named Pedro Saralegui. Saralegui was an excellent pilot.

As part of their routine, agents of the Miami Customs office had noted the frequency of the Lodestar's flights into Miami. They had learned the hard way that any flight of a private plane from a foreign country merited their professional interest. Moreover, Special Agent John D. McCutcheon had made some inquiries among friends in Buenos Aires and had discovered that Pedro Saralegui moved in circles adept at making the fast buck.

So when Germana's Lodestar touched down at Miami International Airport shortly after 7:30 on the evening of May 22, McCutcheon and several of his colleagues were on hand as special observers. They watched as the passengers and crew, including Germana and Saralegui, cleared Customs without incident and left the airport in two rental cars. Then, while other agents trailed the two cars, McCutcheon & Co. made a search of the aircraft. They found three Samsonite suitcases containing what later was determined to be 156 pounds, 11 ounces of heroin concealed in a special compartment behind the mirror in the Lodestar's toilet.

The agents removed from the suitcases all the heroin with the exception of one half-kilo sack in each bag. Sacks of flour were substituted for the seized junk to give the suitcases the proper weight, then the suitcases were returned to their hiding place. The Lodestar was put under twenty-four-hour surveillance.

Customs had quite a wait. It was not until five days later, at 3 P.M. on May 27, that Pedro Saralegui drove up to the airport in a bronze

Mercury Montego, parked the car, strolled leisurely over to where the Lodestar was parked, and climbed into the cockpit. He emerged fifteen minutes later, carrying three suitcases, which he subsequently stowed in the trunk of his rental car. Saralegui was followed by Customs agents as he drove off and onto the upper ramp of the airport's main parking lot. There he left the car, with the suitcases still in the trunk, and made his way to the terminal lobby.

Saralegui strolled about the lobby until 5:30, when he met with a man later identified as Hovsep Caramian, a Uruguayan national living in Buenos Aires. The agents saw Saralegui hand Caramian two keys on a ring. Saralegui, followed by two agents, then took off and departed the airport by cab.

Caramian in turn went to the upper ramp of the main parking lot and drove the Mercury to a parking space in front of National Airlines. He unloaded the three suitcases, got a porter to put them on a dolly, then drove the Mercury back to its original parking space on the upper ramp.

"The guys's nuts," said McCutcheon. "Either that or we're getting another pickup man."

But Caramian was merely a casual type. He was back a few minutes later, followed the porter and his bags to National's ticket counter, checked them through to New York, and bought a ticket on Flight 608 to that city.

"How do you figure that!" said Agent William Mason. "He leaves maybe twenty million dollars' worth of horse on a sidewalk while he parks his car. This is a real cool creep."

Caramian was still cool when he arrived at La Guardia Airport at 12:30 A.M. on May 28. He seemed unhurried to the point of dawdling as he claimed his three bags, consigned them to a porter, and strolled over to rent a Hertz car. But under pressure, he would misplace that cool.

Tailed by two Customs cars, Caramian headed for Manhattan at a leisurely pace. Shortly after crossing the Triborough Bridge, however, his driving became aimless. The Hertz car ducked down side streets and circled several blocks. It made a dash for the West Side Highway and crossed the George Washington Bridge into New Jersey, where Caramian continued his apparently haphazard tour. Finally, when he crossed back into the Bronx, his pursuers had to abandon their hope he would lead them to his receiver. They caught up with him and stopped him in a dimly lit alley near Fordham University, put him in handcuffs, and took him downtown.

Meanwhile, Saralegui had been arrested just after he left the Miami airport in a cab. Germana was picked up in the airport lobby. The other crew member and the six passengers of the Lodestar were taken into custody at various locations in Miami. All were charged initially with smuggling dangerous drugs or conspiracy to do so.

After hearing the stories of those arrested in Miami, Assistant United States Attorney Neil Sonnett dismissed charges against all but Saralegui and Germana, who were held in $300,000 bond each. Subsequently, Germana's bond was reduced to $25,000.

Germana was bewildered and indignant. He told Customs agents he was innocent, that so far as he knew his plane was on a normal charter flight. "I'm in the transportation business—like Pan Am," he told his interrogators. "I've been betrayed by my own pilot." But until the investigation could be completed, the lawmen wanted Germana to stay put so they could locate him without going through the complications of extradition. After all, as part owner of the Lodestar, Germana was responsible until cleared. In reducing Germana's bail, therefore, the magistrate restricted him to the Southern Judicial District of Florida.

As things turned out, the investigation confirmed Germana's story. He had indeed been betrayed by his pilot, Saralegui. But it was not until after Germana had been indicted, along with Saralegui and Caramian, that he was found to be clean.

In any event, Saralegui did the decent thing. Charges against Germana were dismissed at the trial of the three men in August, 1971, at which Saralegui pleaded guilty, absolved Germana of any involvement in the smuggling, and testified for the government. Saralegui also told his Customs interviewers that Caramian had been trying to ship another 100 kilos of heroin out of Buenos Aires and furnished the names of some airplane crew members whom Caramian had contacted about doing courier work.

Saralegui discovered that cooperating with the law can be profitable; he drew four years in prison on charges that could have put him away for five times that long. Or, as Customs' Investigations Chief Harold Smith put it: "The guy is looking at twenty if he doesn't talk."

By trial time the thirty-nine-year-old Caramian was rather better known to Customs than at the time of his arrest. Its probing had identified him as a "moneyman" and "arranger" for a South American syndicate, a big buyer and seller of heroin described by the prosecution as "one of the most prominent figures in the underworld." Caramian offered his own evidence that he was a very important person in the organization. He raised the $300,000 required to spring him from durance vile, then jumped bail even as the jury was deliberating his case. Caramian was no chump; the jury found him guilty on several counts.

Several months later, Caramian caused a flap involving the Defense Department, the State Department, Customs and the domestic enforcer of narcotics laws, the Bureau of Narcotics and Dangerous Drugs. Customs and BNDD agents discovered that Caramian had found refuge in Bolivia and arranged for his extradition back to the United States. On February 24, 1972, he was delivered into the hands of waiting U.S. agents at the La Paz airport, flown by an Air Force C-130 transport to Howard Air Force Base in the Panama Canal Zone, and then returned to Miami three days later. There, on April 12, he was hit with the book—a fifteen-year sentence.

Some Pentagon officials protested that the C-130 had been dispatched on a special mission to La Paz to bring Caramian back without a required clearance in Washington. For their cooperation, the Bolivian police reportedly were promised "30 to 60" revolvers under the foreign aid program.

It was a tempest in a very small teapot. Privately, officials in the office of the State Department's legal adviser reported that the counselor had ruled the procedure was legal because it met the requirements outlined by Bolivian law. The United States, it was said, was not prepared to lecture the Bolivian government on how its own statutes should be interpreted. To the average American observer, the deal probably seemed much more felicitous than the official Washington practice of bending foreign aid policies by financing private jet planes, expensive automobiles and plump mistresses for "cooperating" strong men all over the world.

# 12
# The *Nurmi* Saga

Customs' Investigations Chief Harold Smith liked to say that the case of Errol Bernard Resnick, "respected" businessman and convicted murderer, was prime testimony to his dictum that in police work respectability is subject to the rules of evidence. As a career lawman in the narcotics field, Smith had learned early on that the Customs sleuth who persuaded himself to be taken in by appearances was derelict in his duty. The beefy, hard-eyed Smith was always pounding home this truth, usually in a roar that could be heard in the next county. One day in 1971, for instance, he was discussing several pending investigations with an aide when the aide mentioned that a young man recently promoted to special agent had a lead on a prominent businessman.

"What's the kid say?" asked Smitty.

"Well," replied the aide, "he says the lead seems solid, but the guy is very, very respectable—a pillar of the community."

"That's nice," said Smitty. Then he slammed a huge fist against his desk. "I don't give a goddamn if the guy is Michael the Archangel! Tell that kid to run down his lead and let the facts decide whether the guy is clean. Junk dealers are where you find them these days."

As it turned out, the businessman *was* clean. He hung around with some companions of questionable virtue, but the mutual interest was horse racing, not dope smuggling. Nevertheless, Smitty's point was valid. Drug trafficking in the United States had become billion-dollar big business, and men like Harold Smith had learned the hard way that "respectable pillars of the community" frequently were tempted by such fat and relatively easy profits.

Accordingly, Special Agent Bill Norsworthy of Customs' Miami office took in stride the tip offered him by a longtime informant known as Tom Thumb on a day in early January, 1972. Tom, who moved in circles seldom frequented by Eagle Scouts, told Norsworthy

163

that a couple of Miami firemen had bought a 40-foot Grand Banks yacht for $55,000 and there was gossip around town that the vessel would be used to smuggle in large quantities of marijuana from Jamaica.

Norsworthy merely wondered aloud where a couple of firemen would get $55,000 in cash.

"They got a partner with dough," Tom Thumb told Norsworthy. "Some big-shot movie producer who lives in Golden Beach. This producer is gonna make a movie down here starring Rod Steiger, the star. What I figure is that the producer put up the dough, and the firemen will get a piece of the action for helping to run the boat and keep it up."

Tom identified the two firemen as Daniel V. Boisvert and Harold Hesselrode. Norsworthy made some discreet inquiries and learned that they were both taking fourteen days' leave beginning January 13. As a longtime observer of the local scene, Norsworthy was well acquainted with Golden Beach as an exclusive and expensive bedroom in the Miami Beach neighborhood. It seemed logical to assume that the third man was well financed if he could afford to rent a home in that glittering compound.

Customs agents rode around Golden Beach for a couple of days without locating the yacht—named the *Nurmi* after the Finnish long-distance runner of the twenties. But the vessel, in immaculate condition, finally was spotted by Norsworthy and Special Agent Jack Lynch from a Customs helicopter. It carried the registration number FL3749AN on each side of its bow and was docked alongside a private home at 240 Golden Beach Drive. Through an intermediary, "shopping for rental property," Norsworthy learned that the residence had been rented by one Stephen McCarthy, thirty-five, vice-president of K. M. Films, Incorporated, 1213 North Highland Avenue, Hollywood, California.

A little more legitimate snooping produced the information that the *Nurmi* was registered to one Dennis Kaufman, who later was identified as Dennis Ingham, twenty-nine, "production coordinator" of K. M. Films. Subsequently, it was learned that Ingham, as Kaufman, had brought $55,000 in cash in an attaché case to the boat dealer's office to buy the yacht. According to Tom Thumb, the two firemen had been engaged to find the yacht and instruct Ingham in its operation. The arrangement, said Tom, was that Boisvert and Hesselrode would be permitted to use the vessel when it was not otherwise engaged, in return for maintaining it.

During the surveillance of the house on Golden Beach Drive,

agents saw an MGB sports roadster and a Chrysler sedan parked in the driveway. A check of license tags showed the roadster was registered to Boisvert and the Chrysler to one Joseph B. Layman of Westminster, California. Turning to CADPIN, Customs' computer bank of violators and suspects, the agents learned that Layman had been arrested on a marijuana charge in San Ysidro, California, in March, 1971, and was listed as a "major marijuana trafficker." It developed later that McCarthy had borrowed the car from Layman.

This, of course, was a link—if a tenuous one—to the dope racket. More important to the investigators were documents showing a criminal record running to three pages for Dennis Ingham, and two "known" arrests for Stephen McCarthy.

Now the investigation of the K. M. Films executives became a pursuit; the *Nurmi* suddenly disappeared from its berth alongside 240 Golden Beach Drive sometime during the night of January 12–13. Carloads of agents and the Customs helicopter searched in vain for the vessel for more than three weeks, while Norsworthy and John H. Moseley, special agent in charge, cussed and wished for a surprise gift of a fleet of PT boats.

Norsworthy and Moseley assumed the *Nurmi* had sailed for Jamaica to pick up a load of grass. But they had no evidence against anyone, although they were convinced that if the *Nurmi* was indeed being used for smuggling, the load would be delivered to the Golden Beach house. McCarthy had paid $5,500 for three months' rent of the residence, and the house and its surroundings were an ideal cover for a smuggling operation.

Meanwhile, Norsworthy checked and learned that the two firemen, Boisvert and Hesselrode, had returned to work on January 27. Customs declarations at Miami International Airport revealed that they had arrived as passengers on an Avianca Airlines flight from Colombia on January 26. The pair was put under discreet surveillance, but Customs was not about to annoy either of the men with questions and thus warn the *Nurmi* crew.

The Golden Beach house also was put under twenty-four-hour-a-day surveillance. A 36-foot Customs yacht, equipped with the latest in radar and radio equipment and outfitted to look like a sport fishing boat, was docked across the waterway from 240 Golden Beach Drive. Since the agents could not be seen openly occupying the boat in such an exclusive neighborhood or be seen running back and forth to it without questions being asked, they had literally to sweat it out below deck.

Air and sea patrols continued. Finally, shortly after noon on February 6, the *Nurmi* was spotted by Agents Lynch and Bucky Buchanan from the Customs helicopter in Bahamian waters, south of Cat Cay Island. It was heading in a northwesterly direction—toward Miami. To save fuel, the pilot set the chopper down in a remote area of Cat Cay, where the agents spent the next couple of hours hunting seashells and driftwood. They were aloft again at 2:30 P.M. and sighted the *Nurmi* approximately 15 miles west of Bimini, Grand Bahama Island, heading west toward the Florida coast. The fix was radioed to Bill Norsworthy in Miami.

Norsworthy set up surveillance teams at each inlet into the Miami area and waited. He waited five hours until, at about 7:30 P.M. on February 6, Special Agent Jim Welsh observed the *Nurmi* entering Bakers Haulover Cut from the ocean and then proceeding north on the Intracoastal Waterway. Fifteen minutes later, Special Agents Fred Paesano and Tom Burton saw the yacht passing under the Sunny Isles Boulevard Bridge, and at 8:05 Norsworthy saw the vessel turning into the canal that leads from the Intracoastal Waterway to South Island, Golden Beach.

There were three men aboard the yacht—McCarthy, Ingham, and a man later identified as Keith Meiggs, twenty-four, of North Miami Beach.

While Norsworthy and Jack Lynch watched, the *Nurmi* was carefully docked alongside 240 Golden Beach Drive, with its bow pointing in a northerly direction. After the yacht was tied fast, McCarthy leaped ashore, went into the well-dressed house and turned on the house lights and an outdoor floodlight in the backyard. Norsworthy instructed three carloads of Customs agents, parked at a Howard Johnson's nearby, to move in.

Three agents, Bucky Buchanan, Jim Welsh and Tom Burton, concealed themselves in some shrubbery at the rear of the house. Agents Mike Wewers, Bill LeCates and Fred Paesano covered the front.

Then, as though they had waited for the agents to place themselves, Ingham and Meiggs disembarked, carrying suitcases. A few minutes later, McCarthy raised the garage door from the inside. Standing with his hands over his head, he found himself staring at three lawmen, who identified themselves and asked where the *Nurmi* had come from. "Bimini," replied McCarthy. "What's up?"

Watching from the house, Meiggs and Ingham decided to leave, fast. Ingham ran out the back door, collided with Bill LeCates' broad shoulder and went sprawling into the shrubbery. Meiggs backed out of the glass sliding door of the living room into the barrel of a carbine held by Mike Wewers. All three were arrested and taken away while the *Nurmi* was searched.

What the searchers found was two tons of marijuana, the biggest seizure of pot ever made on the East Coast of the United States. Moreover, it tested out as high-grade flowering tops from Colombia, known as Colombian Gold, and documents aboard the yacht showed the *Nurmi* had sailed from Cartagena in that South American country. The marijuana, contained in seventy-nine big burlap bags, had a street value of $4,000,000; the smugglers' profit would have been around $600,000.

Also seized aboard the *Nurmi* were two publications that suggested to Agent Norsworthy the smuggling trio had been "thinking about going straight and taking up farming." The booklets were entitled *Marijuana—Grow Ur Own* and *The Cultivators' Handbook of Marijuana.*

Whatever their long-range plans, the three had business before a federal court in the Southern District of Florida. McCarthy and Meiggs entered guilty pleas, but Ingham pleaded not guilty and went on trial before a jury and Judge James L. King. When the trial ended, it took the jury only twenty-two minutes to find Ingham guilty on all three counts of smuggling and conspiracy. For the time being, Customs retained custody of an assortment of camera equipment found in the Golden Beach house and three motion picture scripts found on the *Nurmi.*

A few weeks after Ingham's trial, sentences were pronounced on the three convicted defendants. Ingham was hit with three tours in the pen, one of five years and the other two of two years each, to be served concurrently. McCarthy got four years in prison and Meiggs three years. No charges were lodged against the two firemen, Boisvert and Hesselrode. Both had insisted they had merely arranged purchase of the *Nurmi* and had then gone along on the shakedown cruise to acquaint the three defendants with the *Nurmi*'s operation. Moreover, Ingham, McCarthy and Meiggs told the United States Attorney they would testify on the firemen's behalf that they had no knowledge of the smuggling venture.

It was not surprising that a fancy, "respectable" yacht should be involved in the East Coast's record pot seizure. What *was* surprising to the ordinary layman was that Bill Norsworthy & Co. ever managed to bust a seagoing smuggling operation, given the immensity of the problem in southern Florida. In mid-1972 there were more than

240,000 boats of all descriptions registered in the state, and the Florida coast is dotted with hundreds of small, isolated and sometimes deliberately concealed harbors which are a standing invitation to the dope merchant. Thus every seizure and every arrest are a victory, regardless of their size and importance.

While New York operations understandably got most of the headlines, the fact was that in the decade of the seventies south Florida had become the No. 1 entry point for smugglers of heroin and cocaine from both Europe and South America. The neighborhood was used as a stopover and dispersal point for European-processed heroin and as a direct route for the transportation and merchandising of cocaine. Seizure statistics prove the point. In 1971 Customs agents intercepted 539 pounds of heroin and 67 pounds of cocaine in New York, and 464 pounds of heroin and 35 pounds of cocaine in Miami. But as much as half the heroin and cocaine seized in New York entered the United States in the southern Florida area.

Other figures reflected the big-business aspect of south Florida's dope-smuggling enterprises. Between 1969 and 1971 heroin seizures in Miami alone increased a whopping 21,905 percent, cocaine seizures were up 279 percent, hashish seizures increased almost 3,000 percent, and marijuana seizures 90 percent. In January, 1971, more narcotics seizures were made in Miami than in any other American port of entry.

Unwittingly, French authorities in March, 1972, frustrated a long-planned Customs trap for a French shrimp boat loaded with heroin and known to be sailing for Miami. An intelligence report was lying on the deck of Customs' Harold Smith when Marseilles customs agents seized the vessel and discovered 1,000 pounds of pure heroin in its bilges. The report on Smith's desk said the shrimp boat had regularly moved heroin from Marseilles to Miami and was expected to dock in the Florida port within a few weeks.

Smith congratulated the French authorities on the bust, but privately he bemoaned Customs' lost chance of picking up the receiver on this side of the Atlantic.

In Smith's book, that receiver would not have been just another name but almost surely a major-league dealer whose arrest could have forged another link in the chain connecting the American Mafia with narcotics trafficking. Only the organization of Mafia families had the kind of money—in cash—to fork over for 1,000 pounds of horse, worth a resounding $212,500,000 on the street. Thus, had the shrimp boat made it to Miami, there was always the chance that someone would drop a big name or two to save a little of his own hide.

Indeed, the boat's owner, a onetime World War II paratrooper named Marcel Boucan, admitted to French police that he had delivered 220 pounds of pure heroin to Miami during the past year. His admission strongly suggested that if French customs authorities had arranged to have the vessel tailed with its half-ton cargo of heroin across the Atlantic, Boucan's arrest in the United States might have caused him to become even more cooperative with the law. At the very least, U.S. Customs might have pried information out of Boucan that would have provided clues to the identities of some of the syndicate members using South and Central America as staging points between clandestine French processing laboratories and their partners in the "problem area" around Miami.

Part of southern Florida's problem was the fruit of a humanitarian program of the United States government. When Fidel Castro turned Cuba into a Communist dictatorship in the early sixties, America opened its doors to thousands of Cuban refugees and even financed their flight from the tight little island by sea and air. By 1972 there were 290,000 Cuban refugees in south Florida, most of them in Miami and its environs, and many of them have been lured into the high-profit business of narcotics smuggling, thus confirming a prediction made by the man whose rule they fled.

Castro took over Cuba on New Year's Day, 1959. A little more than a year later he told the author in an interview: "Take all the refugees you want. They'll all be criminals. You can have our criminals."

All Cuban refugees are *not* criminals, of course. But enough of them have turned to dope smuggling to make the refugee program unpopular among residents of south Florida and at Customs headquarters. Most Cubans act as couriers, or "mules," for South American syndicates, but a number have set themselves up as receivers and wholesalers with bankrolls earned in more menial employment. Moreover, Cubans are so numerous in southern Florida that Customs intelligence agents find it difficult to pick out the drug smugglers from Latin America in the crowd.

Then there are the veterans from the abortive Bay of Pigs invasion of Cuba in April, 1961. Members of Assault Brigade 2506 have been identified as suspects in a number of smuggling investigations. Customs agents with excellent contacts in the Cuban community report that these men use their well-learned guerrilla tactics to move in and out of Florida by private boat and plane; they are experts in the vital smuggling art of becoming invisible.

They have also dreamed up an almost airtight method of smuggling drugs by air. Two identical two-engine planes are employed. One takes off from a local domestic airport with no customs procedures, then lands at a bigger airport, where the pilot lists a Latin American city as the aircraft's port of departure and submits to a scolding for not having filed a flight plan. Meanwhile, the second plane comes in from the Caribbean loaded with heroin and lands at the small domestic airport after a "domestic" flight.

But because there is such a heavy flow of dope into south Florida, Customs men no longer are surprised to encounter an operation employing hoary ruses that were ancient in the days when the American colonists harried the revenuers paid with King George III's shilling. One of these is the practice of shipping packages of heroin or cocaine by air, unaccompanied by a mule, and frequently the Latin's unfamiliarity with American laws, airline regulations and the language trips him up.

Clearly, that is what happened to one middle-aged Cuban who presented himself at Eastern Airlines in Tampa to dispatch a shoebox-size package to New York. "Do I have to give my name?" he asked the pretty young clerk when informed that the airline required a return address.

The clerk was suspicious; there had been several bomb scares in the preceding two months. She called her supervisor and told him of the customer's strange behavior. By the time the supervisor arrived on the scene the Cuban had taken off, headed for the taxicab rank, so the supervisor decided to open the package under the authority granted airlines to protect their passengers.

Instead of a bomb, the supervisor found six large glassine bags of white powder—about $300,000 worth of cocaine at the street level.

Summoned to the airport, Customs Special Agent Sam Johnson substituted baking powder for the cocaine in five of the bags, then sent the box on to New York after alerting the Customs office there to pick up whoever claimed the package.

Intelligence reports suggested the cocaine could have been smuggled in aboard a Chilean ship then in port, so Johnson led a Customs team to the vessel and mustered the crew for possible identification by the airline clerk. She couldn't finger any of them as the man who had brought her the parcel. But Johnson learned there had been several visitors to the ship, and another agent found a cabdriver who had driven a Cuban from the airport to a hotel that day.

When agents went to the hotel, they discovered the Cuban had moved out. But the landlady told them the Cuban had had a visitor who didn't speak much English. The agents asked her to accompany them to the ship to see if she could identify any of the crew members as the man who had visited her roomer. She refused. "She was afraid of revenge, I guess," Johnson said. "People get scared." But she did say she could pick out the visitor's photograph if she saw it, so the agents returned to the ship with a Polaroid camera and photographed the passport photo of every member of the crew. Back at the hotel, the landlady identified one photo as that of the man who had visited her caravansary twice. Later, she agreed to look at the man in a lineup behind a doctored mirror and identified him again.

The crewman at first denied any knowledge of either the hotel or the boarder, but after a piece of paper was found in his pocket with the hotel's address scribbled on it, he confessed that he had smuggled the cocaine into the United States. He said he had handed it over to the Cuban when the latter visited the ship, then had called at the hotel twice to collect his $1,000 fee. He claimed, however, that he never got the $1,000; that the Cuban had told him he would be paid as the ship passed through the Panama Canal. Understandably annoyed, the crew member tipped off the agents that the Cuban was planning to fly back to South America the next day. The Cuban was picked up as he was about to board the plane, and his New York receiver was arrested when he claimed the package of heroin and baking powder at La Guardia Airport.

"That Cuban was a real dumb ox," Sam Johnson admitted. "He could have given a phony name and return address. But, hell, don't begrudge us a few breaks in this rat race."

# 13

# Sudden Death, N.Y., N.Y.

Like Sam Johnson, who was grateful for the "few breaks" that enabled him to solve the mystery of the shoebox packed with $300,-000 worth of cocaine, Special Agent Irv Weinstein had always appreciated a little help from fate in his investigations. But, also like Sam Johnson, Weinstein knew that in ninety-nine out of one hundred cases an agent had to make his own breaks by assiduous attention to his homework—by squirreling away bits and pieces of information against the day when good fortune took a hand. Sometimes that day was long in coming.

For more than thirteen frustrating months, Weinstein had pounded the pavements of New York City trying to get a solid fix on a cocaine-smuggling ring that he knew was doing a highly profitable business between Latin America and New York. In furtive gin mills and in midnight doorways, he had picked up names he was convinced belonged to leading figures in the conspiracy. His instinct told him the ring must be grossing at least $2,000,000 a year. What he wanted most in his professional life was to meet someone who could lead him to Armando Cardona, Cirilio Ginary, or Santiago García y More.

Weinstein, short, cocky, muscular and wise-cracking, meanwhile spent most of his workdays on the bread-and-butter routine of his unit. Routinely, almost absentmindedly, he mentioned the three names wherever his work took him. He carried the names with him when he was called to Kennedy International Airport about nine o'clock on the night of November 13, 1969, to assist in the investigation arising from the arrest of a passenger on a Lufthansa flight from Santiago, Chile.

During his examination of the baggage of Manuel Olivares-Labra, twenty-five, Customs Inspector Howard Bauer noticed bulges in Olivares' chest. He asked Olivares if he was carrying any merchandise on his person, and Olivares said he was not. Still suspicious, Bauer searched the passenger and found three plastic bags of cocaine taped to his chest. Olivares was placed under arrest and advised of his constitutional rights in Spanish by Customs Inspector John Perez.

Weinstein was interested in whether Olivares had been accompanied by a bodyguard, or "shotgun." He checked the arrival and departure records (Immigration and Naturalization Forms I-94) for all passengers on Olivares' flight—and stopped at the name of one Hector Camacho, a twenty-four-year-old Argentinian. The name rang a bell, but Weinstein didn't know which bell.

Camacho's I-94 form showed his destination as the Hotel Mc-Alpin in New York. Weinstein noted this, but with considerable skepticism; experience had taught him that dope smugglers seldom told the truth about where they were planning to stay. Accordingly, he dispatched a number of agents to check not only the McAlpin but other hotels in the mid-Manhattan garment district.

One of the hotels visited by Special Agents Charles Garside and Edward F. Walsh was the Stanford, near Broadway and 32d Street. There, they learned that Camacho and a companion later identified as Rómulo Jarrin, thirty-two, an Ecuadorian, had been seen in Shelley's Restaurant next door. Meanwhile, another agent reported that Camacho actually had a reservation at the McAlpin Hotel nearby.

Armed with detailed descriptions of the two men, Charley Garside was making his slow, nosy way around the neighborhood when he saw the pair ducking into a subway entrance at Seventh Avenue and 33d Street. He trailed them downstairs onto the platform, and as he approached them to take a make-sure look, they took off down the platform together.

"Together!" said Garside contemptuously. "The stupid bums didn't have brains enough to separate so that maybe one of them would get away."

At any rate, Garside dashed after the two men and cornered them against a staircase as they tried to make for New York's great outdoors. Under the nose of Garside's gun, Camacho produced an Argentine passport and Jarrin one from Ecuador. Meanwhile, Garside was joined by Inspector Perez, who dutifully delivered the required constitutional spiel to the prisoners in Spanish. Then the pair was taken to Customs headquarters at 201 Varick Street for some conversation, if possible.

Camacho agreed to talk. He admitted to Irv Weinstein that he had traveled shotgun for Olivares on the flight from Santiago, and said

Olivares was supposed to have taken a taxicab to the McAlpin Hotel, where he was to deliver the plastic bags of cocaine to Camacho. Camacho reported that on that morning in Santiago he had gone to the apartment of one Mordaqueo Moises Korenfeld, whom he described as a "Jewish *jefe*," to watch Korenfeld tape the bags of cocaine to Olivares' chest. Korenfeld's name was in Weinstein's notebook as a known fellow conspirator of the notorious Armando Cardona, who operated as a kind of general manager for a Chilean heroin and cocaine smuggling ring. Weinstein's information was that Korenfeld, a forty-seven-year-old native Argentinian, handled the mechanics of Cardona's courier system to the United States.

Weinstein and his colleagues wanted Korenfeld because he either knew the ultimate receiver of the cocaine load or could lead the agents to an individual who did. But they also wanted Korenfeld because he was a straw boss for Cardona. If they could get to Cardona, they had a chance of finding out who was running the show for that particular syndicate in South America.

One of the persons Weinstein had talked to about Cardona—a one-time two-bit pusher from Puerto Rico—had summed him up in unofficial language that explained why Cardona had been sought for several months not only by Customs but by the Bureau of Narcotics and Dangerous Drugs, the New Jersey State Police and police in Miami and California. "That bastard Armando," said the informant. "He's a mean bastard. He's a real dangerous son of a bitch. I think he likes to kill."

Perhaps Cardona already had killed. In Customs' files was a gory report from Mexican officials that named Armando Cardona as a prime suspect in the murder of a heroin dealer in Sonora. The victim had been clubbed to death. Then his killer had thrown the body into a car and pushed the car over a cliff. A medical examiner's report stated that at least a dozen blows had been delivered after the victim was dead.

In the United States, Cardona's record so far was only as a known supplier of and dealer in narcotics. He was a handsome, swarthy twenty-nine-year-old physical culture nut, a married man with a stable of pretty Latin-American girls. Curiously despite a preoccupation with his well-built physique, he was a periodic cocaine user, which probably explained why he had a nasty habit of slugging people in the middle of a friendly conversation. Through Camacho and Korenfeld, Weinstein & Co. hoped to arrange matters so that Cardona could test his toughness on them.

At any rate, Camacho now told his interrogators that his orders from Korenfeld were to take the cocaine to his room at the Hotel McAlpin and await further directions from the "Jewish *jefe*," who also was flying to New York. According to Camacho, Korenfeld had told him he would call him at about 2:30 A.M. the next day to arrange the delivery. Camacho identified Jarrin, meanwhile, as a courier employed by Korenfeld in the past; he said Jarrin had turned over to him a shipment of cocaine in his room at the Stanford Hotel in October. Jarrin was formally arrested at this point, and an agent was dispatched to the Stanford to look over the hotel's records. He found a registration card in Jarrin's name dated October 4, 1969, and a bill remitted to Jarrin for lodging from October 4 to October 9.

"What about Cardona?" Weinstein asked Camacho.

"I know him," said Camacho. "He is big man down there. Once I brought some cocaine to him in Mexico City. He is very tough. He can hurt somebody if he does not like them."

Camacho was accompanied to his room at the McAlpin by Special Agents Weinstein, Garside and Desmond Caulfield, and Inspector Perez, the interpreter. There, while the agents listened in, Korenfeld telephoned Camacho at about 3:30 A.M. on November 14. Camacho told Korenfeld that he and Olivares both had passed customs inspection without incident and that he, Camacho, now had the bags of cocaine. Fine, said Korenfeld, he and "Monchie" would come around and pick up the load later in the morning. "Monchie" was Ramón García y More, brother of the Santiago García y More in Weinstein's book.

But it was Korenfeld alone who showed up at 8:30 that morning. When Korenfeld knocked, Camacho asked who was there and the agents heard a voice respond, "It's Mauricio." Camacho nodded. "That's Korenfeld," he told his official companions. "That's his secret name." The agents nabbed Korenfeld as he entered the room and placed him under arrest after a search of his extremely annoyed person produced a slip of paper bearing the notation "Room 1334 Hotel McAlpin." Korenfeld refused to talk, but he did consent to a search of his room at the Belmont Plaza. In a wastebasket, the agents found a scrap of torn paper on which was written in Spanish, "*Mauri, Estoy en el 1334*, Hector," which to the agents meant, "I'm at room 1334 at the McAlpin, Hector Camacho."

Although Korenfeld remained mum, Camacho continued to relieve himself of what he knew. He told of having met in late September or early October an individual nicknamed Tato, whom Weinstein knew as Santiago García y More, and a black named Marcello Díaz. Both men, Camacho said, visited him in his room at the Hotel Stanford and introduced him to María Rivera, also known as María Ginary, common-law wife of still another man who was on Weinstein's black list, Cirilio Ginary. "Tato" and Díaz instructed Camacho to buy a round-trip ticket to Santiago for María, which he did. She then flew to Santiago, and Camacho joined her there a few days later.

Camacho said he helped tape a load of cocaine to María's body in Korenfeld's apartment for delivery in New York to More and his wife, Jorgelina. Camacho also had a nugget of inside gossip for the agents. He claimed that while he was in New York in October, he picked up $8,000 from Santiago García for Korenfeld. Camacho had been told to hand over the money to José Sanchez, also known as Pepe, who would hand-carry it to Korenfeld in Chile. Camacho said he gave the money to Pepe, but that the latter double-crossed Korenfeld and flew to Argentina with the loot.

That was how the investigation stood on November 29, 1969, when Cirilio Ginary was murdered, allegedly by Armando Cardona, in front of the Iberia Restaurant on 47th Street, between Broadway and Eighth Avenue in New York. The theory was that Cardona shot Ginary down because he owed Ginary money for a previous load of narcotics and Ginary was pressing him. There was also bad blood between the two because Cardona, through Korenfeld, had used María Ginary as a dope courier. Witnesses placed Cardona at the murder scene and claimed he fled after the shooting. But New York police picked up María Rivera and Ramón García y More, who also had been present, and held them as material witnesses.

By that time Customs investigators had located María in an apartment on West 87th Street in upper Manhattan—and she was under surveillance when Cardona pumped three bullets into her common-law husband's torso. Weinstein and his colleagues had hoped María would lead them to other conspirators; now they had no choice but to talk to her about those conspirators.

Accordingly, Weinstein and Special Agent E. Meade Feild interviewed María in her cell, and she confirmed Camacho's statement about her involvement in the conspiracy. She said that when she agreed to do some "mule" work for Korenfeld, she was separated from her "husband," Ginary, and needed money badly. She also said that after she had delivered the cocaine load to "Tato" and his "wife," Jorgelina, all three drove to a hotel at West 101st Street and Broadway, where Jorgelina got out of the car and delivered the load to "somebody" living in the hotel.

Both María and Hector Camacho testified for the state before a grand jury, which handed down conspiracy and smuggling indictments against Santiago García y More, Jorgelina Canamera, José Sanchez, Ramón García y More, also known as Monchie, Marcello Díaz, and one Jorge Brieva, Korenfeld's alleged supplier in Chile. Separately indicted were Moises Korenfeld, Manuel Olivares-Labra, Hector Camacho and Rómulo Jarrin.

María was told by Customs to return to her native Puerto Rico and stay there until her presence in court was required. She was under orders to report her whereabouts to the office of the special customs agent in charge in San Juan if she found it necessary to travel from Puerto Rico.

As the situation evolved, María's testimony was not needed at the time of the smugglers' trial on June 2, 1970, because Customs people believed they had the case wrapped up without imperiling the life of a star informant. They were right about the case, but not about María's ability to take orders.

All the defendants pleaded guilty except for Ramón García and Marcello Díaz, who failed to appear for trial and were declared fugitives from justice. Moises Korenfeld got twelve years and the rest drew five-year terms. Korenfeld, of course, had refused to "cooperate." But Irv Weinstein was unhappy. The "mean bastard," Armando Cardona, was still at large.

That was María's hard luck. Two weeks after the trial of her fellow conspirators, the body of an "unidentified female" was found in a vacant lot in the Bronx, torn by gunshot wounds. Weinstein contacted New York police and verified his worst fears; the body was María's. With some help from Customs, the police built up a case against Cardona and charged him with murder. Also implicated, but not charged, was Antonio Flores, whom Customs men remembered from the paella case (Chapter 6). Flores had arrived at the house in Queens used by the receivers of the load of heroin packed in cans of paella shortly after the ring was busted, and knocked fruitlessly at the door. Since Customs had nothing on him, he was allowed to go his way.

But Cardona proved himself an upper-case dope. He managed to get himself arrested on charges of stealing a car under an assumed name, and a routine fingerprint check by New York police established his true identity. It was enough to drive a man mad, and that's what some doctors said happened to Cardona. He was adjudged insane and unfit to stand trial and shipped off to a New York state hospital for mentally ill criminals.

If Cardona, in a sense, beat the murder rap, he unknowingly lent a helping hand to federal agents pursuing the investigation of another case involving one of Cardona's closest pals, Luis Ortega. During his fugitive months, Cardona had done some careless confiding in a pusher who talked too much when he was drunk. As a result, the Feds were able to trap Ortega and one Guido Orsini when they tried to smuggle 80 kilos of heroin into the United States in the upholstery of a sleek Jaguar in September, 1971. Eventually, Ortega and Orsini each were sentenced to twenty-five long years in prison and fined $35,000 in a federal court in New York.

Moreover, the case of Cardona, Olivares, Camacho, Korenfeld, *et al.* was one that provided enough credit to go around. Customs' arrest of Olivares at Kennedy International Airport got the ball rolling, but thereafter there was unexcelled cooperation among Customs, the Bureau of Narcotics and Dangerous Drugs, New York police, the New Jersey State Police and authorities in Florida and California. Despite the sometime squabbling between individuals of various law enforcement agencies dealing with the dope pushing problem, that is the way the real professionals in all the involved agencies like it. As Myles Ambrose, chief of the Office of Drug Abuse Law Enforcement, remarked pointedly when he took over his new assignment in early 1972, "The dope who says he never has to go outside his own outfit for help is a dope."

Ambrose and his successor, Customs Commissioner Vernon (Mike) Acree, could have offered dozens of examples of the profit that accrues from law enforcement cooperation. One of them would have to be the seizure of $400,000 worth of hashish from India in September, 1971. The BNDD prosecuted the case, but it got yeoman help from Customs in tracking down the load.

On August 16, some nosy Washington BNDD agents with good sources picked up intelligence from a periodic informant about a scheme to smuggle 100 pounds of hashish into the United States in a disabled Volkswagen microbus, ostensibly shipped to America for repairs. Hashish is about twenty times as potent as pure marijuana and was then selling on the street in small packages for $200 an ounce.

BNDD relayed the information to the Customs office in Baltimore, to which port the load was reportedly headed—consigned to one William K. Painter of Alexandria, Virginia, care of Tydings Imports Service in Annapolis. The ship, name unknown, that was carrying the microbus was due to stop off at New Orleans. Could Customs employ its resources as policeman of entry ports to identify the ship and take a look-see at the microbus?

Customs could and did. In New Orleans, Agent Bob Harrold went to work checking manifests to try to learn what ships arriving or scheduled to arrive in that port had one or more Volkswagen micro-buses aboard. Fortunately, manifests are filed with authorities when the ship docks and one or two days before unloading commences, so Harrold had a little time. Meanwhile, Customs and BNDD agents were checking elsewhere, and two days later Harrold was informed that the ship could be the SS *Robert E. Lee,* out of Bombay.

Harrold discovered this information was only half right. The mi-crobus in question, a red job, was arriving on another vessel for transfer to the *Robert E. Lee* for the coastwise voyage to Baltimore.

So when the microbus was off-loaded preparatory to its transfer to the *Robert E. Lee*, Customs agents got their look-see at its appoint-ments. They found the Volkswagen was a custom model, with black upholstery and ornate cabinetwork. They also unearthed inside one of the cabinets 123½ pounds of hashish, wrapped in seventy-one tinfoil packages. Most of the hash was removed and replaced with a substitute, and in due time the vehicle was loaded aboard the *Robert E. Lee*. Customs Patrol Officer Cliff Robershaw also went aboard as an "official" passenger, posing as a Defense Department cargo super-visor.

Robershaw rode with the microbus as the ship steamed from New Orleans to Houston and Corpus Christi, Texas, before heading up the East Coast to Baltimore. In Baltimore, Customs and BNDD agents watched as the Volkswagen was off-loaded at the Dundalk Marine Terminal on August 31, and then kept it under twenty-four-hour-a-day surveillance.

The agents' notes, later put into an official affidavit, showed that the microbus was towed to the Tydings Imports office in Annapolis on the early evening of September 3. In the tow truck, according to the agents' reports, were William Warfield Tydings, thirty-one, owner of Tydings Imports, and a second unidentified male. All night long, while the red bus squatted inside a locked chain-link fence, Customs and BNDD men lurked in the darkness and kept an eye on it. Also interested were Tydings and a friend, identified as Gary Patrick Lyons, thirty-four, who patrolled the neighborhood during the eve-ning and night of September 3 and until 5 P.M. on September 4.

At that time, the agents' notes showed that one Mark Lee Lemin-ger appeared on the scene, climbed into the microbus, and began removing the tinfoil packets from their hiding place and stuffing them into a duffle bag. Then the lawmen moved in.

The affidavit, filed by Thomas R. Russo, a BNDD agent, was not made public until February 9, 1972, when Lyons pleaded guilty to part of the indictment—intention to sell a small quantity of hashish. In return, Assistant United States Attorney Michael Marr told Federal Judge Edward S. Northrop in Baltimore that he had agreed to ask for a suspended sentence for Lyons. Marr said Lyons appeared to be the least involved in the plot and had agreed to tell his story to the government.

Besides Lyons, those indicted included Tydings, Leminger and Harold Christian Witherite, Jr., thirty. Leminger and Witherite failed to appear for arraignment, and fugitive warrants were issued for their arrest. Had they known what dispositions would be made of the other two cases, Leminger and Witherite might have stuck around for trial. In Baltimore on July 27, 1972, Judge Northrop placed Tydings on three years' probation and Lyons on two years' probation after their convictions on narcotics conspiracy charges.

The Customs and BNDD agents who had cooperated on the case took time for a collective sigh of resignation and got together again —this time in the Far East—to try to hunt down the big-time supplier who had shipped the microbus halfway around the world.

A lucrative market for hashish had developed in the United States, and if the agents worked hard and had some luck, there was always the chance they would find themselves matching wits with smugglers of superior imagination and daring, as they had in the so-called Lebanese Caper two years earlier.

# ALL-POINTS
# BULLETIN

# 14

# The Lebanese Caper

In the tarnished early morning light of August 29, 1970, two soldiers doing security patrol in the ancient ruins of Baalbek in eastern Lebanon stumbled onto an unexpected and frightening scene. A huge aircraft was squatting on a freshly constructed landing strip in a field near the home of Niaf Masri, a member of the Lebanese Chamber of Deputies. Around the plane swarmed twenty or thirty men armed with automatic weapons.

"Israelis!" whispered one of the Lebanese soldiers in the ear of his comrade.

Approaching as close as they dared, the two soldiers opened fire. Almost on the instant, two trucks loaded with more Lebanese troops roared onto the scene, and for five long minutes the soldiers exchanged fusillades with the intruders. Then the aircraft suddenly roared down the airstrip and took off while the strangers sped away in trucks concealed in a nearby woods.

The intruders were not Israeli guerrillas, but Lebanese smugglers, and the five men who dashed for the plane and fled into the deep gray yonder were not of the Israeli Air Force but American dope traffickers. The Lebanese patrol had arrived on the scene as a consignment of hashish was being loaded onto the plane, and the Americans had flown away without paying for the 648 kilograms of hashish their Lebanese friends had already stashed aboard the twin-engine Martin 202.

Had they known at the time of this violent incident, United States Customs officials would have gnashed their teeth in frustration. Its agents and cooperating foreign police had trailed the Martin 202 all the way to Nicosia, Cyprus. Now the plane had to be found again.

It was found a couple of hours later, flying at an altitude of 9,000 feet over Cyprus, where it was intercepted by British Royal Air Force jet fighters. But then the fighters discontinued their surveillance when the 202 failed to acknowledge radio signals. At this point the fate that bedevils anything mechanical intervened. The 202 started losing large quantities of oil from one of its engines, and its pilot requested permission to land at Herakleion Airport on the island of Crete. Fortunately, Lebanese authorities had sounded the alarm, and the plane was surrounded by Greek police as it taxied to a stop.

Aboard the plane, the police seized the hashish and $51,350 in cash and arrested its five occupants—John Robert Moore, fifty-one, pilot; Philip Irwin Amos, thirty-one, copilot; Kenneth Howard Connell, twenty-nine; David Leigh Mantell, thirty-one; and Robert Franklin Black, twenty-eight. All were charged with "purchasing, possession and transporting hashish, contrary to Greek law." The hashish had a retail value in the United States of between one and two million dollars.

This, then, was the end of a conspiracy to smuggle three and one-half tons of hashish from Lebanon to the United States—a conspiracy stretching from the small town of Carmichael, California, to the Temple of the Sun in Baalbek, which the ancient Greeks called Heliopolis. And its end could be traced unerringly from the concern of a Carmichael father for his daughter. As related in Customs files, the story developed along these lines:

Like so many American parents in late 1968, Harry Reagor of Carmichael was worried because he had seen his daughter, Leslie Ann Reagor, twenty-one, smoking marijuana with Philip Amos and another friend, James Littlepage. He mentioned his concern to his brother, Vincent Reagor, a Deputy District Attorney in Sacramento.

That December, Vincent Reagor had several serious conversations with Leslie Ann and Amos. He warned them repeatedly that their associations and continued use of marijuana would land them in trouble.

Vincent had learned through official channels that Littlepage had been arrested by Customs agents in San Ysidro, California, on October 21, 1968, on charges of smuggling 190 kilograms of marijuana into the United States from Mexico. And in November of the same year, Mexican police had come upon Amos, Littlepage and John Robert Moore as they allegedly were loading 1,000 kilograms of marijuana aboard a small plane at Zihuataneja, in the Mexican province of Guerrero. The Mexican authorities reported that Amos and Moore had escaped in the plane with about 800 kilos of marijuana and that Littlepage had fled on foot.

During a skiing trip, Amos told Vincent he was trying to "get out of the business," but that his partner, Robert Franklin Black, wouldn't let him. Accordingly, Vincent and his brother Harry met with Black at the Brigadoon Motel and tried to convince Black that he was living dangerously. Black laughed it off.

That was in early 1969. On January 17, 1970, Black and some others were arrested by California authorities on charges of possession and sale of marijuana. On February 5, 1970, Leslie Ann Reagor and Amos were arrested by San Francisco police on charges of possession of marijuana; at the time they were living in San Francisco, having been married in late 1969. That was enough for Deputy District Attorney Vincent Reagor. He decided that the only way to save Leslie Ann from prison was to tell what he knew to the law he represented.

Vincent Reagor knew plenty, and he told it all, over a period of months, to Robert Jensen, area supervisor of the California Bureau of Narcotic Enforcement at Sacramento, and to a Customs assistant special agent in charge, Ezra Wolff, in San Francisco.

One of the things Vincent revealed was that Amos had asked to be kept informed of any impending arrest warrants issued by the District Attorney's office. For his services, Vincent would receive $5,000 per smuggling trip; Vincent quoted Leslie Ann as telling him "everyone is going to make a lot of money."

Amos and Black both had taken flying lessons from Moore. Amos admitted to Vincent that he and Moore had been smuggling marijuana in from Mexico, and that they had used Metropolitan Airport in Sacramento to off-load the marijuana because Moore's son was the only attendant on the field after 10 P.M. Amos said he was planning to retire from smuggling after bringing in five more loads.

In early June, 1970, Amos, Leslie Ann and Moore had flown to Miami and negotiated the purchase of a twin-engine red and white Martin 202 plane. Moore and Amos had flown the plane to Sacramento, and Moore had registered the 202 in the name of "M" Enterprises, joking that the "M" stood for marijuana. "When we quit smuggling, we're going to transport crayfish from Haiti to Miami," Amos told Vincent. Harry and Vincent Reagor were given a tour of the aircraft.

Shortly thereafter, Black and his wife returned from Switzerland and plans were changed. The conspirators now would make just one more trip instead of five—to Lebanon and back. Vincent would get $25,000 for warning the group of impending search or arrest warrants. Amos and Moore bought pilot's uniforms, and Black joined them in flying the 202 to Los Angeles because the tie-down fees at the Sacramento Metropolitan Airport were too high. Later, Amos told Vincent Reagor that they planned to buy 4,500 pounds of hashish in Lebanon and fly it back to the United States, where they would land the plane at a small airfield in New Hampshire near a summer home owned by Black's father, a Cleveland industrialist. The hashish would be stored at the airport while Moore and Amos flew the empty plane to Boston to clear customs. Then the hashish would be flown to San Francisco.

At about this time, Amos also mentioned the name of Kenneth Howard Connell, who he said was putting up $250,000 for the venture. Amos had ordered charts of air routes around the world, and he, Moore and Black spent their evenings trying to decide on the best route to Lebanon. Vincent Reagor learned that "final arrangements" had been made for the smuggling expedition.

It was now late June, 1970, and Vincent Reagor told Amos he had "related the facts to the police and that Amos should withdraw from the venture."

Amos, according to Vincent, didn't bat an eyelash; he said he would go along with the expedition as planned. The Customs report, compiled a few months later, would add: "Vincent met Amos twice during the month of July, 1970, but no further plans were discussed regarding the conspiracy." There was never any official mention made of the reaction of Customs officials to Vincent's attempt to keep Amos and the pregnant Leslie Ann from risking further trouble with the law, but at least one agent refused to suffer silently at this leak. "Jesus Christ!" he screamed. "There goes my goddamn son-of-a-bitch of a case."

Officially, Customs kept its cool. Perhaps there was a sort of resigned understanding of Vincent's avuncular concern for his niece and nephew-in-law. Besides, the bureau *did* owe the man something for the information he had provided on the gang's activities.

No one could later explain why the smugglers stuck to a game plan known to the law. But stick to it they did, although the expedition to Lebanon was postponed from July until the end of August, presumably on the theory that the Customs people would naturally assume the trip had been blown and relax their investigation. But Customs stayed on the trail.

Thus Customs agents were in the neighborhood when Moore, Amos, Black and an unidentified male paid a visit on August 14 to the summer home of Black's father, F. Franklin Black, on Belknap Road in Gilford, New Hampshire, near Lake Winnepesaukee. The four men left the Black home late that afternoon.

At about the same time, the Martin 202 took off from Chico Airport in California, and was located by the Federal Aviation Administration two days later at the Lock Haven (Pennsylvania) Municipal Airport. Agents from Customs and the Bureau of Narcotics and Dangerous Drugs set up a 'round-the-clock surveillance of the aircraft, and on August 20 Customs Special Agent Roy Hawk reported that "Moore and Amos were in and about the Martin 202." BNDD officials, meanwhile, cabled their representative in Beirut, Lebanon, instructing him to "determine the attitude of the Lebanon government on allowing contraband to leave Lebanon and reenter U.S."

On August 20, Customs' assistant special agent in charge of the Baltimore office, Ed Lisle, who had been dispatched to Lock Haven, reported to Washington that three auxiliary fuel tanks had been installed in the fuselage of the Martin 202. Each tank, he said, had a capacity of 250 gallons and the flying capability of the aircraft had been increased to approximately ten hours—or 1,820 miles at 189 knots.

Lisle's message added:

"FAA [Federal Aviation Administration] advises three possible routes—U.S. to Lebanon:

"a. Ascension Island—Dakar, North Africa—Lebanon.

"b. Newfoundland—Azores—Africa—Lebanon.

"c. Goose Bay, Labrador—Iceland—North Africa—Lebanon.

"FAA advises that the best route for a clandestine operation would be (a); further, that the easiest and safest route would be (c)."

In Washington, Customs put out an alert to cover all three routes.

The Lebanese government on August 20 reacted with lukewarm enthusiasm to BNDD's cable suggesting that the smugglers be permitted to leave Lebanon with their load of contraband, if any. In a cabled reply to BNDD headquarters in Washington, the Lebanese Internal Security Police said it might be best to make the seizure in Lebanon "in view of the number of countries the aircraft must pass over en route to the United States." Customs, of course, wanted to get the group on smuggling charges, not merely for possession and conspiracy. Accordingly, a second cable was dispatched to Beirut, urging that the contraband be permitted to leave Lebanon and pointing out that U.S. officials were prepared to maintain surveillance all the way and seize the 202 upon its return to the United States.

Customs officials had wrapped up this operation with the United States Air Force command at the Pentagon. The Air Force put it in writing:

"After subject aircraft files a flight plan upon its return to the U.S., the Air Force is capable of and is willing to initiate an intercepting flight that will insure constant monitoring of the suspect aircraft's position. In addition . . . it is noted that the FAA has approximately 736 stations and picket ships, the monitoring capability of which could also be utilized to track the suspect aircraft upon its return to the U.S."

While all this diplomatic horsing around was in progress, the Martin 202 left Lock Haven in the late afternoon of August 20 and landed a little less than an hour later at Olmstead Airport in Harrisburg, Pennsylvania. Moore registered a party of three at the Holiday Inn East Motel in Harrisburg. That night, after dinner, Moore and Amos and an unidentified male repaired to the airport, where they inspected the 202. Chatting with hangers-on at the field, Moore said he and Amos planned to fly to Germany by way of Goose Bay, Labrador. "That's why we've got those auxiliary fuel tanks in the fuselage," Agent Hawk heard Moore say.

The next morning, the three men returned to the airport. After the unidentified male had said some fulsome good-byes and departed, Moore and Amos took off in the 202, heading northeast. They were forced to land in Bangor, Maine, at about two o'clock that afternoon because of fuel line problems; an airplane mechanic at the airport found that the trouble was due to an error in the installation of the auxiliary fuel tank lines. They had been affixed in reverse, causing the auxiliary tanks to overflow.

A less determined pair than Moore and Amos might well have decided to quit there and then. As a Bangor mechanic put it: "They couldn't pay me to fly in that crate across a duck pond." But Moore and Amos had more than their lunch under their belts. The fuel line error was corrected, and they took off again for Gander, Newfoundland—not Goose Bay—followed all the way by the radar tracking equipment of the U.S. and Canadian governments. At Gander, Moore and Amos supervised the taking on of all the gasoline the plane would carry.

Moore and Amos were next scheduled to fly to Keflavik, Iceland, where London took over general supervision and coordination of the tracking operation by radar and fighter planes.

On August 24, London advised that the aircraft had departed Keflavik and was proceeding according to its flight plan to Amsterdam, Holland. Washington had assigned its representative in Rome, Special Agent John J. Molliteri, to fly to Amsterdam. The next day, Molliteri advised that Amos and Moore had been joined by a male using the names Thomas Bryan and Bryan Thomas, also known as Goldfingers. The man was, in fact, Kenneth Howard Connell, the reputed angel of the venture, who had lost his right hand in an argument with an airplane propeller.

From Amsterdam, Amos, Moore and Connell flew to Luxembourg, then went on to Rome, arriving at Ciampino Airport at 10:50 P.M. on the twenty-fifth. Thirty minutes into August 26, the trio flew to Naples, and ten and a half hours later to Athens. They took off from Athens at 3:45 P.M. for Nicosia, Cyprus, where they touched down at 6:20 P.M.

Although Amos, Moore and Connell registered at the Hilton Hotel in Nicosia, that same evening Moore and Connell flew via commercial airline to Beirut, Lebanon, where they met Robert Black and David Leigh Mantell, a strapping Idahoan.

A Customs report laconically narrated the next development:

"On August 27, 1970, Moore, Connell, Black and Mantell were taken to the estate of Niaf Masri, a Deputy of the Lebanese Parliament, located in the Baalbek region of Lebanon. Moore told Connell, Black, Mantell and Shaw Kat El-Masri, Masri's son and the supplier of the hashish, how to construct a dirt landing strip on the estate so that the Martin 202 could land there. On August 28, 1970, Moore returned to Nicosia, Cyprus, and that evening he received a telephone call from Connell, who advised Moore that everything was "ready."

If indeed everything was "ready," a new record had been set in the construction of an airstrip. However, Amos and Moore had faith. They took off from Nicosia in the dark early morning of August 29 and landed an hour later on the new airstrip on the Masri estate— and there encountered their moment of truth.

Only about ten 50-kilogram sacks of hashish, out of the scheduled consignment of three and a half tons, had been loaded aboard the 202 when the fire fight broke out between the loaders and the Lebanese soldiers convinced that they were defending their soil against an Israeli incursion. Less than four hours later, after flying off with the hashish that had been loaded before the gun battle erupted, the five Americans were being interrogated by police at Herakleion Airport on the island of Crete.

Only Moore and Connell did any substantive talking, according to the official Customs report on the arrests. The report, filed by Special Agent Molliteri—who had followed the Martin 202 to its final landing at Herakleion Airport—tells their stories in simple, undecorated prose:

"Moore stated that he and Amos were hired by Connell to pick up 61 bags of hashish and that Connell was the boss of the operation. . . . He further stated that the Airplane belonged to him and that he and Amos were to get $5,000 plus costs for the trip; that they (Connell, Black and Mantell) were going to pay $160 per kilogram and sell it in the U.S. for $1,600 a kilogram. . . . He also stated that he met a Lebanese who took them to the Baalbek area; that, while in Baalbek, on or about August 27, he instructed the Lebanese, Connell, Black and Mantell where and how to build the airstrip he needed to land the Martin 202 aircraft.

"Moore was then shown photographs of several Lebanese male persons by Captain [Antoine] Saadea [chief, Lebanon Narcotics Bureau], and he positively could not identify any of them; however, he believed the photograph of Shaw Kat El-Masri, the son of Deputy in Parliament Niaf Masri, was the person who was dealing with Connell, Mantell and Black. . . . Moore stated he was told he would have no problem landing the plane in the Baalbek area and picking up the hashish because the land belonged to a Lebanese government official, and that the police would not interfere. . . .

"According to Moore, Mantell and Black were supposed to return to the Hotel Phoenician in Beirut after the hashish was loaded in the plane, and Connell was going to fly back to the United States with them; that once they were in the U.S. airspace, he would attempt to get lost in heavy air traffic in the New York-New England area, then land his plane at some small airfield which he had not yet selected, and unload the hashish in a rented truck, which Connell was supposed to have taken care of. The hashish was then supposed to have been driven from the East Coast to the San Francisco area to be sold. . . . Moore then claimed he was on the ground [in Baalbek] less than five minutes and that he made the decision to leave the area in a hurry because of the gunfire. . . ."

Molliteri's report quotes Connell as sneering at Moore's statement that he, Connell, was the "brains" of the smuggling ring. "Connell stated . . . that all of them were equal partners. He then commented that U.S. government agents always think there has to be a boss in every operation of this type. . . ."

After confiscating the 648 kilograms of hashish found on the Martin 202, the Court of Misdemeanors in Herakleion ordered its destruction "upon conviction of the defendants"—a curious bit of phraseology. Subsequently, the court also ordered the aircraft forfeited to the Greek government and confiscated the $51,350 in cash unearthed on the plane. In another curious development—or nondevelopment—reported deadpan by Agent Molliteri, "Efforts to locate and seize the 2,000 pounds-plus quantity of hashish left on the ground at the landing strip have been unsuccessful."

More than ten months elapsed before final dispositions were reached in the Greek government's cases against the five Americans involved. On December 20, 1970, all five were convicted of purchasing, possessing and transporting hashish. Amos, Black, Connell and Moore each were sentenced to ten years in prison, and Mantell to nine years. A month later, the Court of Appeals in Candia, Crete, upheld the convictions but reduced Moore's sentence to nine years, Amos's sentence to eight years, and Mantell's sentence to seven years, and ordered the expulsion of all defendants from Greece upon completion of their sentences. Then, after a new trial in October, 1971, Mantell was acquitted of all charges; Black's and Connell's sentences were reduced to thirty months each; Moore's sentence to eighteen months; and Amos's to fourteen months.

Possibly Greek justice was influenced in thus doling out clemency to the American defendants by an official communication from Beirut. The dispatch carried the information that no criminal action was "contemplated" against Niaf Masri, the Lebanese Deputy, whose Baalbek estate had been used as an airport by the Martin 202's crew, or Masri's son, Shaw Kat El-Masri, alleged supplier of the hashish.

The case of the Martin 202 was the most ambitious example of the use of a private aircraft in a smuggling venture. It also may have been the most foolhardy and the most inefficient. Flying a cumbersome transport plane of questionable trustworthiness almost halfway around the world is one of the hard ways to try to sneak dope into the United States; too many people and too many other better, faster, and immeasurably more sophisticated aircraft are always watching. Amos, Black & Co. of course were relative amateurs, despite their operations between Mexico and the United States. Worse, they were adventurous, a dangerous trait in a smuggler. Their thoughts were too big for both their talents and their experience.

Using a private plane for smuggling ventures has its advantages, including swiftness of transportation and a choice of options when things go wrong. A private plane can always take a detour to another country if trouble looms, whereas a commercial airliner takes the smuggler to the destination ordered by his ticket. Moreover, a private plane can land at interior airfields where there is no customs inspection—an immense advantage. But smuggling by private plane is practicable only over short distances—from, say, Central America, cities in relatively nearby South America, Caribbean ports and Mexico. These routes proved so profitable during the sixties and early seventies that Customs had to add more manpower to its force in and around Miami, not so much to catch the smugglers as to gather the kind of intelligence that would tell the lawmen who was doing the smuggling and when and where to look for an incoming shipment. Such intelligence paid off with one of Customs' biggest hauls during the Christmas season of 1970.

When an Argentinian with the imposing name of Alberto Juan Van Caester flew into Miami International Airport from Asunción, Paraguay, on November 24, 1970, he had no way of knowing that during the past month he had become rather familiar to United States Customs. In the course of its investigation of the so-called Bianchi-Ricord Bust (Chapter 8), Customs had found the name Van Caester, as one agent put it, "sticking out of" several reports on the investigation's findings.

"We knew who he was," said John Moseley, special agent in charge of the Miami office. "We knew he had some creepy friends in South America and that he had visited the U.S. several times in the past couple of years. It added up to the conclusion that Van Caester was a man to watch."

So Van Caester, thirty-eight, and something of a man-about-town, was watched closely as he registered at the Gateway Hotel in Miami Springs and as he met later with Frank A. Martin, an airplane mechanic who moonlighted as an agent engaged in arranging aircraft charters for a number of rental companies. Van Caester's tails also knew that he owed Martin money on a previous account, because they had listened to the gossip of pilots and mechanics at the airports and bars where they gathered.

Customs had unearthed an informant who knew Van Caester well enough to be in the latter's confidence. The informant was in a little trouble with the law, and it was in his interest to pass on whatever intelligence he gathered in his associations with the Argentinian.

Customs could not have had a better in. It shortly developed that

Van Caester wanted the informant, code-named Julio, to join him in a highly profitable heroin-smuggling venture. Julio agreed to do so. Thus through Julio's espionage work and from information gathered as the result of some individual digging by several undercover agents, Customs became a sort of incognito partner in Van Caester's affairs.

Apparently, Julio became Van Caester's alter ego. In any case, he knew everything Van Caester did and was kept informed of everything that was said in the Argentinian's negotiations to further his project. Van Caester denounced the Bianchi group as bumblers and said he'd show them how a job should be done. Back in South America, it appeared, Van Caester had a load of about 150 pounds of a morphine base that he said needed to undergo one more chemical process to convert it to heroin. A chemist in Chicago had been commissioned to handle this process. The load would be shipped from Paraguay to Panama in a DC-3 transport plane with the Federal Aviation Administration registration number N 778 V. Van Caester would bring the load into the United States from Panama by another plane, since the FAA might give the DC-3 special attention.

Accordingly, Van Caester commissioned Martin to fly to Aruba in the Caribbean to arrange for the use of a small plane based there. The transfer of the narcotic from the DC-3 would be made in Aruba and the junk then flown into the Miami area aboard the small plane. Martin flew to Aruba and made the arrangements for chartering the light plane, then returned to Miami.

Customs men working under Senior Special Agent Stephen Csukas learned that the DC-3 had landed at Lima, Peru, with one of its two engines conked out, and that Martin made arrangements to lease another aircraft to fly to Lima and pick up what he believed was lawful cargo and the malfunctioning engine. Csukas learned that Van Caester had ordered Martin to pick up the engine as a cover for the flight to Peru.

The Aruba plan had been scratched, and the substitute DC-3 would proceed back to the United States via Panama and Kingston, Jamaica, with the narcotic stowed beneath the floorboards and the engine tied down over the cache. The plane was to enter the United States at either Miami International Airport or Broward International, then proceed to nearby Opa-Locka Airport.

At this juncture, the Bureau of Narcotics and Dangerous Drugs officially entered the case, although it had been kept informed of earlier developments by Customs. Agents of the BNDD were especially interested in Van Caester's plan to ship the morphine base to

Chicago for final processing, and thus it was important that the bureau take an active part in the investigation from the moment the DC-3 arrived in Miami.

On schedule, the DC-3 touched down at Miami International Airport on the night of December 11 and taxied to the foreign arrival area. Shortly thereafter, the three crew members presented prepared Customs forms to Inspector Maurice Nygard, listing—quite honestly —the only cargo as a sick airplane engine. Customs agents, some of them dressed as cargo handlers and mechanics, were all over the area, but the strategy was to let a delivery be made if possible in order to grab the receiver as well as the courier.

Tension mounted as the crew returned to the plane and asked and was granted permission from the control tower to take off for Opa-Locka. The tension increased when the plane developed engine trouble after taxiing into takeoff position and the pilot canceled his request to fly to Opa-Locka. Then a crew member disembarked and made a telephone call from the Dade County Port Authority building. Thirty minutes later, just before one o'clock on the morning of December 12, a Chevrolet sedan with South Carolina tags drove up to the aircraft, and the crew members took several pieces of luggage out of the plane, stowed them in the car and drove off.

Customs was not interested in the crew members because its investigators had learned through Julio and sources in South America that the morphine base was stashed beneath the floorboards under the engine. So in the loneliness of the early-morning hours, they unstrapped and removed the engine and took up the floorboards, to discover five mustard-colored satchels, similar to mail pouches, each containing a number of packages gaily wrapped in Christmas paper.

When Martin arrived with a truck to pick up the cargo, an agent dressed as a cargo handler delivered one of the pouches to the truck and Martin drove off.

Customs' information was that the delivery would be made to a vacant house on the outskirts of Miami, where the morphine base would be stored until Van Caester could ship it to Chicago. Agents Csukas and Luke Benson had paid a visit to the house a few days before and installed two radio transmitters and certain electronic eavesdropping devices in the basement.

Van Caester had driven to the house in a green Ford Pinto, accompanied by an unidentified male. After Martin delivered the pouch, Van Caester and his companion left and drove off in the Pinto, followed by several unmarked cars occupied by Customs and

BNDD agents. Van Caester drove to the parking lot of the Belmar Hotel in Miami Beach, strolled into the hotel, and then a few minutes later strolled out again and returned to the house.

Meanwhile, Martin had returned to the airport to pick up the rest of the cargo, which agents had told him had to be cleared. By that time the four other satchels had been filled with milk sugar, and Martin was permitted to load them onto his truck and drive off— back to the house.

Van Caester was annoyed. He had made a phone call and had been told by his purchaser that "the money's not ready yet" and to call back in a few hours. He called back at 6 A.M. from a phone booth several blocks away, then returned to the house. Shortly there- after, he and the unidentified male stowed all five pouches in the trunk of the Pinto and drove to Miami Beach, where Mr. Unknown got out at the famous corner of Lincoln Road and Collins Avenue. At about the same time, a man left Room 440 of the Di Lido Hotel in Miami Beach. He was registered as Carlos Rojas of Buenos Aires, but Senior Special Agent Adam Olszewski, who was lurking in the hotel lobby, identified him positively as Carlos Rojas-Colombo, a name on Customs' little list.

Meanwhile, Van Caester was driving around Miami Beach, roar- ing down one avenue, slipping into a side street, circling certain blocks, and generally behaving in the manner of a man who wanted to lose himself. Finally, he picked up Rojas-Colombo and an uniden- tified male, and continued his circuitous maneuverings for several minutes. Then he let off one of his passengers, who immediately got into a 1966 Pontiac sedan. Both cars then were driven off, first heading south and then turning north on Collins Avenue. It was another classic chase in the race between careful smugglers and their patient, if irritable, pursuers. But it was about to end.

At about 7:10 A.M., both cars were driven into the grounds of the Seacoast Towers on Collins Avenue and parked alongside each other. Shortly, the trunks of both cars were opened by Van Caester, two other males and a woman; at such moments of truth everybody always wants to get in on every little act. Two of the mustard-colored pouches were transferred from the trunk of the Pinto to the trunk of the Pontiac.

The delivery had been made.

Customs and BNDD agents converged on the parking lot from all directions to put the three men and their female companion under nice, safe, nonviolent, evidence-securing arrest. At Customs head-

quarters Agent Olszewski's identification of Rojas-Colombo was verified, and the third man was found to be Hibolito Navarro, another
character on the Customs list of interesting people. The woman,
protesting she was merely Navarro's girlfriend out for an early-
morning ride, was identified as Irene Gonzales. Rojas-Colombo, like
Van Caester, was an Argentinian; Navarro and Irene Gonzales were
American citizens from the Bronx, New York, and Hialeah, Florida, respectively.

There was only one surprise. The packages so gaily wrapped in
Christmas paper had seemed to the agents who examined their contents at the airport to contain heroin rather than morphine base. A
laboratory check now confirmed that tentative finding; the pouches
were full of 209 pounds of pure horse, a consignment that would
have sold for a total of between $21,000,000 and $22,000,000 on
the street. At that time, it was the third-largest heroin seizure on
record.

After the arrests, Van Caester had stood apart from the others. He
wore the air of a man who had found himself mixed up with persons
of inferior social standing, and he seemed to want to make friends
with the lawmen, as if desiring to show them that he felt a snobbish
embarrassment *vis-à-vis* the situation.

As it turned out, Van Caester did indeed enjoy a loftier status than
his co-conspirators. He was a member of the Latin-American drug-
trafficking establishment—an individual of value south of the border.
Accordingly, he turned stool pigeon. He testified against Rojas-
Colombo and Navarro at the trial in June, 1971, and was rewarded
with a pretty two-year sentence. He served only a little more than a
year of his term, including his pretrial incarceration, and then was
deported back to Argentina, where a year later he was the subject of
a report by Senior Special Agent Bill Knierim in Washington. Van
Caester, reported Knierim, was alive, healthy and "living it up" in
Buenos Aires.

Obviously, Van Caester was important enough so that the mob
was anxious to protect him from any vengeance seekers. After all, he
was one of those willing to risk their necks by carrying out the actual
smuggling. Obviously, too, he had been ordered by the syndicate to
turn state's witness and sacrifice Rojas-Colombo and Navarro in
order to draw a lighter sentence, himself, so he could return to South
America and go back to work as soon as possible. Rojas-Colombo
and Navarro were merely receivers, who drove their hard bargains
and had no claim on the organization's loyalty. They were hit with

sentences of twenty years each. Whatever suspicions Customs continued to harbor about Irene Gonzales, making a case against her was difficult, and her importance was questionable. At any rate, the United States Attorney declined prosecution and the smuggling charges against her were dismissed.

Meanwhile, the airplane mechanic, Frank A. Martin, was given a clean bill of health. Customs was convinced he had no knowledge of the smuggling conspiracy but—as he sturdily maintained—had suddenly found himself involved in a shady piece of business too late to find a way out. Indeed, Special Agent John Moseley went out of his way to describe Martin as "an honest businessman who had been played for a sucker."

# 15

# King of Smugglers

In the sordid world of dope pushing, Lawrence Fassler had become a living, crawling legend. His airborne marijuana-smuggling enterprise grossed up to $150,000 a week, carrying as much as half a ton of pot per flight into California, Arizona and even New York, from his packing plant in Mexico. He was tough, daring, ingenious, and contemptuous of human life.

Unfortunately for his dreams of empire, however, the husky, broad-faced Fassler had become well known to Customs. His secret, deliberate hunters missed connections a few times as they worked toward building up an airtight case against him, but they finally nailed him on February 2, 1969, with a 15 to 18 years' sentence.

About a year before, in December, 1967, the Customs office in Tucson, Arizona, had Fassler pretty well taped. In the course of its persistent nosing around under rocks, it had collected enough information on the "King of Smugglers" to make him No. 1 on its most-wanted list. To Customs agents pursuing their exhausting investigations, Fassler was a combination Al Capone-Lucky Luciano, with Borgia overtones.

They knew him as a worshiper of that American god, efficiency. He had become the single biggest supplier of pot sneaked into the United States from Mexico, because he thought big. He used airplanes, sometimes owned, sometimes rented, as a railroad uses commuter trains. His aircraft flew at least three times a week, taking contraband toiletries, TV sets, radios and other wanted consumer items south, and returning to the States with their ballast of marijuana. Agent Hugh Marshall called Fassler a "farm-to-market" entrepreneur. He bought most of his pot directly from its growers in the Mexican states of Sinaloa, Colima, Jalisco, and Guerrero, often paying cash in advance for a crop months before harvesttime. He bought it from Mexican border town dealers, who trucked it north to their heavily guarded ranches south of Nogales and around Mexicali and Tijuana.

Fassler also had the right friends. He often entertained local police at his own ranch near Hermosillo, distributing cash and American mercantile goodies at his parties. With this protection added to his own ruthlessness and predilection for violence, he could afford to be utterly merciless to employees who got out of line. Those who worked for him were terrified of him; as one agent of the Bureau of Narcotics and Dangerous Drugs put it: "Unlike most crooks, those mugs wouldn't even talk to keep themselves out of prison." That probably explains why Fassler had been operating for two or three years before either Customs or BNDD even knew his name.

It was Fassler, say both Customs and BNDD men, who first armed his employees. In the fifties, few dealers in dope carried guns. But when Fassler roared onto the scene, rifles, automatic pistols and even submachine guns became a part of their working haberdashery. There followed a wave of mysterious gang murders, hijackings and double-crosses—shortly to become known as rip-offs.

Among other adventures, Fassler was long suspected by federal lawmen of involvement directly or indirectly in the robbery and sometimes slaying of naïve young Americans who ventured into Mexico with a bankroll to make a one-shot killing on pot. In the years before Fassler's heyday, these kids or any other criminally enterprising Americans could usually get away with a onetime transaction on either side of the border. During Fassler's time, they risked being beaten and robbed and occasionally killed. The bodies uncovered from time to time in the border area wilds of both Mexico and the United States were not those of lawmen or professional smugglers, but of amateurs from college and Main Street. Many of the murders went unreported; some of the amateurs simply were never seen again. Lawrence Fassler left the Mexican-American smuggling racket a heritage of violence when he entered prison; he had transformed a relatively safe trade into a jungle of terrorism.

This was the state of the marijuana industry on the day after Christmas, 1967, when Agent Marshall's digging led him to a flight instructor at a Tucson aviation firm. The instructor had rented a plane to Lawrence Fassler four days before for a flight to Phoenix, and the plane had not been returned. A Customs check found the plane in Hermosillo, and the instructor repaired to that bucolic Mexican community to reclaim his property. While the instructor was talking with Mexican police, Fassler and a male companion known only as Jerry arrived and joined the confab. After a few minutes, Jerry took off in a rented car. Fassler later was permitted to go his way, and the instructor eventually was "allowed" to fly his plane back to the United States.

"The Mexican police didn't interfere with Fassler in any way?" Marshall asked the instructor.

"Oh, yes," the instructor told him. "They accused him and the Jerry fellow of buying narcotics in Culiacán and they arrested Fassler at gunpoint. But Fassler talked to them, and I got the impression later, just before I flew my plane back, that he convinced the police he was innocent."

The instructor said that under a seat of the plane Fassler had rented he found a briefcase containing miscellaneous papers and credit cards issued to Fassler, a Tucson telephone number, papers identifying Jerry as one Jerry Lawrence, later found to be Gerald George Lawrence, Jr., of Tucson, and U.S. Navy Reserve documents in the name of a Lieutenant James C. Jelinek. Marshall's report later noted that the instructor had told him Jelinek arrived at the instructor's office "wearing a pistol" and demanded that he be given the briefcase. He paid Fassler's plane rental bill of $231 with three hundred-dollar bills and left with the briefcase, the instructor said.

Meanwhile, Fassler himself showed up to retrieve his Ford station wagon, which he had left parked at the Tucson airfield. Obviously, Fassler had not been incommoded during his stay in Mexico.

None of the people at Customs thought this incident curious; Fassler had all those good official connections and no Mexican law officer was about to hold "The King," or even ask any embarrassing questions of him over the minor matter of keeping an airplane overtime.

But the incident did suggest to Marshall that there was profit in pursuing his interest in Fassler. In various ways, he managed to pick up a report, never verified, that Fassler had bought an airplane in early January, and that in turn gave Marshall another name to conjure with. The name was William Willoughby, a fifty-two-year-old licensed commercial pilot, flight instructor, ground mechanic, and real-estate salesman who had emigrated to Tucson from Norwood, Ohio. Willoughby was a rangy six-footer weighing in at about 175 pounds, with brown hair, cold blue eyes, and a two-inch scar on the right side of his jaw.

Marshall learned that Willoughby had flown Fassler's plane to Mexico on January 23 and had returned to Tucson without notifying

Customs of his reentry into the United States after landing at a domestic instead of an international airport. That was at the least suspicious. On his next flight to Mexico, however, Willoughby did land at an international airport when he returned and dutifully notified customs that he was back on American soil. Marshall also discovered that Fassler and Willoughby were partners in a firm called J. Lynn Imports, Ltd., and that Fassler had shipped 274 pounds of marijuana by airfreight to New York.

That was on February 15. A few hours later, Fassler was arrested by Detective Joe Romano of the Tucson Police Department. "The King" made bail and went his royal way.

That same day, New York police and federal agents arrested one "Tanker" Reisman, a reported Fassler pal, when Reisman allegedly took delivery of 94 pounds of pot shipped airfreight by J. Lynn Imports. On the following day, the shipment of 274 pounds arrived in New York and was duly confiscated by Customs people. Meanwhile, Marshall was annoyed to discover that a shipment of "unknown" merchandise dispatched by Fassler's firm had arrived in Fremont, California, and had been picked up by an unknown female.

Fassler next came to Marshall's attention when he flew to Mexico with Willoughby, Mrs. Fassler and the Fasslers' daughter on March 12, returning on the thirteenth. The party flew to Hayward, California, two days later and then returned the plane to the rental company. Marshall couldn't prove it, but he had what he considered hard information that Fassler had delivered 200 kilos of pot to a Hayward dealer and was under contract to deliver another 1,000 pounds before March 23.

Fassler & Co. kept busy. On March 16 Marshall got a phone call from the San Francisco office reporting that Fassler had also delivered two kilos of cocaine to the Haywood buyer. Meanwhile, gasoline receipt tickets which Willoughby handed over to one June Bonesteel, from whom he had rented a Cherokee 6, showed gasoline purchases made at Tucson International Airport, Marana Airport in Marana, Arizona, and airports at Arizona City, Bakersfield, California, Haywood and Gila Bend, Arizona. It looked as if Fassler & Co. were doing a lively business.

Thus when the unsuspecting Willoughby again rented the Cherokee 6 from Miss Bonesteel under Fassler's known alias, John Prescott, on March 20, Customs had been informed in advance. The Customs agent in charge, Charles E. Cameron, Marshall and Cus-

toms Port Investigator Everett A. Turner repaired to Tucson International Airport to put the Cherokee under surveillance. An hour or
so later, at 10:30 P.M., Customs Agents Jack Hindes and Richard
Warner arrived by private plane from Los Angeles to join the watchers.

Seven long hours later, shortly after 5 A.M. on March 21, the
watchers saw Willoughby drive up to the plane and park alongside it.
He removed all the seats from the plane except for the pilot's and
copilot's and stowed them in his white 1962 Chevrolet sedan, which
he then drove to the parking lot and left there. Willoughby walked
back to the plane and took off.

Marshall, Hindes, Warner and Turner also took off, in the plane
Hindes had piloted from Los Angeles, prepared to follow Willoughby
to his destination. But they lost the Cherokee when Willoughby
turned off all its lights shortly after the aircraft became airborne.
Fretfully, the agents flew vainly around the Tucson area for an hour
trying to find the Cherokee again. Then they flew to Nogales International Airport to await information from agents running surveillance at numerous airports in the general area.

They waited until nearly noon on March 21 before a call came
from Marana, Arizona. The Cherokee had landed at the Inter-Mountain Aviation airfield there and was parked and tied down. Marshall
and his companions took off and were in Marana a half hour later.
They found the Cherokee was still empty of contraband—and, en-
couragingly, of the seats Willoughby had removed at Tucson.

At 2 A.M. on March 22, Jim Shepard, the gate security guard for
Inter-Mountain, phoned Marshall and reported that a blue camper
truck with three male occupants had just entered the airfield. The
truck came into view a few minutes later, and the agents watched
from a darkened hangar as the driver parked it with its rear door
backed up against the plane's left loading door. One of the men in the
truck was Willoughby, another was Patrick O'Neill, a nondescript
twenty-one-year-old with a record of arrests for assault with a
dangerous weapon, false identification, trespassing, auto theft and conspiracy of burglary. The third was unknown to the agents.

The three men appeared to be engaged in some form of activity
around the plane and truck, but it was too dark to make out what
they were doing. At one point, all three jumped back into the truck;
its lights were turned on and it appeared they were about to flee the
scene. But they got out again after several minutes. A few minutes
later, however, the unidentified man leaped back into the truck and

roared off at about 70 miles an hour, eluding the surprised agent who tried to follow him.

Meanwhile, Willoughby and O'Neill had climbed into the Cherokee and taxied to the end of the runway. The guard, Shepard, drove up to the agents in his truck and told them that Willoughby, the pilot, had asked him to turn on the runway lights.

"Not quite," Marshall told him. Instead, the agents piled into Shepard's truck and rode with him to the end of the runway, blocking the Cherokee's takeoff path.

O'Neill stepped out onto the Cherokee's wing. "What the hell's the matter?" he asked.

The agents got out of the truck and told him. O'Neill submitted quietly to arrest, but Willoughby was a touch reluctant, and—as Marshall's report put it—"Agent Warner and CPI Turner were forced to assist Willoughby to step out of the aircraft."

They found 350 pounds of marijuana neatly packed in cardboard cartons. Willoughby and O'Neill were carted off to the Pima County Jail in Tucson and that afternoon were held in $50,000 bail each on smuggling charges. After a few hours' sleep, the Customs men ate hearty breakfasts and then resumed their search for King Lawrence Fassler.

Sometime in May, 1968, a man named Joseph Coll, who worked for the Fassler organization, was murdered in Culiacán, where Fassler operated what Customs people called a "pot factory." There were two stories circulated in official circles as to how Coll met sudden death. One was that Fassler had contracted with a Mexican gunman who worked in the marijuana packing plant to do Coll in because Coll was stealing from Fassler and generally giving the boss a hard time. The other had the verisimilitude of detail and eventually appeared to check out.

The second story was that Coll had fallen in love with a Mexican prostitute and wanted to get married, break away from the organization, and go straight. He went to Fassler and asked to be paid off; Fassler owed him $2,000. Furious, Fassler called in Jerry Lawrence and the Mexican gunman and told them, "Take Joe Coll out and pay him off. I don't want to see him back here." Whereupon, Lawrence and the Mexican reportedly drove Coll out into the country and put two or three illegal holes in his head, then drenched the body with gasoline and set it afire.

Mexican authorities did find the remains of a white male in a desolate spot near Culiacán and reported the body had been cremated.

Later, a California dentist examined the remains and identified them as all that was left of Joseph Coll.

But Fassler remained at large and was doing business furiously. He seemed to have a hand in numberless illicit operations. Once, Fassler and one Richard Charles Bowling made a crash landing in Navojoa, Sonora, and Mexican authorities found about $20,000 worth of electric typewriters which the pair apparently was attempting to smuggle out of the United States. Both were arrested, but Fassler spread several thousand dollars around among Mexican functionaries and beat the rap. Fassler bought one thousand pairs of Levis and twelve business machines from a San Francisco fence for $900 and flew them to an airfield near Hermosillo, where he was again arrested. Lodged in jail in Nogales, Fassler threatened to contact his headquarters in Guadalajara and arrange for the dispatch of a band of armed men to spring him from durance vile. He was released, reportedly after having greased a Mexican judge's palm with $5,000.

A Customs bulletin at the time warned that "Fassler should be considered armed and dangerous inasmuch as he has allegedly killed one or possibly two members of the narcotics ring in Mexico and possibly has a large number of automatic weapons including machine guns and bazookas stored somewhere in Guadalajara."

Indisputably, Fassler was dangerous—as his henchman, Warren Hudson, would discover. Hudson, a pilot, made a sure $5,000 a week flying marijuana north for Fassler, and a big score would pay him as much as $20,000. But Hudson wanted out of the Fassler outfit. He had come to detest Fassler, and besides, he figured he could do even better financially on his own. So he got together with a friend named Gary Sloan, a blond twenty-six-year-old with icy-blue eyes, and they laid plans to rip off an 850-kilogram load of Fassler's pot.

From Mexico, Hudson flew the load to Fassler's ranch outside Tucson, then he and Sloan sold 550 kilos for $29,000 to one of Fassler's steady customers in Oakland, California. They phoned another Fassler customer in San Jose and offered him 2,000 kilos of pot for $100,000; the customer agreed to buy, and arrangements were made for a meeting with the customer and some other buyers at a cabin in the Santa Cruz mountains north of Big Sur.

The San Jose wholesaler rounded up three partners and a member of the Hell's Angels motorcycle gang, and they drove up to the cabin. Sloan and a third recruit to the rip-off operation drove up in a rented car and announced that the pot was in a rented truck down the road. The Hell's Angel went along with Sloan and the recruit to inspect the 2,000 kilos—actually just under 200.

That was the Hell's Angel's mistake. Cocksurely, he opened the rear door of the truck to find himself staring into the barrels of two .45 caliber pistols in Hudson's hands. The rip-off artists locked the Hell's Angel in the truck, made their careful way to the cabin, held up the buyers, and relieved them of $60,000. Hudson complained because one of the buyers had failed to show with another $40,000. But they took the $60,000 and headed for a hideout in Oklahoma. Bored after a month, they returned to California, bought a converted submarine chaser, the *Blue Fin*, and spent three months partying with a procession of assorted females.

But Hudson was still restless. He wanted to buy a converted B-25 bomber to smuggle marijuana out of Mexico, and he drove to Riverside, California, to inspect a plane of that type he had heard about from some casual acquaintances. Sloan, who later turned state's evidence in return for immunity from prosecution, would tell authorities, "I'm sure Warren knew he was being set up by some pros working for Fassler, but he had this ego, man, and he couldn't stop."

In any case, on October 12, 1968, Mrs. Penny Hudson notified the Riverside Police Department that her husband had been kidnapped. Warren Hudson was never seen again.

Customs and a posse of local lawmen finally caught up with Fassler in Concord, California, on February 2, 1969, in a shootout that nearly cost the lives of three Customs agents.

William Willoughby, the fifty-two-year-old pilot, and twenty-one-year-old Patrick O'Neill, who were captured with a planeload of marijuana in the bust at Marana, Arizona, nearly a year earlier, had gone to trial in December, 1968, on charges of unlawful transportation of narcotics and concealment of marijuana. Willoughby had drawn a sentence of two years in prison, and O'Neill an indeterminate sentence under the Youth Corrections Act. Because it is an axiom among Customs agents that "one arrest leads to another," the Willoughby-O'Neill bust undoubtedly provided the bureau with grist for its investigative mill. At any rate, Customs had a pretty good idea of where Fassler would be at a given time.

On February 2, that happened to be the Concord Inn, and Customs arranged a stakeout with the Concord police, headed by Chief James Chambers. On the lawmen's own schedule, Fassler appeared in the hostelry's parking lot, got into a car, and started to drive off.

A car loaded with four Customs agents roared up and blocked the exit to the lot. Three agents poured out of the car with guns drawn. Alex McLennan, thirty-six, a ten-year police veteran, took a quick look and mistook the agents for Fassler men protecting their chief; he explained later that he "believed my life was in danger." So McLennan opened fire, seriously wounding Agent George Gudbranson, thirty, and putting bullets in the leg of Agent David Wilson, twenty-six, and the arm of Agent Leon Jaussaud, twenty-nine.

Despite the confusion, Fassler was cornered and taken into custody. Gudbranson, with critical head wounds, Wilson and Jaussard were rushed to the hospital, where all recovered, although Gudbranson suffered permanent brain damage that resulted in occasional lapses of memory. But Fassler was arrested on smuggling charges, not for murder; it would be months before a California State's Attorney put together a homicide case against The King.

Fassler's car yielded a cache of 1,500 pounds of marijuana, one of the biggest seizures ever in California. Hauled off to jail, he was also charged with various smuggling counts contained in several federal and state indictments handed down during the past year. Fassler was tried on the state charges in May and sentenced to from fifteen to eighteen years in prison. The following September, he drew another fifteen years on federal charges, to be served concurrently with the state sentences.

Meanwhile, on May 12, 1969—a little more than three months after Fassler was busted in Concord—Supervising Customs Agent Melvin C. Johnson in Los Angeles submitted in letter form a report on the continuing investigation of the Fassler organization. The letter, addressed to the Commissioner of Customs, Office of Investigations, Division of Enforcement, contained the following information about and appraisal of the Fassler gang's activities:

"On January 6, 1969, Edward Frank Rose was arrested by agents of the FBI in San Jose, California, on a fugitive warrant. . . . He was interviewed by a Customs agent . . . at which time he related that he was working for Fassler, and since Fassler was a Customs fugitive he would be willing to furnish information and to assist in bringing about Fassler's arrest. A tape-recorded statement was obtained from Rose in which he implicated Warren Hudson, William R. Willoughby, John Doe Ken and John Doe Jim as pilots used by Fassler to smuggle marijuana from Mexico to the United States.

"He [Rose] stated that [Gerald George] Lawrence worked for Fassler in Culiacán, Mexico, and had an office there in which he directed all activities in Mexico for Fassler. He further stated that

Lawrence had approximately 15 Mexican nationals on a weekly payroll and that these Mexican nationals were involved in the packing, buying and shipping of the marijuana. . . .

"In addition, Rose stated that Gary Sloan, Daly Zarbo, Richard Jelenick . . . Joseph Zoel Coll and David Petty, and Joe Doe Littlejohn worked for Fassler both in Mexico and the United States. Their activities included taking the marijuana once it was smuggled into the U.S. to the San Francisco Bay area and delivering it to buyers in that area. Rose further stated that Petty actually arranged for most of the marijuana sales in the San Francisco Bay area, and that one of the major buyers of Fassler's marijuana was William Huttinger. . . . Warren Hudson and Joseph Zoel Coll are believed to be deceased."

(At the time, either Customs or the BNDD had arrested Fassler, Willoughby, O'Neill, Petty, Robert F. Gearey, Glen Lloyd, Allan J. Donchak, Leroy W. Duggan, Teddy G. Beeler, Rose and Mark Lohman. Customs officials believed that the Richard Jelenick named in Johnson's report might be the Naval Reserve lieutenant, James C. Jelinek, who had picked up Fassler's briefcase at the office of a Tucson aviation firm after the firm's representative flew to Hermosillo, Mexico, in late December, 1967, to reclaim a plane Fassler had kept overtime.)

Johnson's letter to Washington also reported he had learned that "Gerald George Lawrence, Jr. . . . was willing to cooperate with Customs agents and reportedly would be willing to testify against Fassler and others involved with Fassler. . . . It is believed that the remaining persons who have not been arrested or indicted can be indicted if some of the co-conspirators would cooperate with the government. . . ."

In Washington, in California and in Arizona, Customs men believed they could do much more than get additional arrests and/or indictments for smuggling dope. They were convinced that Lawrence Fassler had something important to do with the disappearance of Warren Hudson.

So did Richard Huffman, the young Deputy Attorney General in California, Terrence Boren, chief trial deputy of the District Attorney's office of Riverside County, and Agents Ray Cameron and Ernest Halcon of California's Department of Justice. Working seven long days a week and draining every drop of information from Edward Frank Rose and Hudson's rip-off partner, Gary Sloan, they finally wrapped up the damning details of Fassler's successful plot to avenge himself on the double-crossing Hudson.

Their investigation took them back to September, 1968, when

Fassler met with Rose, Jerry Lawrence and Ken Oldright, a twenty-five-year-old pilot who flew pot for Fassler, at the Berkeley Plaza Motel in Berkeley, California. Fassler swung a deal with Oldright whereby Oldright would kill Hudson for a $5,000 fee, plus certain equipment from Hudson's boat, the *Blue Fin*. The boat itself would be taken over by Fassler.

A few days later, Fassler, Oldright and Rose flew to Tucson, where they spent $280 of Fassler's money on a small arsenal at King's Pawn Shop. The armaments included a sawed-off shotgun, a .357-caliber two-barrel derringer, tear gas, a pair of handcuffs and assorted ammunition, plus a guitar case in which to carry their purchases. Oldright already had a .38-caliber pistol and so did his "assistant," Edward Chandler, who later would draw a one-to-five-year sentence in state prison as an accessory to murder.

About a month later, Hudson got a phone call from a man he knew who told him there was an old B-25 converted bomber for sale in Riverside, California. When Hudson said he'd like to look at the plane, the caller put him in touch with Oldright, who told Hudson he and his partner (Chandler) were interested in getting together with Hudson in a smuggling scheme. Hudson arranged to meet Oldright and Chandler at the Ramada Inn in Riverside.

Hudson and his girlfriend, a slender child of sixteen, checked into the Ramada Inn at 8 P.M. on October 13, 1968. Oldright and Chandler were already there, and Hudson phoned their room and invited them over to chat. The three men talked about the plane and also about a building Oldright knew about outside Riverside where marijuana could be stored after being flown in from Mexico. Hudson accepted Oldright's invitation to "go out and look over this place—the electricity is all turned on."

Hudson turned to his girlfriend. "I'll be back in about an hour," he said.

"He'll be back in fifteen minutes," said Oldright.

They were both wrong, but only Oldright knew it. Sometime during the night, said the state of California, Hudson was shot to death and his body disposed of in a manner unknown. The state's case was supported by Rose's sworn testimony concerning the meeting at which Hudson's death was planned. Sloan furnished the motive for the slaying with his testimony that Hudson had double-crossed Fassler, and swore that Hudson disappeared after driving to Riverside to meet with Oldright and Chandler.

There was no dead body, which made it a hard case to make stick in a courtroom. But thirty-two-year-old Richard Huffman skillfully put together the mass of circumstantial evidence surrounding the many activities of Lawrence Fassler, "King of Smugglers," and in April, 1971, Fassler was convicted of masterminding the murder of Warren Hudson and subsequently shipped off to prison for life. Old-right, charged by the state with being the triggerman, disappeared and was believed to be in Mexico, quietly growing vegetables. But a month after the Fassler trial, Jerry Lawrence was convicted of conspiracy to commit murder and drew a life sentence. Both Rose and Sloan were granted immunity in exchange for turning state's evidence against the main conspirators and were set free.

One informant told Richard Huffman he was "sure" Hudson's body had been thrown out of an airplane over that part of Orange County south of Los Angeles. "He was not a credible informant," Huffman told reporters dryly. "His information was third-hand stuff." Besides, by that time the state didn't need his testimony.

# 16

# "Kill Him! Kill Him!"

As chairman of the board of perhaps the biggest and most vicious smuggling ring in the area, Lawrence Fassler was a living illustration of the deadly fact that patrolling the boundary between the United States and Mexico is Customs' most dangerous chore. Agents call it the Violent Border, and an anonymous editorial writer with a poetic gift of phrase once wrote of the neighborhood: "Death Is Over There." It is true that, unlike Fassler, most syndicate bosses prefer to entrust their business to unarmed couriers in order to avoid trouble, but the country swarms with free lances who scoff at such a pacifist way of doing business. They carry submachine guns, sawed-off shotguns, handguns and assorted knives on their travels, and the wise lawman has learned to be ready with his own shooting iron when closing in to make an arrest. On the Violent Border, the rule is not to be caught drawing second.

Saint Joseph's Hospital in Nogales, Arizona, is located about half a mile north of the Mexican border and two miles west of the international port of entry. The neighborhood is isolated, bleak with scrub brush and sand, and to the rear of the hospital the barrier marking the border changes from an eight-foot chain-link fence to an ineffectual three strands of barbed wire only three feet high. A much-traveled dirt road on the Mexican side curves at this point and runs close to the border.

For decades, the area had been a favorite of smugglers, whether bearing narcotics or escorting Mexicans and others seeking to enter the United States illegally. A common method of operation used the hospital as a cover. That is to say, the receiver on the American side parked a car in the lot at the rear of the hospital, then walked down the low hill to pick up the contraband tossed over the fence into the brush by the smuggler on the Mexican side. The car then was driven off without having to undergo the annoying procedures of customs inspection.

Thus Customs Agent Rollin B. Klink was hardly surprised on the night of July 31, 1970, when he received a telephone call at his home, about a five-minute drive from the hospital, that there was a "suspicious-looking" car parked on the lot. What made the car "suspicious-looking" was that, as the caller put it, several human figures were clustered about it, engaged in some kind of busy work.

It was past ten o'clock, and Klink, twenty-eight and conscientious, decided against calling his partner and good friend, Special Agent Horace Cavitt, who lived only three houses away. He and Cavitt had been working long hours for more than two weeks, and Klink was sure Cavitt would be asleep. Besides, it might be a bum tip; people were always seeing "suspicious" figures behind the hospital at night.

Klink drove to the scene and parked his car in front of the hospital, instead of turning into the lot in the rear, where his car, even though unmarked, might cause any would-be smugglers to take alarm and flee down the knoll to Mexican territory. He got out of the car and walked slowly and as soundlessly as possible to the back of the building. There indeed were six suspicious-looking figures about 25 yards away. Five of the figures were carrying duffle bags, and the sixth was opening the trunk of a white Pontiac sedan.

The agent now reminded himself that there was no radio in his car; it was a new model assigned to him only the day before and Klink had an appointment the next day to have the radio installed. Somehow, he'd have to handle this one himself.

One way to handle it was to get back to his car and intercept the men as they drove off onto Route 89, which passed in front of the hospital. But Klink knew his chances of withdrawing without being detected were slim; the lot had been newly laid with peastone gravel, and each footstep sounded like the crack of a whip in the still air. So Klink drew his gun and rushed the six men, identified himself as a federal officer, and told them to get their hands up. When they obeyed, he lined them up against the wall of the hospital and searched them for weapons—"as best I could in a six-on-one situation," he recalled later.

Klink found and confiscated a .22 automatic pistol on one of the suspects, sticking the weapon inside his own belt. Then he started to walk the men around to the front of the hospital where he could get some help from some of the staffers inside. As the procession passed the Pontiac, Klink tried to close the trunk but was unable to do so because it was overloaded with what he now saw to be bricks of marijuana.

At that point, Klink switched strategy. Because he had no way of knowing whether any other smugglers were concealed in the brush, watching the proceedings, he decided it would be imprudent to leave the contraband unguarded. Thereupon, Klink halted the parade and threw a light into the car, satisfying himself that there were no weapons therein—he thought. He then ordered the defendants into the car—four in the rear and two in front. It was Klink's plan to join the two men in the front seat and then force the driver at gunpoint to pull the car around to the front of the hospital.

Three of the men climbed into the rear seat. Then, as the fourth man was about to enter the car, one of the three already seated grabbed a gun from under the right-front passenger seat, leaned across the other two men and yelled to Klink: "Freeze!"

"Oh, bullshit!" Klink bellowed back.

"Kill him! Kill him!" shouted one of the three men still standing outside the car.

There was an explosion from inside the car and a bullet tore into Klink's right cheek. At the same time, two of the men who had not yet got into the car fled down the knoll in the direction of Mexico, and safety. Klink fired one shot into the car with one hand and with the other grabbed the man who had shouted "Kill him!"

Still holding the suspect, Klink backed away to a position about six feet from the Pontiac and crouched at a point just off the right-rear fender. From there he exchanged several shots with the armed man in the car, then dropped back to behind a corner of the hospital wall, dragging the suspect with him. One more shot was fired from outside the car before the rest of the suspects took off down the hill to the border.

A few minutes later, as Klink was escorting his lone prisoner around to the front of the hospital, cars from the Nogales Police Department and the Santa Cruz County sheriff's office roared onto the scene. Klink's partner, Horace Cavitt, also drove up.

But Klink was still in command. He turned over his prisoner to Cavitt, later joined by Customs Agents Mel Paulsen, Charles Timilty and Thomas LeFevere, then drove the suspects' car to the front door of the hospital and went in to get his cheek patched up. Dr. Stephen Letourneaux removed a small piece of lead from Klink's face and took three stitches to close the wound.

Meanwhile, the other agents had secured the marijuana in the trunk of the Pontiac, later found to amount to 88 kilos, and Cavitt subsequently locked the contraband in his own vehicle. The prisoner was identified as one Marco Anthony Páez-Murrieta of Nogales, Arizona; he said he was seventeen years old. Páez also fingered two of the men who had fled, and said the man who had done the shooting was José Luis Romero-Hernandez, twenty-two, of Nogales, Sonora, Mexico.

"I don't know the other two," Páez claimed. "They're nobody. Just mules."

Klink himself had identified Romero. For the past month Customs people had been trying to track down a "Gordo," whom they knew only by sight, and who was wanted for smuggling an average of 100 kilos of marijuana a week into the United States. Klink recognized Romero as "Gordo" when he had the suspects lined up against the hospital wall.

Customs agents and police arrested two fugitives at their homes less than an hour after the shootout. The two pleaded guilty to "an act of juvenile delinquency," and drew indeterminate sentences. Páez, who had urged Romero to "kill" Klink, also got an indeterminate sentence because of his youth. But Romero remained a fugitive for more than two months before he was apprehended by Mexican authorities and delivered into American custody in Nogales, Arizona, on October 16, 1970.

No one did Romero any favors; trying to kill a law enforcement officer has always been regarded in police quarters as an offense second only to kidnapping a child. Romero was charged with smuggling and with assault on a federal officer, and state prosecution also was sought on a charge of assault with intent to commit murder.

Romero pleaded guilty to the smuggling charge and was sentenced to eight years in a federal penitentiary. The United States Attorney's office, concerned about a possible double-jeopardy problem, asked that the federal charge of assaulting a federal officer be dropped, and Romero was tried on the lesser state charge of assault with a deadly weapon. Found guilty by a jury, Romero drew a sentence of nine years, to be served consecutively with the eight-year federal term. Thus he faced a total of seventeen years in prison.

At the state's trial in January, 1972, Klink had his second confrontation with Romero and learned the prisoner had lost none of his toughness. During a break, Klink turned to Romero and asked him, "How's it going? Any problems at Leavenworth?"

"Yeah," replied Romero, "I had some problems. I got into a fight with another inmate. I hit the guy across the face with a chain."

By that time Klink had been promoted to instructor at the Customs Agency Training School at Hofstra University in Hempstead, Long Island, and Romero took note of the transfer. "You're living in New York now, huh?" he said.

"That's right," replied Klink.

"Well, I have lots of friends living in New York," said Romero. "I'll have to have one come and see you some night."

At about the same time, Klink was nominated for and received a Superior Performance Award, carrying a bonus of $200, for his police work in the parking lot of Saint Joseph's Hospital. He also got a congratulatory telegram from Customs' Chief of Investigations Harold Smith. But when Klink met Smith in Washington en route to his new assignment at the training school, there was steel in Smith's greeting as well as in his handshake.

"Klink, you did a goddamned good job," Smith told the agent. "But you dumb SOB, you also broke the first commandment. You went out on a job alone, just because you wanted to be considerate of your partner. In this business, considerate agents sometimes wind up very dead. Remember that, and someday you may be sitting in this office."

But Smith of course realized that the Rollin Klinks and Horace Cavitts were spread ridiculously thin along the 1,800-mile Mexican-American border. Although by 1972 Commissioner Myles Ambrose had beefed up Customs forces everywhere, the bureau still had only 688 people guarding the 1,500-mile boundary from San Diego to Laredo, Texas, plus a classified number of cars, planes, helicopters and boats of assorted size. Electronic sensors had been sown on both sides of the border, and there was a sophisticated radar network to detect planes flying clandestine missions.

Few laymen know that Mexico is a big opium grower. Yet American lawmen estimate that more than two thousand peasants tend poppy fields in the northwestern states of Sonora, Durango, Sinaloa, Nayarit, and Chihuahua. The opium is converted into morphine base and then heroin in laboratories in wilderness areas of Mexico; opium, morphine, or heroin of relatively low purity is smuggled across the border at crossing points in the areas of San Ysidro, Calexico, Nogales, El Paso, Eagle Pass and Laredo. Thence it is moved on to San Diego, Los Angeles, Denver, Phoenix, Albuquerque, Houston, Fort Worth and Dallas.

But only 15 percent of the heroin used in the United States comes from Mexican poppy fields. More is transshipped by Mexican smugglers from France, entering Mexico at the port of Veracruz by sea, or by air through Mexico City. However, Mexico's major dope export is marijuana. It is the source of 90 percent of the pot consumed by Americans, pouring across the border in a flow estimated by U.S. officials at more than 1,000 tons a year. Marijuana grows almost everywhere in Mexico, but the major producing fields are in the states of Sinaloa, Jalisco, Guerrero, and Tamaulipas. Across the border, San Diego and Los Angeles are the principal distribution points for the rest of the country.

By 1972 Mexico had also become a transit point for shipments of cocaine from Latin America, particularly Bolivia and Peru. The stuff is flown in to Mexico City, trucked to border neighborhoods, and then usually flown into the States by private planes. In recent years, too, a substantial amount of amphetamines and barbiturates has come from Mexico, much of it produced in the United States, exported under license to Mexico, and then smuggled back to its land of origin. Unlike the U.S., Mexico has no laws regulating the sale of such drugs.

"How can we stop it?" asked one Mexican official. "Thousands of American tourists and thousands of Mexican workers cross the border every day. They are impossible to screen. You can't search every car and truck, every pedestrian. Where would we get the inspectors?"

Also, there is the increased use of private aircraft.

To nab them, Customs gets considerable help from the United States Immigration and Naturalization Service, which operates a number of airplanes along the long border. For a long time most of these planes were for observation only, but in recent years Immigration has added some pursuit aircraft. Customs itself does its best with its small fleet of helicopters and pursuit planes. But the smugglers can thwart the radar network by flying low, sometimes at treetop level.

The use of boats—everything from a motor-powered rowboat to a seagoing yacht—has become a new problem for Customs. Every weekend, from California and the Texas ports, armadas of ostensible pleasure craft sail out into the Pacific and the Gulf of Mexico. Most are legitimate, but Customs people hate to think about how many are used to bring back heroin or marijuana from their "fishing" and "sight-seeing" voyages. The law says a part-time captain must report for customs inspection on his return, but there is no way to keep track of the hundreds of boats coming home to private marinas along hundreds of miles of California and Texas—and even Louisiana—coasts.

Sometimes luck plays a hand. Two California fish and game wardens on night patrol at Malibu Beach found their attention drawn to two men ferrying sacks ashore from a yacht anchored offshore. The wardens suspected the men were poachers, fishing for lobsters out of season. They found no lobsters in the sacks, but a total of almost a half ton of marijuana. The yacht roared off into the night but was intercepted a few hours later by a Coast Guard cutter when its skipper tried to sneak into the harbor at Long Beach without lights.

The wardens also were lucky personally. Unlike 999 out of 1,000 smuggling couriers from Europe, the transportation corps working out of Mexico tends to play rough. Mules and other deliverymen are often armed, whereas their counterparts from continental countries rarely carry guns or knives or any item a Customs agent might call a weapon. Except for a few congenital brutes with a fondness for violence, they carry nothing on their persons that might persuade a Customs inspector or agent to pursue his examination of their affairs. The axiom is that if an individual is found with a concealed weapon, he gets the "vacuum cleaner treatment"—which includes not only a careful search of his luggage but an investigation of his past and his associates.

Because the dope bosses on the Mexican run operate their businesses with an emphasis on swift punishment of even a suspected traitor, the job of finding reliable informants is a great deal harder than on the European scene. Indeed, some European operators will forgive an informant if he is important enough to the organization to merit absolution. There is always the hope that the competent employee who sings eventually will find his way back to the syndicate (perhaps after doing a little time in prison) and resume a career that means profits for the bosses.

In Mexico, the informant is dealt with summarily, and the penalties for talking are well known, as in the case of one Customs informer, Robert Corenevsky. One day, a Customs agent on the California-Mexico border received a letter postmarked Mexicali, Mexico. The letter contained the personal papers of Corenevsky and a note: "Here is his papers. He made one phone call too much. Our regrets to his widow. Gracias."

So U.S. lawmen have to work in other directions. One of these was the 1970 Operation Intercept, which sent Mexican officialdom—and thousands of American tourists—into a mass fit of rage. A report of a special task force to President Nixon declared that narcotics smuggling across the Mexican border was "increasing at an alarming rate," and criticized official Mexican law enforcement efforts as "totally inadequate in the face of the problem."

So Customs launched Operation Intercept, in which travelers to the United States from Mexico were subjected to intensified searches at the border. The traffic snarl was horrendous; cars were stacked up for miles, for as long as four hours. But the operation was a success. Its objective was not so much to arrest drug smugglers as to jolt the Mexican government into action, and this Operation Intercept succeeded in doing. Within a few weeks, the United States and Mexico had agreed on a bilateral program to combat drug traffic, called Operation Cooperation. The United States agreed to tighten security on its side of the border; Mexico agreed to hunt down drug traffickers with its Army as well as its police.

Since then, as many as 10,000 Mexican soldiers have launched drives into the boondocks, sweeping across mountain and plain in search of opium and marijuana plantations. Mexican Air Force planes dropped hundreds of leaflets to farmers in remote areas warning them to get out of the narcotics business, or else. Mexican police have smashed several heroin rings and demolished a few heroin laboratories. Marijuana was destroyed in public bonfires in a number of city and village squares. The United States provided military aircraft, sensory devices and electronic eavesdropping equipment to aid the Mexican effort.

Yet the Mexican problem remained. One reason was that so many peasants continued to be lured by the cash crops of poppies and marijuana. Another was the shortage of trained manpower in the law enforcement field. Mexico is not a rich country, and although the government expanded its Federal Judicial Police, or Federales, from 250 men to more than 400 and turned increasingly to its Army for sweeps into the wilderness, its force was lacking in expertise. And corruption continued to plague the campaign. There are crooked cops in every country, and Mexico has more than its share. The top narcotics hoodlums have plenty of money, and they spend it lavishly to buy protection from the country's ill-paid policemen and military.

Meanwhile, on the American side of the boundary, Customs agents did what they could with the weapons at hand—including the remarkable patience and perseverance that is one of the trained Customs agent's chief stocks in trade. In one case, scores of agents participated in a 3,300-mile pursuit of a station wagon loaded with marijuana that started in Calexico, California, and ended in North Bergen, New Jersey.

An informant in Mexicali tipped off Special Agent Paul Martin in Calexico that the Ford station wagon would be coming through the border on a certain September night, "headed for New York." In line with the policy of trailing a carrier for as long as possible and, ideally, to the receiver, a nationwide system of chase and surveillance was hastily organized.

When the station wagon carrying two Cubans crossed the border, it was tailed discreetly by four Customs cars, with one Customs car leading the way. The two Cubans stopped off for the night at El Centro, 14 miles from the border, and so did the agents—although they bedded down in a separate motel. There followed a wandering trip through California that took three days. Then the smugglers headed northeast into Utah and Wyoming, where they picked up Interstate 80 to Chicago.

It was a chase beset with problems. For the most part, the Cubans drove no faster than 50 miles an hour, which made the pursuit manageable. But refueling was a problem; the agents couldn't stop at the same gasoline stations the Cubans patronized, but had to drop back and then hit the throttle to catch up, or race on ahead. One car loaded with agents had a tire blowout at 105 miles per hour but fortunately no one was hurt and the car was otherwise undamaged. In Chicago and Cleveland, the pursuers were joined by agents from offices in those cities; they also picked up reinforcements at several points in Pennsylvania.

The station wagon pulled into a service area on the New Jersey Turnpike, and one of the Cubans made a telephone call. Meanwhile, agents in New York and Newark were alerted to watch for the wagon. Ninety-six hours from Calexico, the Cubans arrived at a house in a quiet neighborhood of North Bergen.

The house was the residence of Ángel Roberto Millan, a Cuban known as a major marijuana wholesaler but at liberty because no law enforcement agency had been able to put together admissible evidence against him. This time, the pursuing Customs agents did the trick. Millan directed the Cubans to pull the station wagon into his garage. Then, as he started to close the garage door, the Customs men moved in. They seized Millan, the two Cubans, and half a ton of prime marijuana concealed in a compartment cleverly constructed beneath the bed of the wagon. At the time, it was the second biggest marijuana seizure ever made by any U.S. law agency, and it showed what could be done with adequate manpower skillfully and painstakingly employed.

Eventually, Millan drew five years in prison. Back in San Diego, a co-conspirator named Carlos Theodore Hecht got six years. Antonio Estrada-Díaz and Hermenegildo Cárdenas, who led the Customs agents on the 3,300-mile chase, fared much better. Estrada-Díaz drew a relatively easy two years in prison, and Cárdenas was placed on five years' probation.

# 17
# The Big Chase

Four thousand feet over the nighttime landscape of Arizona, Customs Agent Harold L. Diaz was taking what most men would consider a perilous gamble. His two companions, one of them at the controls of the Piper Cherokee, were confessed dope smugglers, headed for the airport at North Las Vegas, Nevada, to deliver a cargo of 528 pounds of marijuana to their bosses. To be sure, the delivery was to be "controlled"—that is to say, made under Customs surveillance and supervision—and Hal Diaz expected to find some official help when the plane landed; besides, his companions had agreed to cooperate with the law. Moreover, Diaz was armed and they were not. Still, he was outnumbered, and a lone armed man is in only uneasy control of a situation when he is flying a long way up from the ground.

Diaz could take some comfort from the knowledge that the Cherokee was being tailed by a light Cessna piloted by another Customs agent, Jack Hindes. Presumably, Hindes would see to the apprehension and punishment of Diaz' companions if they turned desperate and somehow managed to overpower him. But Diaz might not live to testify at their trial.

At any rate, the situation was Diaz' responsibility. It had been his case for more than a month, since the afternoon of January 5, 1968, when he filled in one of those Customs "Memorandum of Information Received" forms that open with the printed line "I have received information that. . . ."

Under that line, Diaz had typed two terse paragraphs:

"Nick PAPPAS and Alan GREEN of Las Vegas, Nevada, are attempting to smuggle approximately 400 kilos of marijuana from Culiacán, Sinaloa, Mexico, into the United States by private aircraft.

"The pilot is unknown at this time; however, prior to the actual smuggling, the informant will attempt to obtain the pilot's name, and

220

the number and description of the aircraft to be used. It is believed at this time that the marijuana will enter the United States through the Nogales Valley, Nogales, Arizona, which is a known radar dead-spot."

The contraband was to be delivered to Nick Pappas, forty-three, heavyset, with the look of an old-time movie tycoon in his heavy horn-rimmed glasses, and Alan Green, a crew-cut, youthful-looking twenty-six.

Both Pappas and Green were "known" narcotics dealers—the lawman's frustrated term for people he is sure are in the racket but who have never been caught at their trade. Diaz could remind himself that Green also was known as a quick-draw artist who knew how to handle a firearm and enjoyed exhibiting his art. There had better be lots of help when they landed. Hindes, of course, would be on the Cherokee's heels, but Diaz could only hope that reinforcements would reach them in time.

It was a good case, Diaz could tell himself as the Cherokee knifed through the night. Customs had had it taped from the beginning, thanks to Diaz' "handling" of Jack Bernard Smith. Entered in the FBI's records as Number 233488G, Smith had been arrested the previous November on a charge of conspiracy to smuggle marijuana, and his case was still pending. Diaz had gone to work on him, informing Smith that he was already aware of the involvement of Pappas and Green in the racket. Customs eventually would put the arm on the two men, Diaz told Smith; why shouldn't Smith get some credit for lending a hand? Smith didn't have to be told that his cooperation, at the very least, would not damage his own case. So Smith had talked—and through Smith, Diaz and Customs had been in on this one from its very inception. Smith talked for the first time, profitably, when he informed Diaz that Pappas and Green had asked him to help make the arrangements for smuggling 400 kilos of marijuana into the United States from Mexico by private airplane.

On January 8, 1968, when Smith and Pappas had discussed the problem of locating a reliable pilot in a Las Vegas drugstore, Diaz and Agent John Enochs were in the drugstore and observed the meeting, and Smith later told them what had been said, including mention of previous loads of marijuana Smith and others had delivered to Pappas and Green. Three days later, Smith and Pappas met again at Smith's home, with Diaz listening in on their conversation via eavesdropping equipment installed with Smith's written consent. Then on January 24, Smith, Pappas and Byron Hahn traveled to Calexico, California, in Pappas' car and tried to locate a pilot named Donald Johnson, who allegedly had done some marijuana smuggling as a free lance. The trio was photographed by a Customs operative from the Calexico office.

Johnson was finally located a week later through a friend in Mexicali, Mexico. He telephoned Smith, and a meeting was set up for February 9 in Los Angeles. Again with Smith's consent, Diaz hid a microphone in an electrical outlet box in Smith's room at the Holiday Inn near Los Angeles International Airport, and then sat in an adjoining room and listened to and taped the conversation among Smith, Johnson and Pappas. The upshot was that Johnson agreed to fly the smuggling trip, and Pappas paid him $420 for expenses and to cover a deposit on a rented plane.

The next day, Smith and Pappas were photographed by Customs agents as they boarded a flight for Tucson, Arizona, with a connection to Culiacán, Mexico, via Aeronaves de Mexico. In Culiacán, Pappas bought 300 kilos of marijuana from a Mexican dealer. Smith returned to the States and tried unsuccessfully to reach Green by phone; meanwhile, Pappas was inspecting the airfield at Culiacán.

Smith finally reached Green the next day, and Green gave him a phone number for the pilot, Johnson, at the Flamingo Motel in Phoenix. Johnson told Smith he had lined up a Cessna 210 plane for February 14, but that the weather was bad and he wanted to deliver the load to Las Vegas during daylight. But Johnson had no luck; the manager of the Sun Valley Aviation Company in Phoenix, from which he had reserved the Cessna, refused to go through with the deal on the ground that the plane's owner needed it for his own use. Johnson went to three other aircraft rental companies, then wired Green that there would be a delay of three or four days in getting a plane.

Johnson never did succeed in renting a plane. Pappas was annoyed at the delay; he returned from Mexico on the evening of the nineteenth and complained to Green that because of Johnson's dillydallying the dealers in Culiacán had to keep moving the marijuana from house to house to avoid police suspicion. At about that time, Green told Smith that Byron Hahn "has a piece of this but Cliff's was the first money in it." Green apparently referred to Clifford Isbell, thirty-two, another Las Vegas operator.

Green and Pappas finally found another pilot, Bobby Bates. They also got a plane, a Cherokee 300 from Phoenix Aviation at Phoenix Airport. Customs' monitors taped all the arrangements, including

Pappas' telling his girlfriend "the kid has got a plane." Bates did look like a "kid," with his crew-cut hair and open face, and later, when the chips were down, he would act like one.

Smith, Bates and Green left Las Vegas at five o'clock in the morning on February 22 in Green's car and arrived in Phoenix early that afternoon. There, they met Donald Taylor, and Bates and Green rented the Cherokee 300. Bates made a brief checkout flight in the plane, and then he and Green flew from Phoenix to Deer Valley Airport, about 40 miles from Phoenix, where they were met by Smith and Taylor. While Customs agents watched, Taylor transferred several plastic gasoline cans from his truck to the airplane. Smith, Green and Bates then flew back to Las Vegas.

The next day, Bobby Bates bought 43 gallons of aviation gasoline from the (Harold) Hughes Tool Company at McCarran Field, which he had funneled into the plastic cans. He and Smith then flew the Cherokee to the dirt landing strip at Parker Canyon Lake and hid the cans of gasoline in the scrub growth that surrounded the strip. The plan was to fly to Culiacán, pick up the marijuana, then fly at an extremely low altitude across the border at a point which, because of its hilly terrain, would be dead to radar. The plane would then land at the Parker Canyon strip, refuel, and proceed to another prearranged airfield for the rendezvous with Pappas and Green.

As far as Smith was aware, neither he nor Bates knew which of two airfields—one in Searchlight, Nevada, and the other in Jean, Nevada, just west of Las Vegas on the Nevada-California line—would be used. The instructions, as given to Smith by Pappas and Green, were to make several passes over Searchlight and wait for a signal—the turning off and on of a car's headlights. If no signal was given, they were to go on to Jean.

At any rate, the smuggling trip was now on. Bates and Smith took off in the Cherokee at two o'clock in the morning on February 24 and flew directly to Culiacán, where they picked up the load of marijuana and a small sample of heroin. They flew back over the border and touched down at Parker Canyon Lake at 4 P.M. the next day. That was when the fun and games began.

Diaz and Hindes had rented a Cessna 210 and had flown from Las Vegas to the border area at which Bates and Smith were expected to cross on their return flight from Mexico. Their plan was to stay airborne in the neighborhood so they could tail the smugglers' plane when it crossed the border. But the smugglers were late, and Diaz and Hindes had to go down to a Nogales airport to refuel. As soon as they landed, Diaz called the Nogales Customs office to report his whereabouts. Several minutes later, the office called him back to report that Customs agents staked out at Parker Canyon Lake had radioed in that the smugglers' plane had landed there.

The Parker Dam area is a mesa covered with mountain grass and small scrub growth, only slightly larger than sagebrush, and with outcroppings of huge rocks. The airstrip sits on a finger of the mesa pointing toward Mexico, with the dam at the end of the runway. None of the few scattered vacation cabins in the area was occupied. Because Diaz feared a shootout (Green and Pappas had told Smith there would be a "fire fight if any cops get in our way"), Customs had enlisted the help of eighteen deputies from the Clark County, Nevada, sheriff's office. There was also a narcotics squad, a detective detail and a number of uniformed police. Most of this force was staked out at Searchlight, the presumed delivery place, with a smaller detail at Jean, and the rest at Parker.

At Parker, the lawmen were hidden in several wooded areas about 50 yards from the landing strip. When Bates and Smith landed, they jumped out of the Cherokee and went to work refueling the aircraft from the plastic cans they had cached there the day before. By prearrangement, Special Agent Jack Dennis emerged from the woods and strolled toward the men. Dennis was carrying a shotgun and wore hunter's garb.

He engaged in some small talk with Bates and Smith about the weather and the fact he hadn't had any luck. "I may as well tell you, if you flew in to do some hunting there ain't much game around here tonight," Dennis said. Both men ignored him except for some absent-minded monosyllabic mutterings.

When Dennis got close enough so he could see the marijuana sacks in the plane, he went into action. Pointing the shotgun at the men, he informed them they were under arrest. Meanwhile, the other lawmen converged on the plane. At about the same time, Diaz and Hindes arrived in their Cessna.

For his own hide's sake, Smith played the role of a genuine suspect, submitting with a Hollywood-like snarl to being handcuffed. With Bates all ears, Diaz gloated over Smith. "Well, we finally caught you with your pants down," he said. "We may not have had you very good before but this time we've really got you." Then he told Smith, "If you're smart you'll cooperate; you don't have any choice."

Smith, after putting on a brief act of defiance, finally caved in and told Diaz, "Okay, if you give me a break on the other case."

"Fine," Diaz said. "But remember, you've got a right not to say anything, and anything you say could be used against you. Also, you've got a right to have a lawyer present during questioning, and if you can't afford one, the court will get you one free. Also, if you talk without a lawyer, you can stop talking at any time."

"Cut the crap," Smith told Diaz. "I'll talk and I'll go through with the delivery." Then he turned to Bates: "How about you, Bobby? You don't have any choice either." By this time young Bates was trembling, ripe for conversion. He started to say something, but Diaz cut him short to deliver the same constitutional spiel he had given Smith.

"All right," Bates said, "I'll go along."

Both Bates and Smith then told Diaz they had been hired by Pappas and Green to pick up the marijuana and a heroin sample and fly it into the United States. Both said the delivery would be made at either Searchlight or Jean.

Following the book, Diaz and other agents flew Smith and Bates to Nogales, where they were fingerprinted and photographed and signed waivers of their right to an immediate appearance before a United States commissioner. About three hours later, Diaz, Bates and Smith were airborne in the Cherokee and Agent Hindes in the Cessna—headed, they thought, for the rendezvous with Pappas and Green at either Searchlight or Jean.

At this point, Smith gave Diaz some bad news. Bates had told Smith that Pappas and Green had instructed him to bypass both Searchlight and Jean and fly directly to North Las Vegas. Further, they had ordered Bates *not* to inform Smith of this change in plans. Until then, according to Smith, Bates had been unable to summon up enough courage to spill the beans.

That posed a problem. Both Searchlight and Jean were crawling with law enforcement people, but no alert had been given for North Las Vegas. Diaz did the only thing he could do; he got on the radio to Agent Jack Enochs in Searchlight and told Enochs to "get to North Vegas—like an hour ago. That's where the delivery will be made. Drive like hell."

Then, to waste a little time, Diaz ordered Bates to make passes over both Searchlight and Jean. "We're gonna make sure nobody is giving any signals," he told Bates. There were no signals given at either landing strip, and the Cherokee flew on to North Las Vegas but—under Diaz' orders—in something less than a straight line.

Enochs, meanwhile, had piled into Hal Diaz' car with three other lawmen: Frank Perez and John Davis, Clark County sheriff's deputies; and Bob Eyman, a Customs staff assistant later promoted to senior special agent in the Washington office. The car, an Oldsmobile confiscated from a drug trafficker, was equipped with two portable radios, one operating on Customs' frequency and the other for communication with the Clark County sheriff's office. Frank Perez did the driving because he was familiar with the roads and general terrain. Enochs rode with him in the front seat, manning the two radios; Davis and Eyman sat in the back.

As the car roared off, Enochs got on the sheriff's radio and asked that as many "black-and-whites"—police cruisers—as could be spared be dispatched to the Thunderbird Airport at North Las Vegas. Then everybody settled down—nervously.

Nervously, because Perez took seriously the admonition that time was of the essence. Traveling for the most part over two-lane paved roads through the desert, Perez kept his foot hard on the accelerator. For more than half the 60 nighttime miles to North Las Vegas, the Oldsmobile's speedometer needle hovered around 130 miles per hour; Perez said later he had to "slow down" to 80 miles per hour going through towns.

Because it was after 11 P.M., traffic was relatively light. But there were several close calls and one hair-raising near-accident.

After about ten minutes on the road, a big trailer truck loaded with steel girders made a U-turn across the highway. Perez downshifted into third gear and quick-turned the wheel to the right. The Oldsmobile flung itself off the road in an 80-mile-per-hour lurch onto the desert. The car started to spin, then fishtail, kicking up a cloud of sand. But Perez eased the machine under control and got it back onto the highway in a half leap—with the accelerator again pressed to the floor.

Enochs, who swore he had to swallow his heart twice, turned to Eyman and Davis in the back seat. "You guys are gonna have to pay for those fingernail scratches on the ceiling," he told them. Later, Enochs would say, "If it wasn't for Frank Perez, Customs would have given me a grand funeral." And Eyman bought Perez a trophy inscribed for "Driving Skill." Meanwhile, Enochs kept his finger off the siren button, even when the car was passing through towns. He figured that at the speed they were traveling the siren's screech would do more harm than good. He wanted other cars to get out of the way, and a driver's first reaction upon hearing a siren is to freeze.

Almost incredibly, Enochs and his companions beat both planes to Thunderbird Airport. They had been parked for about five minutes when the Cherokee carrying Diaz, Smith and Bates landed. Enochs had used the time to get on the sheriff's radio again and instruct the deputies in their cruisers to locate themselves in various small hangars in the service area, where it was dark and they could observe without being seen themselves. The deputies, more than twenty in all, were armed with sawed-off shotguns.

As the deputies were stationing themselves, Enochs spotted what he thought was Green's new Pontiac sedan parked in a canteen area near an entrance to the runways. He had the Oldsmobile parked on a service road where they could keep the car under surveillance.

Bob Eyman had run out to greet Diaz, Agent Hindes and the informants, Smith and Bates. Together, the three agents escorted Smith and Bates to the airport building so Bates could telephone Pappas and tell him the marijuana had arrived. But Bates had gone to pieces; he was trembling and virtually incoherent—apparently he, too, had heard about Green's reputation as a quick-draw man. So Bates was walked to one of the police cruisers in a hangar and stashed away for safekeeping. Smith then phoned Pappas and told him all was well and to "Come and get it."

To set things up, Diaz and Eyman commandeered the FOLLOW ME truck used to guide landing aircraft and spent the next ten minutes cruising about the airport, stopping from time to time to fiddle with tied-down planes.

Pappas and Green arrived at the airport and parked their car alongside Green's Pontiac, as Enochs had anticipated. Both then got into the Pontiac and drove out onto the airport apron, pulled up to within a few feet of the Cherokee, then backed up to the right-hand door, where Smith was standing. Smith unlocked the Cherokee's door and the three began transferring the marijuana from the plane to the Pontiac's trunk.

Diaz and Eyman promptly drove up to the Cherokee in their FOLLOW ME truck.

"Can we give you a hand?" yelled Eyman.

"Nope," yelled Pappas. "Everything's under control."

"Well, just doing our job," yelled Eyman. "We want to make sure the plane is tied down all right."

Eyman jumped down from the truck. "I'd better clean that windshield on your bird," he told Pappas.

That was the signal for Customs men and sheriff's deputies to move in. There was no fire fight, despite Green's and Pappas' threats to wipe out "any cops" who got in their way. Both surrendered without a struggle and submitted to a frisking job that produced two handguns—a .38-caliber Smith and Wesson revolver and a .32-caliber Colt automatic.

Indeed, Diaz would testify that the men seemed resigned to their fate. He quoted Pappas as telling Green, as they sat on the airport concrete, "Well, we can't be caught much worse than this, with the stuff in our hands." Green looked at him sadly. "Yeah," Diaz heard him reply.

Enochs, Perez, Eyman and Davis had to borrow a ride into town. Diaz' Oldsmobile wouldn't start, and later it was discovered the clutch and transmission had been blown during the wild race from Searchlight to North Las Vegas. Asked about his plane ride with Smith and Bates, Hal Diaz played it straight. "That Bates," he said, "is a goddamn lousy pilot."

Two months later, a federal court disposed of "The Case of the Midnight Chase." Pappas was sentenced to ten-year prison terms on each of two smuggling counts, the terms to run concurrently. Green drew six years on each count, also to run concurrently. Bobby Bates, the kid pilot, and Clifford Isbell, described as the gang's principal "banker," each got five years in the pen. Charges against Byron Hahn, another alleged banker, were dismissed for lack of solid evidence.

The letter to United States Attorney Bart M. Schouweiler in Las Vegas agreeing to dismissal of the charges against Hahn was signed by Oscar W. Polcuch, agent in charge of Customs' district office in Terminal Island, California. As commander-in-chief of investigations in his area, Polcuch technically was in charge of the successful roundup of the Pappas-Green ring, and it was he who had insisted that his agents proceed cautiously and with superior manpower and weaponry. Polcuch had reason to preach what might be called aggressive prudence. Some years before, when he was a brash young Narcotics Bureau agent, Polcuch had learned that some of the mobsters involved in drug trafficking on the U.S.-Mexico border could play very rough.

At that time, Polcuch was assigned to go underground in Mexicali, Southern California. The game he was after was one of Mexico's top hoodlums, Jesús Demara, alias Chiguili, who bossed a big opium and heroin operation and who enjoyed being called the Al Capone of Mexico. His undercover role was a natural for Polcuch, a glib talker and smooth operator with an air of detachment toward danger.

Polcuch hung around the seedier gin mills in Mexicali, employing discreet language but managing to make it plain that he would like to make contact with some junk salesmen. On occasion, he flashed a fat roll he boasted contained $25,000; actually it was made up of $2,500 in small bills wrapped around a wad of paper. Eventually, Polcuch was directed to Jesús María Reyna-Celaya, alias the Professor, who Polcuch had heard was a merchant of the right type. Polcuch found the Professor in a saloon, sipping tequila—and ignored him. Instead, the agent asked about two men named Martínez and Tapia, who ran a competing operation.

The Professor pricked up his ears and introduced himself to Polcuch. He described Martínez and Tapia as gangsters and suggested it would be better if Polcuch did business with him. Polcuch went along; all he wanted, he told the Professor, was some high-quality opium. An hour and a bottle of tequila later, a deal had been arranged whereby Polcuch would buy thirty cans of opium from the syndicate represented by the Professor. The opium would be delivered by the Professor on the American side of the border in exchange for $6,000.

But the deal fell through. The Professor tried to be subtle and hired a pretty girl named Eva Pérez Cruz to drive the opium through a Customs check. Purely by happenstance, a Customs inspector stopped Eva, found the opium, and escorted the courier off to the pokey. Polcuch had had no time to warn authorities the opium was coming across the border.

So Polcuch had to try again. This time, the Professor said it would be better if Polcuch met the big boss, "our own Mr. Capone." Polcuch grumbled, but inside he was delighted; he sorely wanted a personal look at Capone junior. The encounter took place in a luxurious house in the high-rent district of Mexicali, where the door was opened by a maid in starched uniform—and two hoods brandishing tommy guns. The Mexican Capone, Jesús Demara, a big, heavyset man in his late forties, was guarded by three more bodyguards wearing automatic pistols as he sat drinking coffee in the dining room.

Demara ordered Polcuch frisked and seemed annoyed when he found the agent was wearing a gun. Polcuch shrugged. "This is a dangerous business, señor. I am a careful man." Demara grinned and assured Polcuch the gun would be returned to him when he left, "if you leave."

After some small talk designed to sound Polcuch out on his connections, Demara seemed convinced that the agent's credentials were authentic. He agreed to sell Polcuch 110 5-tael cans of opium for

$25,000; 5 taels are equivalent to 6⅔ ounces. The opium would be delivered at a point on the All-American Canal north of the border known as the Woodbine Check.

Three times in the next two weeks Demara set up meetings to settle details of the delivery, and three times Demara postponed them. Finally, Demara contacted Polcuch by telephone and told him all arrangements had been completed and that the opium would be delivered at seven o'clock that night at the Woodbine Check. Polcuch had to work fast to make his own arrangements, for an ambush.

Woodbine Check was an obstruction, or drop, in the All-American Canal spanned by a small concrete bridge. At the bridge, the canal was about 50 yards north of the border on a parallel line with the boundary. Roads ran along the border on both sides. The canal banks were covered with brush and young trees and offered good cover. But the country north of the canal was flat, with no cover but an occasional clump of stunted trees. It was not an ideal spot to try to conceal official bushwhackers. Moreover, Polcuch knew the smugglers were heavily armed.

But the lawmen did what they could. Customs Patrol Officers John Lynch and Francis Merkt were stationed in an unused building about a quarter of a mile down the road from Woodbine Check. From there, they could observe the scene with binoculars, rifles at hand. But it was out of the question to use more than one car; there was virtually no traffic in the area, and even one extra vehicle would make Demara's men suspicious. So Customs Agent Kenneth Grant hid in the trunk of Polcuch's car. The rear seat was removed, and Customs Agents J. P. Sheehan and Fred Parkerson and Narcotics Agent Bill Craig piled into the cavity. A blanket was thrown over them and then four large suitcases. All the officers had pistols, and they also were armed with four riot guns and a 30-30 carbine.

Polcuch drove off for the rendezvous. He arrived at Woodbine Check at one minute after seven o'clock and stopped about fifty yards from the bridge. At the bridge, on the American side, were three men armed with automatic pistols. One of the trio was Demara, another was Pablo Martínez Gálvez, a Demara errand boy. In the middle of the bridge stood a man named Loreto Sánchez, fondling a rifle.

Polcuch walked over to the Mexicans and saw three burlap bags on the ground at their feet.

"Where's the money?" asked Demara.

Polcuch said he had to examine the goods. He deliberately opened the bags and checked a couple of cans at random in each bag. "Okay," he told Demara. "Bring it along. The money's in the trunk of the car."

As Polcuch reached the car, with the Mexicans about twenty feet behind him, he turned to Demara. "The money's in the trunk," he said again.

That was the signal Grant was waiting for. He scrambled from the trunk, while inside the car suitcases toppled as Craig, Sheehan and Parkerson made clumsy escape from their hiding place.

By this time, the Mexicans at the bridge had been joined by several others and had started firing.

But both Polcuch and Grant were young and agile, and they ducked and dodged between bullets, miraculously escaping sudden death. Polcuch shot one Mexican in the stomach with two bullets. Someone else got Martínez as he was running for the bridge. Demara and another man retreated up a footpath that crossed the bridge as Sánchez opened fire with his rifle from the middle of the span. Seconds later, a rain of fire poured down on the scene from the upper road on the Mexican side, where Demara had stationed a couple of men to cover his retreat. As he fled, Demara engaged in a running fire fight with Parkerson, standing at one side of the car.

From the building a quarter of a mile away, Lynch and Merkt opened fire on the riflemen on the upper road, and a shot from Merkt's weapon caught one of the riflemen and spun him around. He crawled away into the brush. Rifle and pistol fire continued intermittently for nearly an hour, with the Americans huddled in the heavy foliage on the bank of the canal and the Mexicans skulking on the upper road on their side of the boundary.

When darkness fell and put an end to hostilities, more than two hundred shots had been fired at Woodbine Check. Polcuch's expert guess was that three of the smugglers had been wounded. None of the Americans was so much as scratched, although Polcuch's car had been ripped by ten bullet holes. All the smugglers had escaped but Martínez, who had lain quietly after being hit. "The Al Capone of Mexico" was over the border, and shortly after midnight the chief of police in Mexicali, Juan Meneses Adarga, was shot to death. One report was that he had refused to furnish a convoy to the smugglers.

Jesús María Reyna-Celaya, the Professor, did something dumb several weeks later. Apparently fearful that Demara would hunt him down for his involvement in the bust at Woodbine Check, he crossed the border one night into the United States—instead of losing himself in the wilds of Mexico's backcountry. He took a job in a meat-packing plant in Hemet, California, and there he was picked up by federal agents a year after the big fight. He drew ten years in the pen.

# 18

# Five Tons of Pot

As long as civilized human beings cling to their inalienable right of privacy and protection against unreasonable search of their persons and dwellings, the controversy will rage over the employment by law enforcement agencies of wire tapping and other electronic means of surveillance—and properly so. Dictators' prisons have always been well filled with political opponents incarcerated because their harmless privacy was invaded.

But there is also the question of whether persons engaged in a conspiracy to commit a crime should enjoy the privacy necessary to their plotting. The answer has to be in the negative, providing always that the law has knowledge that a conspiracy is afoot and can submit to a judge evidence convincing enough to cause him to issue a temporary court order permitting electronic investigation of the suspects.

In the pursuit of dope smugglers, there have been numerous cases that could not be broken simply because there was insufficient evidence of a conspiracy to warrant an eavesdropping order. Other cases were solved only because Customs agents were able to listen in on the plotting. Such a case was that which resulted in the seizure in California in May, 1971, of five tons of marijuana, at the time the largest single such confiscation in the history of American law enforcement. The investigation, which led to the eventual arrest and conviction of eleven persons, including a well-known and prosperous San Diego lawyer, was conducted almost entirely by means of a tap on the telephone line of a well-to-do wig shop owner and man-about-town.

The cast of suspects was varied, a melting pot of society from the professions to the casual milieu of the handyman:

Richard Michael King, also known as Richard Michael Hansen, Mike Johnson and Mike Brady, forty-two-year-old wig shop owner and entrepreneur, suave and well dressed, something of a gourmet, described by friends as a "semiswinger" with charisma, smuggler and general manager in charge of transport.

James Leo Olson, also known as Captain Jack and Jimmy, thirty-six-year-old skipper of the *Mercy Wiggins*, last known address Captain Cook, Hawaii. Customs would charge that Olson worked for a flat fee; in this particular case he allegedly was to have been given the *Mercy Wiggins*, appraised at a value of $31,000.

John Ferris Pope, fifty-three, of Kealakekua, Hawaii, and Sparks, Nevada, charged with being a transporter.

Virginia Marie Pope, wife of John Pope, fifty-two, a crew member.

William David Baldwin, "Bill," also known as John Jacent Martin, William Bliss, Red Wilson, Robert Henry Redford and Paul Smith, thirty-one, alleged supplier of the marijuana from his ranch in Mexico. Baldwin, who was still a fugitive in 1972, allegedly used two aliases to lease houses in California for the duration of the smuggling venture, and although he was reported to be in San Francisco at the time of the bust, he went unrecognized by Customs agents. Customs fingered him as the moneyman, with a piece of the distribution operation in the United States.

James Russell Vukich, twenty-five, of San Diego, a handyman.

Carole Jean Swisher, also known as Carole Jean King and Carole Jean Hansen, twenty-seven, King's girlfriend, assistant and alter ego.

Paul Angelo Vesco, Jr., a thirty-year-old attorney with a prestigious practice in San Diego, a good friend of King-Hansen. Vesco, described as another swinger, was charged with conspiracy to smuggle marijuana and drawing up false documents for the two yachts involved. Customs also charged Vesco with advising King on how to beat the law and alleged that he arranged the leasing of certain land at Hidden Harbor, California, where the marijuana was to be delivered.

John Edward Fahlen, about thirty, eventually arrested in Hawaii, a kind of first mate to "Captain" Olson.

Robert Craig Light, thirty, of Seattle, Washington, alleged to be a free-lance smuggler who had asked King to bring some pot into the United States for him.

Michelle Dee Thieda, also known as Miki, twenty-five, of La Jolla, California, a girl-of-all-chores.

Gordon Ardell Maack, also known as Gordon Ardell Jones, thirty-eight, of Kailua, Hawaii, an "engineering mechanic" on the yachts.

Information received from a variety of sources strongly indicated not only that these suspects were involved in pot smuggling but that they were linked in a conspiracy to do so. But securing a conspiracy conviction requires evidence that the accused persons knew one another and were in communication in a more than casual fashion. Thus Customs' urgent need to listen in on what the suspects might be saying to one another.

According to Customs' records, it was one of the few times the bureau had used a wiretap. The scoreboard told the story of the tap's success: Eleven arrests, eleven motions to suppress the electronic evidence denied, eleven convictions.

The most vital wiretap was on King's San Diego telephone, listed in the name of his alias, Richard Michael Hansen. By early March, John E. Van Diver, special Customs agent in charge in Southern California, and Paul Martin, senior resident agent in San Diego, were convinced that the arrival of a big shipment of pot was imminent. A wiretap on King's phone was the only way they could keep in touch with the gang's activities and get continuing fixes on the two yachts, *Andiamo* and *Mercy Wiggins*.

Every scrap of information Customs had been able to pick up said that King was masterminding the multimillion-dollar smuggling venture by telephone in his San Diego apartment. His *modus operandi*, it was learned, was to arrange a deal with a supplier in Mexico, and then by ship-to-shore telephone relay directions to the crews of the *Andiamo* and the *Mercy Wiggins* as the two vessels sailed about in neutral Pacific waters, moving in and out of various West Coast harbors. The major problem, then, was pinpointing the exact movements of the two vessels so that lawmen could be waiting when the marijuana was off-loaded on American soil.

Martin phoned an old friend for help—Senior Special Agent Doug McCombs of Washington headquarters. Initial approval was required from Attorney General John Mitchell before submitting a request for a wiretap to a federal district judge in California. The timing was crucial. Customs wanted to begin eavesdropping on King's line as soon as possible; at the same time Martin and McCombs agreed they had to make sure the tap was not installed prematurely, lest the mandatoiy twenty-day period expire before the *Mercy Wiggins* or the *Andiamo,* or both, returned to American waters.

McCombs got busy on liaison with the Justice Department in Washington, making sure he knew whom to see and what paper work was involved. Martin worked with Justice Department attorneys attached to a special narcotics division in San Diego, preparing the necessary papers, motions, affidavits and orders for the wiretap request. But when the crucial moment arrived, there was no time to risk using the mails. Martin grabbed the documents and flew to Washington, arriving at Dulles Airport at 6:30 on the morning of Friday, March 19.

McCombs met Martin's plane at Dulles. They had breakfast, then drove to the Justice Department and hurried to the office of one of Mitchell's assistants with whom McCombs had been working. McCombs tossed the papers on the desk.

"This is what we've been talking about for the past two weeks," he said. "How about getting this to the Attorney General so we can get Paul on a plane back to California?"

Mitchell signed the request that afternoon, and Paul Martin took a 6 P.M. flight back to California. He got the court order the next morning. Customs people had alerted the telephone company that a tap probably would be approved, and it was installed less than an hour after Martin's appearance in court. Agents Erson E. Kern and Richard R. Lackey manned the earphones in a recently rented apartment two blocks away. Thirty seconds later they overheard Richard King, as Richard Hansen, discussing food and fuel supplies with James Leo Olson, captain of the *Mercy Wiggins,* somewhere at sea off Sacramento. In Customs' log, King thereafter would be referred to as Hansen, since the telephone was listed in that name and so was the authority for the wiretap.

Paul Martin had learned that on March 5 Hansen received a telephone call from Olson via an overseas operator in which the vessel from which the call was made was identified as the *Casandra.* This was the code name for the *Mercy Wiggins,* which at the time of the conversation had been located at Hidden Harbor, Sacramento. Olson allegedly had told Hansen that "all is cool in the situation here."

On March 21, the day after the wiretapping order was issued, Customs' eavesdroppers heard Hansen take a call from an unidentified male who said he would be arriving in San Diego on United Airlines Flight 347 at 11:23 A.M. About an hour later, Hansen received a call from "Carole," and in the course of their conversation told the caller he had just talked to "Bill."

Hansen was tailed to the San Diego Airport, where he met a person described in the official report as "a white male adult, 5'10", 165 pounds, dark hair, mustache, wearing dark sun glasses, with unusually even white teeth. Subject appears to be in his early thirties."

Then, according to the Customs logbook:

March 22, 7:55 A.M. Delta Truck Lines called Hansen and asked for General Marine Import-Export. They had three inflatable boats with COD charges of $1,164.34 due. Hansen stated he was General Marine Import-Export and payment would be in cash.

8:45 A.M. Hansen called Pacific Southwest Airlines for round-trip reservations on Flight 59 to Sacramento with open return.

8:55 A.M. Hansen placed a call to James Olson. Olson related that he had the *Mercy Wiggins* inside the harbor and that there was plenty of water and no problems. Olson stated they still had a little digging to do in some places. Hansen stated he was arriving on PSA at 1:25 P.M. that day and asked Olson to meet him at the airport.

Switching to personal surveillance, Martin flew to Sacramento on the flight taken by Hansen, and then Martin and Agent Leon Jaussaud flew over Hidden Harbor and took photographs of the *Mercy Wiggins*. Hansen returned to San Diego the next day, and at 5:02 P.M. the Customs log showed he took a call from Paul Vesco, who said he had called Hussong (a yacht broker) and told him that Hansen had authorized payments from the funds Hansen had there. Hansen told Vesco he had just returned from "up north," and that they would have no problems up there—"the only problems we'd have, if anybody's aware of . . . so keep your ear to the ground."

Hansen's telephone conversations kept his eavesdroppers busy. On March 24 and 25, they overheard eighteen calls considered interesting enough to record in the book. John Pope called, and he and Hansen discussed the Hidden Harbor docking site. Hansen told Pope to send "Johnny" (John Fahlen) down to San Diego that day. Hansen called Kettenberg Marine to inquire about some auxiliary fuel tanks he had ordered and was upset when he was told they had not arrived. About fifteen minutes later, Kettenberg returned the call and told Hansen the tanks would be delivered there by noon. Hansen told one Bobby Jones he had a big deal that would take about two months to consummate and asked Bobby if he was interested. Bobby said he wanted to make some quick money and that Hansen "pretty well had that down pat now."

Hansen called Shreve and Hayes, customs brokers, to inquire about getting boat papers for a trip to Mexico; he said the name of his vessel was the *Andiamo*. He called Kettenberg Marine again about his fuel tanks, and there was background conversation on Hansen's end about the "price of stuff, and quality." He called the Mexican consulate to inquire about a visa, and Shreve and Hayes again about his boat papers. Hansen identified himself as John Pope and listed the crew as consisting of John Pope, Virginia Pope and John Fahlen; he said they planned a voyage to Acapulco via Manzanillo.

John Pope called his daughter in Sparks, Nevada, and asked her to send her mother's passport airmail special delivery to the Marina Hotel in Newport Beach, California. Hansen called San Diego Scales Service and inquired about scales with a capacity of from one to 100 pounds. He called Carole and asked what she had done with the "hash."

On March 26, at 9:25 A.M., Hansen got a collect call from Jim Olson, who said "they" arrived the night before and had cruised down by the *Andiamo* that morning and woke up John Fahlen. Hansen told Olson he would be up the next day. Paul Martin located the *Andiamo* at Villa Marina, Slip 38, Newport Beach, and had it photographed. Later that afternoon, Hansen called Paul Vesco at his home and asked if Vesco had "gotten the ten grand." Hansen said he had to go up the coast and "see how things were." He told Vesco he hadn't heard from "Bill" yet. Vesco asked if "Bill" had "already purchased," and Hansen replied "Not actually. . . ."

Customs men observed the *Andiamo* departing Newport Beach at 11 A.M. on March 28. Aboard the vessel were three persons whom the agents identified as John and Virginia Pope and John Fahlen. The *Mercy Wiggins* pushed off from Newport Beach at 6:15 P.M.; aboard her were James Olson, a woman believed to be one Miki Thieda, a red-haired male believed to be Gordon A. Jones, a tall man with a mustache, wearing an orange hat, believed to be Richard Hansen (King), and a woman with long light-brown hair. Hansen called Carole at his home and told her he had arrived at about 2 in the morning on March 29.

That same morning, Customs agents aboard their own craft located the *Andiamo* anchored at the Coronado Islands, about 17 miles south of San Diego in Mexican waters. The *Mercy Wiggins* was found at the accommodation dock of the Bali Hai Hotel in San Diego, but sailed late that afternoon on a course for Mexico. Carole took a call at the Hansen home from Hansen's son, Mike, and told him his father was in Seattle on a business trip and would be back in about a week.

It was at about this time, apparently, that Richard King, as Hansen, decided to disguise the smuggling operation as the innocent comings-and-goings of a documentary film company. He spent considerable time on the telephone getting prices on metal signs, and shortly his Customs tails observed him driving a Volkswagen camper bearing signs which read: DEL MAR FILMS—WILDLIFE AND DOCU-MENTARIES. Those aboard the 57-foot *Mercy Wiggins* and the 36-foot *Andiamo* (valued at $16,000) posed as both documentary film makers and charter operators for fishing and diving parties. Besides the camper, King-Hansen also owned a Volkswagen Karmann-Ghia and a trailer, and Virginia Pope owned a 1971 Toyota pickup truck. Later agents would learn that King-Hansen was using a 24-foot fiberglass inboard-outboard boat named the *Wild Goose*. The organization had plenty of transportation.

The wiretap on the Hansen telephone was maintained for forty-nine days; an extension for fifteen days was granted by the court on April 9, and seven-day extensions were granted on April 23 and April 30. During that period, eavesdropping agents intercepted 1,114 communications involving 77 persons, and heard 897 "incriminating" conversations. The cost to the taxpayer was $1,000 for apartment rental and electronic supplies, plus $11,000 for manpower— four Customs agents at $7,500, two stenographers at $1,000, and two Justice Department attorneys at $2,500.

It was not an exorbitant tab, as samples from the Customs logbook showed. There were conversations between Vesco and King-Hansen about money matters and numerous calls by King-Hansen to the *Mercy Wiggins*, which enabled Customs to keep a fix on both that yacht and the *Andiamo* on their wanderings in American and Mexican waters. King-Hansen learned that Johnny Falcon (John Fahlen) had broken his foot and might have to be evacuated from the *Mercy Wiggins*. Agents heard Olson tell King-Hansen, "The diving party with Bill didn't come off as the water was too rough and dirty." The Bill mentioned was King-Hansen's Mexican supplier, William David Baldwin.

On April 12, Paul Vesco called and asked King-Hansen, "Has he got five toes or four and a half?" King-Hansen replied that John Pope had told him, "There's only going to be four and a half." From the information they had at hand, Customs' sleuths translated toes as tons of marijuana. The same day, Olson called King-Hansen from the *Mercy Wiggins* to report the yacht was fueled and watered and that John Fahlen's foot wasn't broken after all and he'd be able to help out.

Two days later, King-Hansen got a phone call from "Bill" (Baldwin), who told him, "It will probably be Friday or Saturday now as we are going to do it all in one time instead of two more. . . ." King-

Hansen said somebody had told him there would be only "four guys and a kid in the charter." (To Customs, four and a half tons of pot.) "I think we'll get an extra for ourselves, an extra half," Bill told him. "I had a little cash so I thought I might as well go ahead and use it for us." Bill also advised King-Hansen that he should "start thinking about another vessel because there is 10 all together at one place for next time, as time is running out in a couple of months and that is going to be it until next year."

A few hours later, King-Hansen called Jim Vukich about "somebody talking about" King-Hansen being in the "pot business." King-Hansen told Vukich, "I hope you talked them out of that," and Vukich replied, "I told them if you ever were I never knew about it." King-Hansen also called San Diego Camera Company and Roger Tilton Films, looking for props. An incoming call from "Bill" in Mexico concerned payoffs to Mexican federal officials. Paul Vesco called King-Hansen later and asked "if the fish got away or did they get more of the same." King-Hansen said he had heard from Bill and "he [Bill] got together with them [apparently the Mexican officials] and it may be the best thing that could happen. . . . They were very, very big in Mexico."

On April 18, at 7:30 A.M., Bill called again from Mexico and said "they had practically made it, and they were only about four hours away." Everything would be on for that night, Bill added; he would get the party on board. Next day, Olson called from the *Mercy Wiggins* to report that he and Bill "had a very good day." Olson said he measured the draft of the boat and figured four feet; "however, Bill said four and a half feet." (Customs' translation, four and a half tons of pot.)

Aboard a Customs boat on April 29, Special Agent Peter Grootendorst observed both the *Mercy Wiggins* and the *Andiamo* about 14 miles west of Mexico's Todos Santos Islands, on a northbound course. U.S. Navy four-engine Electras joined the three Customs boats and a Coast Guard cutter in surveillance of the two vessels. King-Hansen's Karmann-Ghia showed up on Sea Horse Street in Ventura, California. A parade of official cars sped into the San Francisco area in anticipation of the two vessels' arrival.

The *Andiamo* showed first, entering San Francisco Bay at the Golden Gate and proceeding past Sausalito in a northeasterly direction. Agents Kern and William E. Waggoner, Jr., boarded the cutter *Point Barrow*, and the cutter took off to intercept the *Mercy Wiggins*. It was now the afternoon of May 3, and the weather was bad, with dark clouds almost at water level and rough seas. On dry land,

Customs agents followed King-Hansen's Volkswagen camper to a market near the St. Francis Yacht Harbor in San Francisco. In the camper were King-Hansen, Vukich, Bob Light and Miki Thieda.

Back at sea, Customs and naval planes and helicopters were giving lawmen aboard the pursuing boats the positions and movements of the *Andiamo* and *Mercy Wiggins*. As the *Andiamo* crept into San Francisco Bay, the *Mercy Wiggins* was lying about 20 miles off Half Moon Bay in international waters. Shortly after 6 P.M., in the roiling waters, Customs Special Agent David G. Wilson and Coast Guard Petty Officer George Jackson boarded the *Andiamo* and took into custody the yacht's only two passengers, John and Virginia Pope, who did not resist arrest.

But those on the *Mercy Wiggins* were not about to give up without making a run for it. The yacht turned north from its easterly heading and raced toward the open sea. During the twenty-minute pursuit, lawmen in covering aircraft saw what appeared to be books and papers being thrown overboard from the smugglers' craft. When the cutter finally overtook the *Mercy Wiggins*, Agents Kern and Waggoner took no chances. They had their sidearms out and cocked as they boarded the yacht.

"Please, gentlemen," Captain Jack Olson told them, "you don't need guns. We are professional smugglers, not gangsters."

The other half of Olson's "we" was Gordon Maack. Agents arrested Richard Michael King-Hansen, Miki Thieda, Jim Vukich and Bob Light outside the camper near St. Francis Yacht Harbor. Carole Jean Swisher-King-Hansen and the lawyer, Paul Vesco, both were arrested nine days later—Carole at her home and Vesco at the U.S. Federal Courthouse in San Diego. Johnny Falcon Fahlen somehow managed to make it all the way back to Hawaii before he was picked up in early June, 1971.

When Vesco was found guilty, the presiding judge, Leland C. Nielsen, provided a touch of unexpected pathos. Tears welled up in his eyes as he described Vesco as a personal friend and a promising young attorney whom he had observed from Vesco's earliest days before the bar. At sentencing time, Judge Nielsen was more composed. He remarked that as a judge he had an obligation to the people of the community and could not countenance Vesco's avoiding imprisonment for his crime. However, it could not be said that Nielsen threw the book at the promising young lawyer. Although he sentenced Vesco to three years in prison, he suspended all but ninety days of the term.

Nor did the other defendants suffer cruel and unusual punishment.

King-Hansen drew five years in prison on each of four counts, to be served concurrently. Olson got five years on one count and one year each on three other counts, to be served concurrently after his five-year term. Fahlen drew two years and so did Pope. Maack got a year and a day. Jim Vukich and Bob Light each were sentenced to two years, with only ninety days in custody. Virginia Marie Pope and Carole Jean Swisher-King-Hansen were placed on probation for three years, and Miki Dee Thieda drew two years' probation.

But Customs counted the bust a victory for its own case on behalf of electronic sleuthing. Working under the strict and continuing supervision of the court, the bureau had proved it was possible to catch dope smugglers with little more than a set of earphones.

Richard Michael King, Paul Vesco, *et al.* were sentenced in January and March, 1972, which might have accounted for the penalties most law enforcement officials involved regarded as extremely lenient. By that time marijuana had become, if not respectable, at least a tolerable nuisance to many Americans. Senator George McGovern, Democrat of South Dakota, had called for its legalization under controls similar to those for alcoholic beverages, and Senator Harold Hughes, Democrat of Iowa, shortly would come out in favor of amnesty for persons serving prison sentences for using pot. Neither proposal at the time seemed to have a chance of being adopted by the Congress, but it was a fact of life that the country had grown to view the use—but not the sale—of marijuana much as it did boozing during the life of the Eighteenth Amendment.

Looking back, most experts in the field suggest that there was the same tolerance from the very beginning for the hundreds of thousands who were caught up in the amphetamine—or "speed pill"—craze of the sixties. Most of the speed users were college students or other young people, of course, and Americans have always been a mite softheaded about the antics of their children.

But the people at Customs were constrained both by law and by personal predilection to take a more puritanical attitude toward the problem. Not only was it their sworn duty to catch and convict peddlers of speed pills, but they had the professional lawman's built-in antagonism for smugglers of every description, and particularly for those who dealt in harmful merchandise. Besides, the smuggling of amphetamines from Mexico and Canada was a nuisance they didn't need; they had their hands full dealing with the heroin, cocaine and hashish pushers.

Thus a Customs agent named Melvin Moore, stationed in San Ysidro, California, only a long stone's throw from the Mexican border, could summon no kindly feelings for Henry Brulay. In December, 1965, Moore had collected information indicating that Brulay, who ran an income tax service in San Ysidro, had smuggled five tons of speed pills into the United States during the previous twelve months. In retrospect, Moore would reach the conclusion that Brulay made a substantial contribution to the amphetamine craze which had its beginning at about that time. Certainly, Brulay's enterprise had become big business before he was caught.

Almost as bad, in Moore's book, Brulay was a former U.S. Customs inspector on the Mexican border and consequently a defector from the camp of the mandatory righteous. A hail-fellow sort, Brulay passed back and forth across the border as a privileged former club member, lavish in his first-name greetings to his ex-colleagues. As Moore put it, rather wistfully: "In this job you suspect everybody, but you've got a right to think a guy who used to work for the bureau is cleaner than most."

At any rate, Moore was a trifle shocked by reports that large shipments of amphetamines from Mexico City to Tijuana were finding their way into Brulay's hands. From an informant, he got his hands on a quantity of the round white tablets marked with a cross, and a test showed they were indeed amphetamines. Bills of lading showed the consignee was using the name David Fierro, and Moore learned that Fierro drove a black 1956 Chrysler sedan bearing a California license plate. Moore was not surprised to discover that the vehicle was registered in the name of Henry Brulay of San Ysidro and that the address on the registration was that of Brulay's income tax service office.

To the sidelines reporter, the fascination of the Brulay case was in its utter lack of conventional fascination. No one would ever make a "French Connection" movie of Mel Moore's operations in pursuit of evidence substantial enough to bring into a courtroom. He spent most of his time sitting behind a desk, a drudge to paper work and the telephone. Even when he left his office, it was not with gun drawn to fight it out with sinister suspects or to embark on a wild chase of his prey, but to interview more-or-less innocent bystanders, businessmen, other law enforcement officers and congenital gossip mongers, and to pore for hours over dry commercial records.

The work was not only tedious and mind-numbing; it consumed many man-hours. For nearly two months, Moore worked an average of 14 hours a day and dined at his home only three times. As Senior Special Agent Irv Weinstein was wont to remark, drily, "There are times when you can feel that divorce lawyer breathing down your neck because you have to forget temporarily that you've got a wife and a couple of kids." Aside from domestic problems, Mel Moore also had to face the fact that there was no Mexican law against the mere possession of speed pills. When the crunch came, he could only hope for cooperation from officials south of the border; he had no right to expect it as a matter of course.

Moore collected every possible scrap of information that even suggested Brulay was part of a smuggling conspiracy. In the process, he crammed a file folder with the records of sixty-three telephone calls Brulay had made or received to or from San Ysidro, Tijuana, Mexico City, San Diego, Los Angeles, Scottsdale, Arizona, and El Cajon, California. At the Tijuana airport, he made copies of six bills of lading for "drogas secas," or nonliquid drugs, and "pharmaceutical products" from Mexico City for which Brulay was listed as consignee. He recorded the license numbers of forty-three "suspect cars" seen in "suspect neighborhoods."

Brulay also had a *pied-à-terre* in Mexico—an apartment over the Mercado González at Third and F streets in Tijuana. Moore could not personally get into the business of surveillance in an area of Mexican jurisdiction, but he managed to engage a small corps of free-lance sleuths to keep him informed of Brulay's movements. At the most generous, the movements were suspicious. During the first two weeks of January, 1966, Brulay made several trips to the Tijuana airport to pick up shipments dispatched from Mexico City by one "Antonio Larrea." On at least some of these occasions, Brulay was observed removing the shipments from the trunk of his black Chrysler sedan and stashing them in the garage of a residence on Calle Bernal in Tijuana.

Moore was interested in Brulay, but he was also interested in tracking down the receiver—if the receiver was not Brulay himself. To Moore, Brulay appeared as strictly a middleman, the one who picked up the speed shipments and stashed them at the Calle Bernal rendezvous for eventual smuggling into the United States.

But operating incognito in a foreign country is a ticklish business, and by January 23 the inevitable had happened. Moore's free-lance tails told him neighbors had complained to the Tijuana police about their lurkings in the vicinity of Brulay's apartment and the house on the Calle Bernal. Clearly, the surveillants' position had become untenable, so Moore called them off and the case was handed over to the Mexican Federal Police.

To Moore's delight and relief, the Mexican lawmen acted with swiftness and dispatch. They arrested Brulay less than forty-eight hours later and lodged him incommunicado in a cell at the headquarters of the Mexican Secret Service. They also seized 2,217 pounds of speed pills with a street value in Los Angeles of $226,760. Tijuana Police Chief Jesús Medina subsequently invited Agent Moore to assist him in the continuing investigation of the case and made arrangements for Moore to interrogate Brulay in an attempt to learn the name of the receiver.

Brulay's story, according to Moore's notes, was that he had met a man named David Fierro in the bar of the Foreign Club in Tijuana about a year before and that Fierro had offered to pay him $20 for each load of speed pills Brulay picked up for Fierro at the Tijuana airport. Brulay claimed he himself had never smuggled any of the pills into the United States and had no idea who did. He did admit he was aware the pills were destined for Los Angeles and that he knew the racket returned huge profits, but insisted he had never asked for more than $20 a load.

Considering the circumstance that the Mexican government, under the nation's laws, could find Brulay guilty of nothing more reprehensible than residing in Mexico illegally, the cooperation of Mexican authorities was estimable to a point beyond the call of duty and international amity. After notifying American officials in advance, they shipped Brulay back to the States, and he was met by Customs agents on schedule in San Ysidro. Three months later, a jury took only thirty minutes to convict Brulay of conspiracy to smuggle 2,217 pounds of "hypnotic drugs" into the United States. He drew five years in a federal penitentiary for, as Chief Medina put it, "thinking he could get away with anything in my country."

# 19

# The Swellheaded Leopard

From the St. Louis office in the spring of 1971, a message came clattering into Customs headquarters in Washington from Special Agent Sidney C. Bowers. The St. Louis office was investigating the background and present activities of Frank August, also known as George Murray Kimbrell, who was suspected of sneaking heroin concealed in "tiger skins" into the United States from the Far East. August, said Bowers' message, could be the head of a smuggling ring which both St. Louis and Chicago agents had been investigating for some time.

"What the hell next?" Commissioner of Customs Myles Ambrose asked of no one in particular as he read the message. "Now we've got to believe tiger skins!"

But by that time Ambrose and Customs men everywhere had learned to believe anything. On a quick trip to Afghanistan, one agent had encountered a shepherd who showed him how to slit the skin of a sheep and slip in a wad of opium before herding the beast across the border into Iran. To Ambrose, therefore, the case Sid Bowers was working on was important mostly as another indication that Asian smugglers of dope were still trying to make a dent in the American market.

At the time, only about 5 percent of the illicit junk entering the United States was coming from across the Pacific, almost all from Southeast Asia. Eighty percent of the heroin consumed by Americans still originated in Turkey, and about 15 percent in Mexico. But American diplomatic pressure was cutting back production in Turkey, and the Turkish government had agreed to ban the cultivation of poppies after 1972. There was the obvious danger that as the flow from the Middle East was reduced, the demand would grow for opium and heroin from Burma, Thailand, Laos and the Yunnan province of Communist China. Besides, the American market in South Vietnam was dwindling with the withdrawal of U.S. troops.

Most American authorities in a position to know about such things had long dismissed as a propaganda canard charges by the Soviet Union that Communist China, as a part of official policy, manufactured narcotics and unloaded them on the world market to hasten the decline of its enemies. There was no evidence of a massive and calculated campaign by Peking to flood non-Communist countries—and the Soviet Union—with debilitating junk.

As a high official of the American intelligence community put it: "The story would make good propaganda, but we just don't have any evidence to back it up. With our spy planes and our satellites we'd certainly be aware of any large-scale, illicit opium and heroin industry in mainland China. There is some illicit trafficking, of course, but there's no proof that it is organized by the Peking regime."

However, Yannan province is hundreds of miles away from Peking, and like half of mainland China's provinces, it was still ruled by the Army. Oriental generals have been known in the past to fatten their pocketbooks by providing protection for dope merchants, just as some American politicians protected rumrunners in the 1920's and early thirties.

Moreover, a book published in January, 1973, again raised the untidy specter of a Communist Chinese government officially encouraging the illicit narcotics trade. *The Cairo Documents,* written by Mohammed Hassanein Heykal, an internationally known Cairo editor and friend of Presidents Nasser and Sadat, submitted some remarkable statements Heykal attributed to Premier Chou En-lai when the two dined together in Alexandria in June, 1965.

Wrote Heykal: ". . . when talking about the demoralization of the American soldiers in Indochina, Chou remarked that "some of them are trying opium, and we are helping them. We are planting the best kinds of opium especially for the American soldiers in Vietnam. Do you remember when the West imposed opium on us? They fought us with opium. And we are going to fight them with their own weapons. We are going to use their own methods against them."

At any rate, in "The Case of the Swellheaded Leopard," the main source of opium in Southeast Asia was the border area where China, Burma, Thailand and Laos converge. Most of the crop was coming from Burma, with the main transit routes through the Thailand hills to Bangkok, and thence by trawler to Hong Kong. Opium from Laos was being flown to South Vietnam and to the Gulf of Siam.

From these regions of semiwilderness the illicit transportation lines carried out between 400 and 600 tons of opium a year. Burma was simply incapable of putting a stop to production; most of the opium grows in tribal neighborhoods over which the Rangoon police has never had much control. Moreover, the tribesmen are a rough lot, and the undermanned Burmese police agencies are not inclined to mix it with them. In some areas of Burma and Laos, Chinese Nationalist soldiers who went into exile after the war with the Communists hire out as mercenaries to guard the opium caravans of ponies winding their way into and through Thailand. These Chinese also operate their own poppy fields and thus collect twice from the industry.

Government attempts to stamp out production were complicated by two factors. First, many of the tribesmen were special protégés of the U.S. Central Intelligence Agency because of their fierce resistance to Pathet Lao and North Vietnamese troops in the Communist-held areas. The CIA had never considered it an official obligation to try to persuade the tribesmen to stop growing the opium, which forms much of their livelihood. Then there is political and military corruption.

In Laos, Army units cultivate, harvest and sell opium poppies and processed opium, and much of it is transported by Royal Lao Air Force planes. In Thailand, government officials extending into the Cabinet have been linked with the dope traffic. The police must be paid off, at an average of $5 per kilo of opium at each checkpoint between the borderlands and Bangkok. A State Department spokesman acknowledged the problem: "If narcotics agents nose around too closely, they're going to uncover some links to pretty high places." Among these places was the palatial residence of the sister of a Southeast Asian head of state, who ran a morphine laboratory.

In 1972, a fleet of thirteen trawlers—each with a capacity of 3.5 tons of opium—was moving opium from Thailand to Hong Kong. The fleet was operated by a consortium of Thai government officials and businessmen whose names were well known to United States Customs, the State Department and the Justice Department's Bureau of Narcotics and Dangerous Drugs, but nothing could be done about it because the Thai government was either unwilling or unable to initiate prosecution procedures. Yet Secretary of State William P. Rogers and Thai Foreign Minister Thanat Khoman had signed an "understanding" in September, 1971, providing for "immediate action" against the dope traffickers. Several months later, the State Department informed the Thai regime through the embassy in Bangkok that "continuation of illegal traffic in drugs, particularly heroin, will have a serious impact on American support of the national effort." These were strong words, but unfortunately it was in the national interest to keep the anti-Communist Thai government on its economic feet.

In Thailand, and in South Vietnam as well, the pressure on government officials to "cooperate" with the heroin industry was intense. Salaries even for high-ranking officials were relatively low, and it has always been a way of life in Southeast Asia for bureaucrats to improve their life-style by pocketing bribes. And, of course, once the heroin peddlers have bought legal protection, they hold the club of exposure over the heads of their governmental conspirators. Meanwhile, the heroin gangs invested some of their huge earnings in buying arrangements from corrupt authorities in the Philippines to transfer their operations to that country against the unlikely day when Southeast Asia became too hot for them.

For Americans at home, the tragedy of these profitable operations has been the victimization of U.S. military forces in the area, particularly in South Vietnam. Official estimates were that as large a proportion as 20 percent of all American troops had become heroin addicts at the height of the American presence in Vietnam. Ironically, during 1971 and 1972 the military's biggest casualty figures resulted from heroin addiction, not from combat. Between August and December, 1971, there were 90 deaths caused by overdoses of heroin. The death rate in this category for 1972 was estimated in the fall of the year as heading for the 200 mark.

In Vietnam, American servicemen always could get heroin of a high degree of purity on any street in Saigon and other big cities. The horse was pure and it was cheap—only $2.50 for a quarter of a gram, and as little as $1.50 for an eighth of a gram. Some of the heroin was provided by dealers among the one thousand or so military deserters who did a thriving business, especially in a Saigon slum known as Soul Alley, which was always off limits to U.S. personnel and where even the toughest MP's hesitated to venture.

A report on a special around-the-world study mission by Representatives Morgan F. Murphy of Illinois and Robert W. Steele of Connecticut quoted United States agents on the spot as identifying the czar of the Bangkok heroin industry as one William Herman Jackson, a former GI. Jackson, in 1971 and early 1972, was operating the Five Star Bar in Bangkok, patronized chiefly by black U.S. servicemen. Jackson, said the report, "recruits patrons of the American Star Bar as heroin couriers to the United States and utilizes other active duty military personnel to ship heroin to the United States through the Army and Air Force Postal System."

Some of this heroin undoubtedly was being consumed by addicted Vietnam veterans who had returned to their American communities. In his report to the House Foreign Affairs Committee in March, 1972, of a comprehensive study of drug abuse in the United States, Congressman Seymour Halpern of New York said there were approximately 60,000 addicted veterans. Halpern noted that as of November, 1971, Veterans Administration drug treatment centers had treated 9,542 addicted former GI's and that 6,014 were veterans of the Vietnam War.

"It is safe to assume," said Halpern, "that only one out of 10 has come forward for such treatment, which would even be a conservative estimate. Thus, if that ratio applied, the number of addicts who have returned from Vietnam could surpass the staggering estimate of 60,000 . . . and could be well over 90,000." Meanwhile, authorities on the drug problem in the Customs Bureau and the Bureau of Narcotics and Dangerous Drugs feared that the addicted veterans could turn on as many as 3,000,000 others in a five-year period. Many of the new addicts would be women of childbearing age, since one out of four of the nation's addict population was female, and they in turn could be expected to produce heroin-addicted infants if they continued their drug habit during pregnancy. Thus through the "Asian Connection," the effects of the Vietnam conflict would inflict damage on the next generation.

Much of the heroin was smuggled into South Vietnam from Bangkok by Thai soldiers either returning from leave or beginning a tour of duty in South Vietnam. Most of these soldiers traveled by U.S. military aircraft, and the customs procedures in Vietnam were so casual as to be virtually nonexistent. Thai soldiers also mailed heroin through the postal system set up by American authorities for Thai military serving in Vietnam. This loophole was at least partly closed in mid-1971 when a U.S. Customs Group was established to assume responsibility for all military customs operations in Vietnam and to direct the processing of personnel and their accompanying baggage arriving in or leaving the country.

But the problem in South Vietnam, as in Thailand, was complicated by the involvement of high government officials and military officers. Investigators for U.S. Army Intelligence, Customs and the BNDD in late 1971 furnished Ambassador Ellsworth Bunker with the names of more than fifty high- to middle-ranking Vietnamese officials and military brass alleged to be doing business with the heroin bosses. But although the possession and sale of heroin are illegal in South Vietnam, the Saigon regime took no action.

"What can we do?" asked a State Department official. "How can President [Nguyen Van] Thieu clean up a country where most of his government is on the take?"

Meanwhile, Washington kept pushing its Southeast Asian allies to take the problem seriously, holding Japan up as an example of what can be done to curb illegal drug trafficking. By taking a tough stand, the Japanese since 1964 had reduced their heroin addict population from more than 50,000 to only about 8,000. A convicted peddler is assured of spending at least ten years in prison, and there is no bail permitted in narcotics cases.

Moreover, Japanese law made disposition of such cases swift as well as sure—much swifter, for instance, than the plodding prosecutions in the United States. A suspect must be charged within 48 hours, but the police can hold him for 10 days, during which preindictment investigations are conducted. At the end of 10 days, the prisoner is turned over to the prosecutor, who has another 10 days to bring the accused to trial. If necessary, the prosecutor can request an additional 10 days for further "unusual" investigation before commencing trial. Thus a suspect can be held for 30 days without bail.

But, then, corruption in Japan has never been the problem it is in Southeast Asia. No government in that area exercises any really effective administrative or political control over the wild and hilly regions where the heroin-producing poppy is grown. Besides, in Thailand and Laos the military is supreme, which in the context of the heroin problem means that any group of officers with enough rank can take over the processing and smuggling operations while thumbing its exalted nose at the politically inconsequential police forces. No common garden variety of cop in either Thailand or Laos is about to match muscle with any member of the military brass.

One day, for example, residents of a suburb of Bangkok watched with suspicious fascination as a helicopter made several landings and takeoffs outside a godown, or warehouse, at which it unloaded a number of large packing cases. One nosy neighbor called the police, who raided the warehouse looking for contraband liquor and were embarrassed when they discovered the contraband was fresh opium. Their embarrassment was understandable: Only the Army and border police operate helicopters in Thailand.

This was the situation in January, 1971, when the Customs Bureau in Washington received a routine request from the Interior Department's Bureau of Sport Fisheries and Wildlife. Would Customs establish a lookout for imported tiger skins from the Far East? Tigers were on the list of endangered species whose importation into the United States was prohibited, and investigators for Sport Fisheries and Wildlife suspected tourists were smuggling in the skins concealed in their luggage, or by mail.

On March 12, Frank August arrived in Honolulu from Bangkok and was questioned by Customs inspectors, who wondered why he made so many trips to the Orient. August, twenty-five, had served with a United States Marine unit in Vietnam and had since changed his name from George Murray Kimbrell, a fact that intrigued the inspectors. They decided a search of August's person was justified under what might be called the "constant traveler" rule. No contraband was found, but in one of August's pockets were receipts for two "tiger skins" he had mailed to his mother in St. Louis.

To anyone ignorant of the Customs investigations in St. Louis and Chicago, the encounter between Frank August and Customs inspectors in Honolulu would have seemed trivial. The inspectors themselves were merely performing a routine duty in taking an official interest in a man who traveled frequently between the United States and the Far East. To them, Frank August was an employee of a service company that repaired helicopters in Southeast Asia. They could not have known, as mainland investigators did, that August was friendly with some curious types in Laos, Thailand and Okinawa and that he had been arrested in Okinawa on a charge of possession of marijuana.

At any rate, what followed this simple encounter was the untangling of a web of events and circumstantial coincidences that led to a smuggling ring, a syndicate of dope pushers in Chicago and St. Louis, and two prostitute rings—all connected with Frank August's comings-and-goings between the United States and the Orient.

Little things contributed to the mass of evidence: the receipt for the parcel August had mailed to his mother in St. Louis, a receipt for passport photos, a motel bill here, a list of telephone calls there. It seems safe to say that, but for the persistence and investigative expertise of Agent Sidney Bowers and a gaggle of other Customs men, these coincidences would have gone unnoticed or dismissed as meaningless.

"Don't you know it's illegal to import tiger skins into the United States except in special cases?" August was asked.

"Hell, no," August replied. "A friend said he had two tiger skins he was willing to give me, so I took them and mailed them home."

August was permitted to continue his trip to the United States for reasons satisfactory to Customs investigators in Chicago and St. Louis, who had been checking on the activities of an assortment of individuals suspected of involvement in illicit drug trafficking. The probers were not so much interested in August's "tiger skins" as they were in making a case that would stand up in court. In developing that case, their investigation suggested that Frank August, born George Murray Kimbrell, was a leading figure in a smuggling ring aimed at the neglected American market.

As of March 12, the investigators were able to reconstruct their case back to October 12, 1970, when George Kimbrell quit his job for a private American company in Okinawa and traveled to Bangkok, the picturesque Thai capital. Their notebooks told the following story:

Kimbrell left Bangkok on October 21, 1970, and returned to the United States. A couple of weeks later one Carol B. Morris, later identified as Betty Carol Aleshire, a known heroin user, traveled from Chicago to St. Louis for a business appointment with Agnes Brittain, who had been released without prosecution on a charge of keeping a bawdy house the previous February. Brittain told Aleshire that she had a chance to buy a substantial quantity of heroin at a low price and asked Aleshire if she would sample the horse and give an opinion as to its quality.

On instructions from a bartender in a St. Louis saloon, the two eventually repaired to the Brittain home, where they were shortly joined by two men. The younger of the men identified himself as Frank and introduced his companion as his father. "Frank" produced a pound of heroin, which Aleshire tested by "snorting"—that is, by sniffing it up her nostrils. She rated the heroin as high grade, whereupon Brittain bought the stuff. "Frank" took Aleshire's phone number in Chicago and said she'd be hearing from him.

She did, on or about November 19, when "Frank" showed up in Chicago with a man he called Aaron Gray and identified as his half brother, and a third man named Speed. "Frank" gave Aleshire about a spoonful of heroin and asked her to find some buyers in the Chicago area for "some big loads." When, after a few days, Aleshire failed to come up with any buyers, the three men left Chicago and returned to St. Louis. There, in early December, George Murray Kimbrell changed his name to Frank August.

Early in December, Aleshire found a prospective buyer—Lee Clinton Finger, a Chicago black with an arrest record that included convictions for rape, burglary and narcotics dealings. Aleshire met Finger through Doris Groth, a reported prostitute, with whom she was living and who was Finger's girlfriend. Finger agreed to buy, and on three days in December phone calls were made from the Aleshire-Groth apartment in Chicago to a number in St. Louis listed to Kenneth DeClue, brother-in-law of Frank August.

Meanwhile, Frank August had passport photographs taken, showing him wearing eyeglasses and a goatee and mustache. August and Aaron Gray went to Chicago in mid-December and met Finger at the Aleshire-Groth apartment, where August sold Finger a pound of heroin.

The chase now became an international affair. August flew to Bangkok in late December and returned to the United States via Honolulu a week later. On January 10, 1971, he checked into the Tides Motel in Chicago and made three phone calls to the Aleshire-Groth apartment. The next day he was joined by Mr. and Mrs. Aaron Gray.

While in Chicago on this trip, August sold Finger another pound of heroin and gave Aleshire an ounce of the stuff for her own use. He made another one-pound sale to Finger on January 16. August went back to Bangkok on the twenty-first, and on January 21 and 31 telephone calls were made from Bangkok to August's home phone in St. Louis.

August returned to Chicago on February 11 to sell another pound of heroin to Finger, make a round of phone calls, and a further sale. Once again, on February 27, August flew to Bangkok and thence to Okinawa. It was on his return from this trip on March 12 that he was searched by Customs inspectors and surrendered receipts for the two "tiger skins" mailed to his mother. Then, during the last week of March, a parcel from overseas addressed to Aaron Gray was delivered to the Afton, Missouri, home of Mrs. Ima DeClue, Frank August's sister. Later, too late for action, Customs authorities learned that Gray and August arrived at the DeClue home and August opened the package, revealing a black leopard skin, which he took with him.

August apparently didn't know the difference between a tiger skin and a leopard skin. He might have escaped official scrutiny had the receipts mailed to his mother's home described the skins correctly.

In any event, August was still at large and so was everybody else on the lengthening list of suspects. No one had been caught accepting delivery of even a few grains of heroin. But the suspect list now included the name of Donald Graine of Bangkok, who wrote Frank August in late March: "Today I sent out 9 ozs. It went by APO [Army Post Office] insured, so you'll be getting it within seven days. . . . You can wire the grand to this address. Thank you again and again perpetually! Don."

Meanwhile, three parcels mailed from Bangkok and intercepted by United States postal authorities were opened and found to contain leopard skins with from one and a half to two and a half pounds of heroin in the heads. Finally, on April 30, Customs agents intercepted a parcel addressed to Aaron Gray at the Kimbrell address. Instead of the tiger skin declared, there was another leopard skin— with two pounds of 99 percent pure heroin in its head. On the same day, a BNDD agent bought several ounces of heroin from a lesbian madam in St. Louis; she said her source was in Bangkok.

The case appeared to be closed, or ready for closing, but Bowers wanted to talk to the half brother, Aaron Gray; no one seemed to know where he was. Frustrated in his attempts to get someone with the goods in hand, Bowers got a search warrant for Ima DeClue's house in Afton, and she turned over to a party of agents still another parcel, addressed to Frank "Kimbull."

"We haven't opened it," Mrs. DeClue told the agents. "We don't want any part of it." Bowers opened the package and found the inevitable leopard skin, this one with one and three-quarters pounds of heroin packed in the head. Bowers finally tracked down Aaron Gray in a bar, and a Customs team of interrogators questioned both Gray and Mrs. DeClue about the flood of leopard skins received through the overseas mails. Meanwhile, back at the office, a warrant was sworn out, charging Frank August with attempting to smuggle heroin into the United States.

Mrs. DeClue insisted she had nothing to do with whatever the agents were interested in. She claimed that she had no reason to expect any parcels either for Frank August or from him, that he had never lived in her home, and that she had no idea of his whereabouts. Aaron Gray admitted he had had a leopard skin for about two weeks but it had then "disappeared." He also admitted August had asked about the skin, but clammed up when he was asked if he had given the skin to his half brother. He said he wouldn't say anything that might get Frank into trouble.

The agents had more success with Marie McClure, a waitress at the Tick-Tock Tavern in St. Louis. She quoted Frank August's father, Murry Kimbrell, as saying Frank was involved in peddling dope and that his suppliers were two girls in Thailand and Okinawa. On occasion, Marie told her interrogators, Murry Kimbrell said Frank mailed packages to St. Louis from Thailand and Okinawa and then flew back to the United States and picked them up.

Investigators from the Justice Department's Bureau of Narcotics and Dangerous Drugs also made a score. Late in April, 1971, two undercover agents bought 41 grams of heroin from Agnes Brittain and quoted Brittain as saying her supplier operated out of Thailand. Subsequently, Brittain was taken over by the BNDD to introduce its undercover agents to other heroin dealers.

Yet it was not until September 23, 1971, that a federal grand jury in Chicago indicted nine Americans and two Thai nationals for conspiracy to peddle heroin in the United States. Those named included Frank August, Lee Finger, Donald Graine, Aaron Gray, Doris Groth and Agnes Brittain of the original cast; Johnny Allen Lanpheare, Kenneth Matson and Clyde Penrose, who allegedly operated out of Southeast Asia; and the Thais—Preecha Leeyarug and Boonlert Kun Bum Roong, both of Bangkok.

Lanpheare had been arrested as a courier for Frank August and Boonlert Kun Bum Roong, also known as Young Chalee, and Matson as a combination bodyguard and decoy for Lanpheare on the latter's flight to the United States. Graine also allegedly worked with August and "Young Chalee" in Thailand. Preecha Leeyarug was described by Customs investigators as "perhaps the largest heroin trafficker in Bangkok, with operations directly affecting U.S. servicemen and the United States. Preecha admittedly makes large payoffs to corrupt Thai police officials to continue in business." He was arrested in Bangkok on October 23, 1971, by Thai police and BNDD agents as he delivered 700 grams of heroin to a BNDD informant.

Frank August and three other American defendants were tried in St. Louis and drew the stiffer sentences. August got fifteen years; Aaron Gray twelve years; Donald Graine ten years; and Agnes Brittain a mandatory five-year term. In Chicago, Lee Finger got five years; Lanpheare and Matson were placed on five- and four-year probation, respectively, under the Youth Corrections Act, but the charges against Doris Groth were dismissed. Earlier, Clyde Penrose drew a ten-month sentence after a trial before the Koza branch of Naha District Court in Okinawa. Betty Carol Aleshire, the heroin addict, was not prosecuted. She voluntarily entered Cook County Hospital in Chicago for withdrawal treatment and thenceforth cooperated with Customs agents in the complicated 10,000-mile investigation.

# 20

# The Golden Triangle

Customs' painstaking pursuit and eventual conviction of the Frank August gang was a conspicuous example of what the law can accomplish on the American side of the world with a little cooperation from authorities in Southeast Asia. That is to say, it was a blow against the smugglers who bring heroin into the United States and thus a notch in the bureau's gun. But by the fall of 1972 the major problem remained to be solved: how to get at the source of the increased flow of illicit narcotics from the Golden Triangle, comprising parts of Burma, Thailand and Laos, and, possibly, a few hundred square miles of no-man's-land inside Communist China.

In 1971 the Golden Triangle was the source of 58 percent of the 1,200 tons of illicit opium produced throughout the world. Even if the Turkish ban on growing illegal opium, which went into effect on January 1, 1973, turned off the spigot in that part of the world, the Golden Triangle alone could grow and process enough opium to supply twice the number of American heroin addicts—estimated at the end of 1972 at upwards of 560,000.

Accordingly, the problem was to find, seize and put out of business the Golden Triangle's big-time narcotics entrepreneurs—men like Lo Hsing Han.

The legend was that no one but two or three of Lo Hsing Han's straw bosses had ever seen the man. There was no physical description of Lo in any governmental dossier, no photographs in the "believed-to-be" files. He was believed to be Chinese, born in the southern province of Yunnan, but many Golden Triangle experts claimed he was Burmese. He was estimated to be as young as twenty-two and as old as sixty. Lawmen from Bangkok to Washington agreed that Lo was an operator of superb organizational abilities and a charismatic leader.

Operating from the small Burmese town of Tachilek, just across the border from Thailand, Lo Hsing Han was No. 1 among those syndicate chieftains who made up the first link of the chain that ended with the dope pusher on American street corners. In 1971 Lo was credited with arranging for the production, sale and distribution of more than 300 tons of opium, morphine base from which heroin is processed, and pure heroin. The infrequent raids of local authorities had no effect on Lo's operations; he had sold his merchandise on the spot and it was the dealers who were caught on their runs to Bangkok, Saigon and Hong Kong.

Lo benefited hugely from the chaotic state of affairs within the Golden Triangle. With the tacit approval of the Burmese government, he recruited, organized and equipped an army of at least one thousand men. Rangoon, harassed by bands of Burmese Communist guerrillas, okayed Lo's army because it sought his help in fighting the guerrillas. Instead, intelligence reports charged that Lo reached an accommodation with the guerrillas in exchange for a noninterference policy toward his opium operations.

American military experts admitted that Lo's army was the best equipped and most cohesive fighting force in the mountainous area. Composed of assorted hill tribesmen, dacoits, Yunnanese, Haws, Shans and deserters from Nationalist Chinese troops who fled China after the 1949 Communist takeover, Lo's forces were armed with American M16 rifles, mortars, grenade launchers and even a couple of tanks, originally supplied to the Lao Army but diverted to the black market in Thailand.

Lo was buying his opium from hill farmers and transporting it to his own refineries by packhorse and mule caravans. His army provided an armed escort to prevent rival bands from hijacking the opium. He also had a piece of the so-called legitimate border smuggling action, using his pack trains to transport airplane parts, black-market machinery, textiles, rice and electronic equipment into Burma. The Burmese government seemed powerless to interfere because of a lack of police and military manpower. Thai officials refused to cross the border for fear of creating an incident with Rangoon.

In the vast underworld which is the Golden Triangle, opium is transported by tribesmen from Burma's Shan and Wa states to the walled city of Kengtung. From there, its custodians boldly turn down the Burmese road system to Lo Hsing Han's "capital" of Tachilek, where Lo established at least eight heroin-processing plants. From Tachilek, the dope takes two routes, one across the border into Thailand and thence over the Thai network of roads and trails, the other east to a point where Burma, Laos and Thailand come together. It crosses into Laos from Burma at Muong Hi village, then flows down to the Yao tribes' center at Nam Keun on the Mekong River, where refineries handle opium from both Burma and the Ekaw and Lahu tribes in Laos.

Most of the dope caravans were protected by Lo Hsing Han's troops. But other tribesmen hired themselves out as free-lance guards. Protection also could be bought from the Do Ko private army in Burma's Shan state, which otherwise was engaged in fighting Chinese Communist-organized Ekaw tribesmen, and the official Shan army, which made war on Burmese government troops. With their protection money, the various bands bought United States arms in the black market.

As the drug-busy year 1972 neared its end, therefore, increased attention was given the Southeast Asian production line. Most U.S. antinarcotics agencies, including Customs, agreed publicly or privately that the rivulet of heroin from the Golden Triangle had increased its flow and there was danger that it could become a roaring stream. There also were admissions that the amount of high-quality heroin being smuggled into the United States from Southeast Asia was greater than previously had been realized. Intelligence officials of Customs, the Bureau of Narcotics and Dangerous Drugs, the Central Intelligence Agency, the State Department and the Defense Department noted that the situation was being reviewed with particular focus on Southeast Asia as an alternate to the Middle East as a source of supply. But almost all the experts also agreed with Nelson G. Gross, the State Department's Coordinator for International Narcotics Matters, that "certainly no more than 10 percent of the heroin presently flowing into the United States originates in Southeast Asia."

Meanwhile, a flow of United States intelligence reports hinted strongly that Corsican traffickers in France, in alliance with Mafia forces in the United States, had established an "Asian Connection" to assure a continuing supply of heroin for the American market if other sources were shut off.

One report, issued by the Bureau of Narcotics and Dangerous Drugs, said that much of the heroin from Southeast Asia was being smuggled into the United States by "essentially apolitical Chinese entrepreneurs operating out of Laos, Thailand and Hong Kong. The heroin is sold to ethnic Chinese seamen, many of whom may be organized, who jump ship once their vessels dock in the United States." The BNDD report said further investigation "may reveal the substance of long-standing hitherto unverifiable reports of a 'Chinese Corsican' connection between morphine base from the Orient and the chemical expertise of the Marseilles area."

To most experts, this meant involvement of the American Mafia, which since the middle sixties had maintained a close and profitable relationship with the Corsican-dominated drug syndicates in both Europe and South America. Indeed, some American officials were inclined to find substance in testimony given a Senate subcommittee in June, 1972, by Alfred W. McCoy, a Yale candidate for a PhD in Southeast Asian history and author of the controversial book *The Politics of Heroin in Southeast Asia.*

McCoy told the subcommittee that beginning in 1965 "members of the Florida-based Trafficante Family of American organized crime began appearing in Southeast Asia." He specifically named Santo Trafficante, Jr., purported heir to the global syndicate established by Lucky Luciano and Meyer Lansky, as having traveled to Hong Kong and Saigon in 1968, apparently to arrange a mutually profitable accommodation with Southeast Asian traffickers. McCoy also claimed he had been informed by Lieutenant Colonel Lucien Conein, a retired agent of the Central Intelligence Agency, that in 1969 "there was a summit meeting of Corsican criminals from Marseilles, Vientiane and Pnompenh at the Continental Hotel in Saigon."

Customs Commissioner Mike Acree put it this way: "There is some logic in assuming that our own home-grown Mafia would be interested in the production of opium and heroin in Southeast Asia. They are, after all, deeply interested in the fat profits that accrue from dope trafficking, and they will go wherever those profits can be made. Customs has known for years that the Mafia has a well-established Corsican Connection."

Acree might have added a comment that was hardly news: to wit, that only the Mafia had the money, the expertise and the personnel to exploit fully the Southeast Asian heroin sources. In the meantime, Customs, the BNDD and the relatively new Drug Abuse Law Enforcement Office (DALE) already had their hands full trying to deal with the free lances engaged in smuggling dope from the Golden Triangle into America. Adding a tragic footnote to the Vietnam War, many, if not most, of these free lances were present or former American military personnel—men like William Herman Jackson, a black retired Army sergeant.

Jackson, forty-five at the time of his arrest, had made a bad name for himself with the Army's Criminal Investigation Division while he was on active duty in Europe during the fifties. According to CID files, he was then boss of an organization made up predominantly of former noncommissioned officers which employed civilian cardsharps to fleece military gamblers at various bases located on the Continent. Jackson's gang allegedly was also involved in the sale of counterfeit military orders and identification cards.

In 1967 Jackson moved part of his operation, including himself, to Vietnam, but within a few months he was deported for narcotics and black market activities. Late that same year, Jackson and some pals opened Jack's American Star Bar in Bangkok, purportedly as a front for his assorted illicit operations. Jackson was ordered out of Thailand in 1968, but apparently he knew somebody because the deportation papers were never served on him. At the same time, Jackson was reported to have wangled introductions to several major heroin suppliers in the Golden Triangle in order to deal with them directly and thus avoid what might be called finder's fees. At first, Jackson used couriers, usually recruited at his bar, to body-carry three to five pounds of horse into the United States. Some of these couriers were deserters or AWOL's, to whom Jackson furnished military ID cards and fake travel orders; some were comely females from the native population.

Later, Jackson cozied up to military personnel at the U.S. air base in Bangkok and at various military supply centers, and began using military cargo aircraft to smuggle out his heroin shipments. A 20-pound shipment of heroin dispatched by the Jackson gang was intercepted at Walter Reed Army Hospital in Washington, and another 17 pounds were intercepted at Fort Monmouth, New Jersey.

Then in February, 1969, Jackson and one of his partners, Leslie Atkinson, took off from Bangkok aboard a U.S. Air Force plane after showing fake travel orders. On a tip from Customs headquarters in Washington, relayed from an agent in Bangkok, Jackson and Atkinson were picked up several days later in New York City by agents of the Bureau of Narcotics and Dangerous Drugs for possession of 22 pounds of 85 percent heroin. Subsequently the charges against both men were dropped because of conflicting evidence offered by government witnesses.

In the meantime, however, Jackson continued to run his organization in absentia from his home in Norman's Trailer Court in Goldsboro, North Carolina. Jackson had not settled in Goldsboro to enjoy its springtime explosion of azalea blooms. Four big military reservations are located in the area: Pope Air Force Base, Seymour Johnson Air Force Base, Fort Bragg and Camp Lejeune. Customs, the BNDD and local law enforcement agencies maintained a surveillance of Jackson's home from November 15 to December 15, 1971, under the direction of Howard Wright, Customs' senior resident agent in Wilmington, North Carolina.

All this information, including records of a dozen telephone calls Jackson made to Bangkok, convinced Wright and his colleagues that Jackson was still in business. But they lacked the kind of evidence that would stand up in a courtroom, and they were busy trying to tie up loose ends when the break came in the person of a confidential informant employed at U-Tapao Airfield outside Bangkok. On December 28 he contacted Special Agents Gayle R. Braithwaite and Robert L. Brooding of the U.S. Air Force Office of Special Investigations and told them an interesting story.

The informant, code-named Pacer, said he had been approached by Air Force Sergeant Sylvester Serles, also known as Mumbles and Boop, a twenty-four-year-old supervisor in the records section of his squadron, who offered him $500 to schedule a package out on a TWA flight leaving the next afternoon. Pacer agreed and did the necessary paper work to assure that Pallet NR 8005, on which the package would be loaded, would be put aboard the TWA flight to Travis Air Force Base in California.

The next day, Braithwaite and Pacer were at the airport to watch an Air Force Sergeant put the package on the pallet. Several minutes later, Braithwaite had the package removed from the pallet and found that it contained numerous plastic bags filled with a white powdery substance. After taking a sample of the powder, Braithwaite resealed the box, and it was returned to the loading pallet and eventually loaded on the aircraft. Within a few hours, Customs offices in Sacramento and San Francisco were informed that a package containing about 20 pounds of heroin would arrive at Travis Air Force Base that night.

The flight arrived on schedule, and four Customs agents were there to meet it. The box, addressed to Project Fast Pace, at Lowry Air Force Base in Denver, was off-loaded and placed in a warehouse at the base, with Customs Special Agents Charles L. Deatrick and Alvah M. Henley maintaining surveillance. Subsequently, the box was opened and a test showed the powder was indeed 85 percent pure heroin. When the package arrived in Denver, the heroin was removed and largely replaced with soap powder. Meanwhile, Customs was informed that there was no Project Fast Pace in Lowry's official records.

After the box was repacked, it was sprayed with a fluorescent powder visible under a black light. Then, before the box was resealed, agents stashed two electronic transmitters among the plastic bags. One of the transmitters gave an intermittent tone every three seconds until the box was opened, at which time the tone became constant. The second transmitter emitted a constant series of tones which could be followed by a directional finder to locate the box if it was moved.

Several days passed while the trap was being set, and it was not until January 7 that the package was stored in Hangar No. 2. Four days later, both transmitters stopped operating. A few minutes later, the package was found to be missing from its storage bin in the hangar. Two airmen who had been working in the hangar were hauled in and traces of fluorescent powder were found on their hands and clothing. But they claimed they thought the box contained smuggled stereo equipment and said that when they saw the bags of heroin, they got scared, dropped the box, and took off. Both were arrested but subsequently released.

In any event, the box was gone. Customs agents later learned it had been picked up five minutes after the two airmen fled the hangar. As one agent put it: "Color our faces red on that one. It couldn't have happened, but that's just when it does."

However, Customs still had Sergeant Serles back in Bangkok, and on January 8 Pacer signed a sworn statement in which he quoted Serles as telling him the missing package contained heroin, "the hottest selling stuff in the world." At first, Serles insisted he didn't know what was in the package, although he admitted sending it and two innocent "test" packages to the States. A few days later, however, in the company of his lawyer, Serles told all and fingered Jackson as the mastermind of the smuggling organization.

Serles said he and a serviceman friend, Johnny Trice, had "discussed" smuggling heroin to America, "and it was understood between us that we would try this if the opportunity arose." Then, in August or September, 1971, Serles said he had contacted Jackson and told him that he (Serles) could slip narcotics through the Air Force freight system. Jackson told Serles to "be cool" and said he'd be in touch later. A month passed, and Jackson got in touch. "He was interested in my proposition," said Serles, "and had found a contact in the United States who could remove the shipment I sent from the cargo system. As a coincidence, the man Jackson identified was the same Johnny Trice I had discussed the matter with before."

At any rate, Jackson ran two test runs through the Air Force freight system. However, Trice, at the other end, had had a change of heart and refused to accept either shipment. Meanwhile, Serles had been introduced to Andrew Price, forty-five, Jackson's nephew, who became Jackson's contact man with Serles. Price delivered packages of heroin to Serles and from time to time gave him money to recruit Thai helpers. Jackson promised Serles $15,000 for each heroin shipment safely delivered to the United States.

Although Serles said he didn't know Price's last name until he was shown photographs of Price and Jackson after his arrest, he unhesitatingly identified Price as the individual who served as a kind of supervisor in the field for the tycoon, Jackson. It was Price, Serles said, who gave him the packed and sealed box, which Price told him contained "trash," used in the first test run.

"After each shipment, I would give the shipping document to Andrew Price," Serles told his interrogators. "I assume he telephoned it or had it carried to the United States for identification of the package when it arrived at the destination."

Sergeant Johnny Trice was located at Tinker Air Force Base in Oklahoma and immediately agreed to cooperate with Customs' investigation. He said he had "come down with cold feet" after returning to the United States and had decided it was "immoral" to traffic in dope. Trice confirmed Serles' statement naming Jackson as the smuggling ring leader and also implicated one Gerald Gainous, thirty-seven, an Air Force master sergeant stationed at Seymour Johnson Air Force Base in Goldsboro. According to Trice, Gainous was Jackson's "representative" in the United States, charged with setting up receipt of the packages of heroin. It was Gainous who forwarded information concerning shipping manifests and instructions as to how to pick up the heroin shipments. When he got cold feet and decided not to go along with the conspiracy, Trice told a grand jury Gainous informed him that if he cooperated, he would "make some big money . . . you're playing with the big boys."

Serles was arrested on January 16, 1972, and Price on January 22, both in Bangkok. Jackson and Gainous both were arrested in Goldsboro on January 21. Three months later, Jackson was hit with the book; he was sentenced to thirty years in prison. Price drew two fifteen-year sentences, to run concurrently. Serles got eighteen months. Convicted on one count of conspiracy to smuggle, Gainous got a break. The Denver judge agreed to postpone sentencing until October, 1972, when Gainous would become eligible for an Air Force pension. But the judge did Gainous no favors at sentencing time; he sent Jackson's American contact man off to serve ten years in a federal penitentiary.

Then in December, 1972, the name of one of William Herman Jackson's old buddies popped up in the most grisly narcotics investigation of the decade. Assistant United States Attorney Michael E. Marr in Baltimore reported that Leslie Atkinson, who had been picked up with Jackson in the abortive New York trafficking case in February, 1969, had been aboard a military transport plane searched by federal agents when it landed at Andrews Air Force Base, outside Washington.

The search was conducted after confidential informants had tipped off authorities that 20 kilos of heroin had been secreted inside the corpses of two United States servicemen bound for Dover Air Force Base in Delaware. The plane was diverted to the Andrews base, and civilian and military agents with dogs trained to detect hidden drugs took the plane apart and searched the passengers. A pathologist opened and searched the two bodies, but no narcotics were found.

Marr, who made the identification of Atkinson, described him as a man "who we know to be part of the conspiracy." But Atkinson, a retired Army sergeant, was not arrested; obviously whatever Marr "knew" about Jackson's pal was not enough to make a courtroom case. But the feds did hold Thomas E. Southerland, thirty-one, of Goldsboro, North Carolina, on charges of impersonating an Army sergeant, possessing forged travel orders and counterfeit official identification papers, and making false statements to Customs agents. Southerland, subsequently indicted on nine assorted criminal counts, was described as a "functionary" in a conspiracy to smuggle heroin into the United States in the cadavers or coffins of American servicemen killed in Vietnam.

There were hints dropped in some official quarters that Jackson also knew something about this macabre conspiracy. If so, it lent credence to the prosecution's contention that the operation had been carried out for as long as eight years. There was also Atkinson's link with Jackson in the New York case, but at the time of Southerland's indictment Marr would say only that Atkinson and Southerland "were seen in Honolulu acting in a friendly fashion together. They were also staying in the same hotel in Honolulu." Meanwhile, Customs, the Bureau of Narcotics and Dangerous Drugs, and military authorities launched a full-scale investigation which Pentagon officials said they were certain "will produce shocking results."

William Herman Jackson, whose criminal career spanned two continents, was the first big catch of 1972 in Southeast Asia's flourishing narcotics underworld. Several months later, police in Saigon nabbed another American expatriate whom they charged with having achieved major-league status. He was Joseph Berger, sixty-six, who allegedly had worked the opium and heroin fields for sixteen highly successful years and who was arrested after bringing in a haul of 400 pounds of opium from Thailand, according to the South Vietnamese charge sheet.

Moreover, Saigon authorities crowed that Berger had fingered a mysterious Chinese known as the Phantom, described as Lo Hsing Han's only authentic rival in the Golden Triangle's complex of dope-running barons. Berger reportedly had arrived in Saigon in June, 1972, for a summit meeting with the Phantom, and after his arrest he identified the Phantom when the latter arrived at the Saigon airport two days later. Saigon police identified the Phantom as Wan Pen Phen, who, according to his Saigon police dossier, was responsible for transporting 4,500 pounds of opium a month through Thailand and Laos.

Back home on the streets, federal agents also made two big scores, both in New York City. The first came in late 1971 when a Philippine diplomat and his Chinese companion were arrested in their room at the Lexington Hotel on the Upper East Side. Agents found 38 pounds of a brand of highly refined heroin known as Double Uoglobe in their luggage. Double Uoglobe is processed in Laos and was a big favorite with American servicemen in South Vietnam when that market was at its height.

Then, in the late summer of 1972, federal agents nabbed four men, including Kenneth Kankit Huie, sixty, self-styled "unofficial mayor of Chinatown," and Tim Lok, thirty-five, nicknamed the General for his military posture. The arrests were made with the help of two undercover narcotics agents who posed as big buyers and who were led by the General to a cardboard box in a Chinatown sportswear shop found to contain fourteen plastic bags filled with 20 pounds of "Pure No. 4" heroin from Thailand.

Clearly, the Lo Hsing Hans and other big-league operators in the misty hills of the Golden Triangle were getting their stuff into the United States in increasing quantities now that their captive market of American GI's had all but disappeared. The heroin flow from the Orient might still be insignificant compared with that pouring in from the Middle East, Europe and South America, but every indication suggested that it had become part of the problem in Washington's global war against dope.

# 21

# How Much Hope?

In Marseilles, an Irish "tourist" hands a French official an envelope containing $2,000 in French francs. Half an hour later, the Irishman's wife leaves a Greek ship carrying two suitcases and is casually waved through customs. Inside the suitcases are plastic bags containing 10 kilos of morphine base which, when processed into 10 kilos of heroin at an illicit Marseilles laboratory, will retail for $2,250,000 on American streets.

A sealed truck from Italy gets the same friendly treatment at the French border, but this time no money changes hands. Under European customs agreements, such cargo-carrying vehicles more often than not are permitted to cross frontiers after a mere inspection of their papers. Secreted within the cases of macaroni carried by the truck are 40 kilos of morphine base.

Such incidents illustrate America's biggest problem in its all-out war on illicit trafficking in drugs. The United States Customs Bureau, the nation's first line of defense, does what it can to keep dope out of the country, but it is powerless against the corruption of government officials and lax law enforcement abroad. Even if corruption were reduced to zero, the lack of manpower in most foreign countries makes any efficient crackdown on smugglers virtually impossible. Indeed, in the United States itself, no more than a tiny percentage of persons and carriers can be searched every year. In any case, the enormous profits earned by the smuggling kings and their underlings mitigate any successful campaign against corruption. A Turkish farmer receives $22 for enough opium to produce heroin worth $220,000 at retail. There is money enough in that vast profit margin to pay fat bribes all along the line from Turkey to New York City.

Obviously, then, only international action on a cooperative scale can make any meaningful global progress in stamping out drug addiction. If the sixteen-year-old high school boy in Toledo or Paris is

269

to be protected from the slow death of the junkie, law enforcement officials in the United States and France must work with lawmen around the world at least to reduce and, if possible, stamp out the supply of illicit dope. Despite the lofty prose emanating from United Nations headquarters in New York, there was little hope of mounting such an international campaign when dope addiction was of major concern only to the United States. But in the late sixties and early seventies, drugs suddenly became a problem in other countries of the world, notably Great Britain, France, West Germany, Belgium, Italy and the Scandinavian nations. The drug problem worsened in India and Iran and even surfaced, to a minor degree, in the tightly policed countries of the Eastern European Communist bloc—the Soviet Union, Hungary, Rumania and Czechoslovakia.

Seizing upon these developments, the United States took the initiative in a wide-ranging effort to persuade UN members to face reality. That effort, conducted through diplomatic and law enforcement channels, produced a decision by the UN Economic and Social Council on May 20, 1971, to conduct a plenipotentiary conference in Geneva the following March to consider amendments to the Single Convention on Narcotic Drugs. The convention included ninety member states; it was adopted on March 30, 1961, and became effective on December 13, 1964.

In essence, the convention operates through two bodies—the United Nations Commission on Narcotic Drugs and the International Narcotics Control Board (INCB). The commission is a policy-making body; the INCB administers the system of controls and is charged with issuing quotas on the amount of legal opium to be produced, imported and exported by member nations.

Each party to the convention was required to submit to the INCB estimates of the amount of opium to be consumed for medicinal and scientific purposes, as well as the amount to be held in stock. Using these figures, the INCB computed the amount to be produced in specially designated countries and later reviewed the statistical report each nation was responsible for filing annually, listing production, manufacture, consumption, stocks, imports, exports and confiscation.

But the parent United Nations gave the INCB too weak a mandate for its job of controlling the growing illicit traffic in narcotics—estimated in 1972 at from 1,200 to 1,400 tons of raw opium convertible into 120 to 140 tons of heroin. No provisions were made for a comprehensive information network to aid the INCB in determining drug quotas, the use of investigatory powers aimed at member states suspected of violating the pact, and the imposition of meaningful sanctions against offending states. In fact, Congressman Seymour Halpern, Republican of New York, charged that the INCB had been "under-utilizing the weak mandate it does have to monitor international traffic in drugs, and has seemed prone to maintain a policy of live and let live rather than to offend member states by pointing a finger at their failure to adhere to treaty requirements."

Halpern was no amateur. A member of the House Foreign Affairs Committee, he had led a study mission to eleven countries involved in illicit drug trafficking and later was named a member of the United States delegation to the Geneva conference to amend the Single Convention. In the interim, he had been an indefatigable fighter for international drug control.

Halpern singled out Turkey as "a glaring example of the INCB's failure to carry out one of its most basic responsibilities." Turkey was one of the nations authorized to grow opium for export in order to fulfill legitimate worldwide needs. But this authorization was contingent upon local enactment of an enforceable licensing law to control production. It was not until 1971 that Turkey finally put a licensing law into effect, as a result of diplomatic and financial pressure by the United States. Yet no penalties of any kind were imposed on the Turkish government by the INCB, and no embargo against the importation of Turkish opium was even recommended.

It was in order to bolster the investigatory and enforcement powers of the United Nations, therefore, that the United States launched its campaign to amend the Single Convention. Named to direct the effort was Nelson G. Gross, the State Department's Coordinator for International Narcotics Matters. A year in advance of the Geneva Conference, Gross's task force had prepared a draft of suggested amendments and began presenting and explaining these proposals to more than one hundred governments. As Halpern wrote in the May 1, 1972, issue of the *New York Law Journal*, "The result of this lengthy series of missions was the development of a new international consensus on narcotics control . . . which both defines drug abuse as a critically dangerous contagion to which no country is immune, and, at long last, equips the INCB with sufficient power to adjust world opium production to scientific and medical demand while preventing diversion to illicit channels."

Halpern was referring to the work of the Geneva conference of March, 1972, which adopted the American amendments as cosponsored by twenty-nine other nations. The vote was 71 countries for, none against, with 12 abstaining. The abstainers included the East European Communist bloc—the Soviet Union, Bulgaria, the Byelorussian Soviet Republic, Czechoslovakia, Hungary, Mongolia, Poland and the Ukrainian Soviet Socialist Republic—which is congenitally suspicious of any American proposition on any subject. (Although, as Gross said later, "The Russians promised to vote for the amendments. I don't know what happened.") Other abstainers were Burma, Panama, Algeria and Cuba, also for political reasons.

The amendments appeared to attack all the loopholes inherent in the original Single Convention. They gave the INCB responsibility and authority to join the fight against illicit trafficking and put at its disposal information from a wider range of sources, including the UN and various intergovernmental and nongovernmental organizations with competence in the drug field. They authorized the board to recommend that technical and financial assistance be provided to governments cracking down on trafficking within their borders. The INCB may recommend to the UN General Assembly that an embargo be imposed on the import and export of all drugs by a violating nation, and if there is evidence that any country is permitting diversion of drugs into illicit traffic, the board may order that the country reduce its production in the following year. The amendments also applied to narcotics offenses the same improvements in the area of extradition applied in multilateral conventions to air hijacking and other offenses against civil aviation.

Guided and cajoled by the United States, the UN member nations had done their job at Geneva. But the results of the new and strengthened Single Convention on Narcotic Drugs would not be felt for years, even with no allowance for foot dragging on the part of some of its signatories. The immediate problem remained, and the assignment of trying to keep it from becoming worse and perhaps cutting it down to size was still a matter for lawmen everywhere. It was an assignment of enormous magnitude.

For instance, there is the case—again—of Turkey. Under intense pressure from the White House and a flood of Congressional bills aimed at cutting off economic aid to Turkey if it continued to flood the black market with opium, the Turkish government agreed in June, 1971, to halt the growing of poppies after the 1972 harvest. In return, the United States said it would provide some $35,000,000 in foreign aid funds to compensate the Turkish government for the loss of foreign exchange from legitimate opium sales.

Turkey's acquiescence to American demands has come under considerable criticism from some Turkish politicians and caused a surge of anti-Americanism. There was skepticism that Turkish police would fully enforce the ban because it would cause the loss of under-the-table payments from opium buyers and dealers. Moreover, there is a difference of opinion among experts over the policy of checking heroin smuggling by halting the growing of opium poppies around the world.

Notable among those who found it unrealistic was President Nixon's top hand in the war against drug trafficking, Myles Ambrose, who called the concept "one of those magic-wand statements born in ignorance." Ambrose had been promoted from his post as Commissioner of Customs to chief of the Drug Abuse Law Enforcement Office established to combat drug traffickers at the street level, so he could hardly be described as an antiadministration type.

Testifying before the National Commission on Marijuana and Drug Abuse, Ambrose said, "I think our children's children's children will be looking forward to a long life before we see opium-growth cessation at the source." Ambrose rejected estimates that 80 percent of the heroin reaching the United States came from Turkish opium fields. In fact, he said, 60 percent of the world's opium supply was grown in the rugged Shan states of Burma and in remote and mountainous corners of Laos and Thailand, where governmental control is nominal at best.

Ambrose's own figures may have been subject to rebuttal, but he had an argument in pointing out the difficulties involved in trying to halt poppy growing worldwide. A 1972 study commissioned by the Ford Foundation found that United States heroin addicts consumed only 1.5 percent of the world's opium supply—a percentage that could be cultivated on five square miles of land. And besides the threat from Indochina's Golden Triangle, there were movements in Mexico, India, Afghanistan, Pakistan and other countries to move in on Turkey's former monopoly. For the first time, agents of U.S. narcotics agencies reported the operation of a heroin laboratory in the Philippines, and the Nixon administration announced plans to appeal for cooperation through diplomatic channels to the governments of fifty-seven countries suspected of harboring either illicit opium growers or heroin-processing plants.

Most U.S. intelligence studies agreed that about half of the world's total raw opium supply is produced in India, Pakistan and Afghanistan. One Central Intelligence Agency report placed total world opium production at a whopping 2,500 tons per year, compared with the United Nations estimate of 1,200 to 1,400 tons, another indication that statistics on the subject tend to be a sometime thing.

Nevertheless, it is necessary to work with the statistics at hand, and the official U.S. government studies calculated that India produced about 200 tons of illegal opium a year. Most of this dope enters the domestic market, produced by upward of 550,000 addicts, but there is almost immeasurably more money to be made by converting opium to heroin, and India could become a major supplier of the American market if the big European syndicates include the subcontinent in expansion plans for the Far East.

In Pakistan, intelligence reports noted that lax law enforcement encouraged illicit traffickers by permitting easy access to illicit opium grown by autonomous tribes in the northwest areas, amounting to about 175 tons a year. Official corruption also was blamed for Pakistan's failure to suppress the drug trade, although the reports acknowledged that Pakistan authorities were forced to move carefully against the growers for fear of stirring up a politically sensitive region of the country. Afghanistan was said to produce between 100 and 125 tons of opium a year, cultivated mainly by Pushtun tribesmen in the eastern parts of the country. Smuggling is a way of life in Afghanistan; most of the opium crop is sneaked out of the country in caravans protected by mercenaries.

Unfortunately for the United States and, to a lesser extent, the rest of the Western world, the big profits to be made from international dope trafficking suggested that Afghanistan might become a new source for the heroin merchants in New York, London, Paris and Amsterdam. Already, by the end of 1972, the Afghan operators were shipping two tons a month of what most experts considered the best hashish available to the United States, Canada and western Europe. With the Turkish ban on cultivation of poppies threatening the supply of opium, there was the fear that the Afghan hashish smugglers would switch to dealing in opium to fill any vacuum that might be caused by Turkey's more or less serious enforcement of the poppy-growing ban.

Lawmen from several countries who had sought cooperation from the Afghan government in trying to stem the flow of hashish were convinced that the Afghans were making no significant attempt to stem the outflow of either hashish or opium. Indeed, there were diplomats along Embassy Row in Washington who openly charged that the Afghan government itself was engaged in the narcotics traffic and that powerful individuals in King Mohammed Zahir Shah's official family were reaping huge profits from giving the trade their personal protection. Bribery is also a way of life in Afghanistan. When two Americans were arrested during a raid on a hashish-processing plant in the summer of 1972, their escape was arranged through a bribe of $3,000 to an Afghan official, and they fled with passports supplied to them by Dr. Timothy Leary's Brotherhood of Eternal Love.

Iran not only had produced a new crop of narcotics addicts, but had become a potential mass transit area for illegal dope moving from South Asia toward Europe and the United States. Shah Mohammed Reza Pahlevi legalized the production of drugs in 1969, after a fourteen-year ban on opium output, explaining the step as aimed at halting a drain on his country's foreign currency reserves through smuggling. Since then, Iran has registered about 90,000 drug addicts, but this number represents only one-fourth of the estimated 400,000 drug users in the country.

But for the United States and Europe, the danger was that Iran would become another means of pouring illicit dope into their cities. Already, more than 170 tons of Afghan and Pakistani opium are smuggled into and through Iran every year, and in late 1972 substantial quantities of Indian opium, plus some heroin, had begun to flow into and through the country. Iran is only a short walk from Turkey, stepping stone to the lucrative heroin-processing centers of Europe.

Contemplating these developments, President Nixon displayed some dollar muscle. He announced in September, 1972, that he was prepared to cut off economic and military aid to all countries that willfully contributed to America's narcotics problem. Nixon described heroin traffickers as "the slave traders of our time . . . they are traffickers in living death. They must be hunted to the end of the earth. They must be left no base in any nation for their operations."

Meanwhile, what for decades had been considered the unthinkable had happened in Switzerland: the sanctity of numbered bank accounts was breached. The Swiss Ministry of Justice announced several months earlier that it had frozen more than $500,000 hidden in secret Swiss accounts by international drug traffickers. It was the first time authorities had acted against the use of Swiss banks by dope smugglers. Although some cynics suggested that the highly confidential Swiss banking system still protected millions of dollars in junk money, the official U.S. view was that the move signaled closer cooperation between Bern and Washington on matters pertaining to dope trafficking. "I'm not going to haggle," said Customs Commissioner Mike Acree. "We'll take all the help we can get. The idea is to put the squeeze on those creeps, and one of the ways to squeeze them is to let them know they won't be able to put their hands on their profits if they get caught."

America indeed could use all the help it could get. Although the government spent a record $453,100,000 to battle drug addiction in fiscal 1972, compared with only $65,200,000 in fiscal 1969, the Bureau of Narcotics and Dangerous Drugs reported that the number of addicts had jumped in the three-year period from 332,000 to 559,000.

Most tragically, children continued to be numbered among the victims of the now not-so-new drug culture. In Fairfax County, Virginia, a suburb of Washington, undercover narcotics agents turned up an organized heroin ring operated by a thirty-eight-year-old man and employing seven pushers ranging in age from seventeen to twenty-two. In New York, school officials announced that the city's 900 schools had 7,783 known or suspected heroin addicts and users in 1971. More than 58,000 pupils—about 5 percent of the overall enrollment—were known to be or suspected of using various hard or soft drugs.

A survey conducted for the National Commission on Marijuana and Drug Abuse revealed that 6 percent of the nation's high-school-age youth—a figure much higher than previous estimates—had used heroin at least once. The figure meant that 1,500,000 Americans between twelve and eighteen and 700,000 Americans over eighteen had tried heroin, and it did not include hard-core heroin addicts who were not picked up by the survey.

The police chief in Chapel Hill, North Carolina, told a United Press International pollster that there were 150 heroin users—80 percent of them teen-agers—in his town of 30,000.

In Chicago, a fourteen-year-old boy was arrested on a charge of knifing a pedestrian to death when the man refused to give him his wallet containing $4.56. The boy said he had been on heroin for more than a year and needed a fix. A medical examination confirmed his story.

In New York City, Human Resources Administrator Jule M. Sugarman told a news conference that the disruption and cost generated by the increasing number of dope addicts on relief threatened to paralyze the city's welfare system. Sugarman estimated the cost of supporting addicts on welfare at $80,000,000 a year and increasing at the rate of $300,000 a month.

"Every time I give a check to an addict," a New York welfare caseworker told the New York *Times*, "I say to myself, 'I just paid for a fix.' But I also say, 'I just kept someone from being robbed.' "

Two days before, a disgruntled junkie had ambushed a supervisor on the street and thrown lye in his face. The junkie had been trying to enroll at a welfare center and got tired of waiting in line. The heroin on which he was hooked was traced to a street pusher, then to a dealer, and then to a wholesaler. His last packet of horse had cost the addict $5. It was part of a shipment smuggled into the United States by a French Corsican who had bought the heroin in Marseilles for $120,000 and sold it to his receiver in New York for $1,000,-000.

And still the hard drugs poured into the United States. Southeast Asia's new global connections with international syndicates grabbed a lot of headlines, but Europe and South America remained the major sources of supply to the American market; indeed so heavy was the flow at times from these two continents that it suggested a state of oversupply. Taking note of this, Customs Commissioner Acree was prompted to remark wryly, "There's no need for any American addict to start raising poppies in his backyard." Meanwhile, locating the poppy fields around the world was no longer a problem; U.S. spy satellites were finding and photographing them from the Andes to Teheran.

There was even the argument that Americans were traditionally and peculiarly attracted to the use of hard drugs—that it was part of the American way of life. This thesis came from two Yale professors, Dr. David Musto, assistant professor of history and psychiatry, and Alan Trachtenberg, associate professor of English and American studies, in a *Yale Alumni Magazine* article.

Musto and Trachtenberg pointed to the "enormous use of drugs in this country in the Nineteenth Century," and added the reminder that the use of heroin and morphine in the United States "has been so great, compared with other nations, that some American scientists around World War I called heroin or morphine addiction 'the American Disease.' " They went on to cite a federal government study during the World War I period which reported the average consumption in America was thirty-six grains of opium per capita, whereas in France it was three grains and in Germany only two grains. Said Musto: "We have called the addict un-American, and yet it is a characteristically American problem and it has been perceived as characteristically American by other nations, which couldn't understand why we kept demanding that they plough under their poppy fields when they didn't have this problem."

What, then, was the long-range solution? The Drug Abuse Office's Chief, Ambrose, who said, "It's nonsense to me to keep reading these stories about how we're going to stop poppies from growing," saw the only hope as a continued, massively financed harassment of smugglers and big-time dealers aimed at upsetting the supply systems and reducing the availability on the street. Ambrose, Acree and John Ingersoll, head of the Justice Department's Bureau of Narcotics and Dangerous Drugs, agreed that an all-out harassment campaign, by reducing the heroin supply, at least would discourage nonusers from experimenting with the drug and also have a substantial impact on addiction.

In sum, such a campaign, supported by diplomatic pressure, would make it more difficult for the addict or experimenter to buy hard drugs. In theory, this would cause more addicts to turn to methadone maintenance or other treatment programs—perhaps even through a controlled and policed system of offering free methadone on the street.

But there was more that had to be done. The devastating problem had to be attacked from all sides. Government would have to take on the expensive job of stepping up research on various types of other drugs to combat the addict's craving. New investigative methods had to be found for spotting potential addicts so that preventive measures could be taken. The problem had to be approached on the basis of its sociological, physiological and psychological roots to come up with a better answer to the question of why Americans turn to dope. There were those longtime experts in law enforcement and medicine and on both sides of the aisles in Congress and state legislative bodies who believed that the drastic last resort was imposition of the death penalty for hard drug traffickers. There were those pessimists who maintained that America had no choice but to sweat out the problem and hope for the best, that the United States' "total war" on heroin was too little and too late.

"I won't buy that," said Mike Acree. "Every time a law enforcement agency here or abroad seizes a load of heroin and makes an arrest or arrests we are chiseling away at the problem, making the traffic in illicit drugs a little harder and a little more dangerous and a little more expensive. The idea that we should sit on our hams, that we should surrender to this worst of all crimes, is preposterous."

Public opinion in 1973 seemed to agree with Mike Acree. Governor Nelson Rockefeller of New York won the support of those interviewed in a nationwide Gallup Poll when he recommended that all convicted pushers of hard drugs and addicts convicted of violent crimes be sentenced to life imprisonment, with no parole and no plea bargaining—that is, pleading guilty to a lesser charge to save the state time and money. Shortly thereafter Mayor John Lindsay of New York City, not celebrated as a hard-nosed law enforcement type, proposed that the mandatory minimum term for a Class A felony be increased from fifteen to twenty-five years. More important, Lindsay urged that parole procedures be strengthened so that felons would serve at least one-third of their maximum sentences instead of only one year before becoming eligible for parole. The dope pusher facing a certain eight-plus years in prison before parole might decide that selling watered stock was safer than peddling heroin.

Then in March, 1973, President Nixon offered his hard-line "solution." He asked Congress to enact legislation which would "put heroin pushers in prison and keep them there" by providing mandatory life sentences without parole for offenders with a prior conviction for a drug felony. At the same time, Nixon reiterated his opposition to legalizing the possession, use, or sale of marijuana and inveighed against "softheaded" and "permissive" judges and probation officers who "are more considerate of the pusher than they are of his victims." He asked that Congress require federal judges to "consider the danger to the community before freeing on bail a suspect for heroin traffic."

Writing in *New York* magazine in November, 1972, on crimes perpetrated by blacks against blacks, the black author Orde Coombs had this to say:

"No question of crime can be raised without exploring dope addiction. It must, quite simply, be recognized that in the black ghettos of our country, heroin addition is no longer something that happens to people across the street. It is an epidemic that has consumed the best and now threatens the rest. If we were menaced by bubonic plague or smallpox, our response would be immediate. We would quarantine the victims and end the epidemic. This is what we must now do to the addicts in our midst. They must be swept off the streets and placed in addiction villages in the deserts of the West. And the pushers of heroin must know that once they are caught they will spend the remainder of their lives in the dungeons that we call prisons.

"If the liberals cry about constitutional rights, chase them back to Scarsdale, for they do not quake every time they saunter out of doors. Of course, I know that if this is done to addicts, it can be done to alcoholics, to homosexuals and to all blacks. But we can only fight one battle at a time, and we are fighting, now, for our lives. . . ."

Much the same solution had been laid before the platform committees of both major political parties in Miami Beach a few months earlier by the new Citizens Crusade Against Crime, Incorporated, many of whose members were speaking out in outrage against murders in their own families.

Said the Crusade, in a plea ignored by both Democrats and Republicans: "Drug addiction is a serious factor in crimes of violence as well as a contagious, epidemic disease which is spread by addicts. It has created a social problem so complex that there has been no agreement on how to deal with this danger. We think reasonable men should be able to agree that every addict—beginning with the thousands on welfare rolls—should be identified as a dangerous disease-carrier and placed under social control and supervision until he is cured."

Within the Administration the quarantine was viewed as impractical because of its possible threat to civil liberties. But in the spring of 1973, President Nixon sent to Congress his proposal to place enforcement of anti-narcotics laws under a new agency within the Justice Department—the Drug Enforcement Administration. The reorganization plan collected under the agency's umbrella the Bureau of Narcotics and Dangerous Drugs, the Customs Bureau's drug investigation force, the Office of Drug Abuse Law Enforcement (DALE), and the Office of National Narcotics Intelligence. The President named Myles Ambrose, the forty-five-year-old chief of DALE, to organize the DEA and act as its temporary administrator, and announced that some five hundred Customs agents would be transferred to the new unit.

Nixon argued that a seven-fold increase in the drug enforcement funds in the previous five years had not been adequate to combat "the resilience of the international drug trade," that a single agency with overall authority and responsibility was the only answer to the problem of stemming the flow of illicit narcotics into the United States. He thus acknowledged that his "all-out global war on the drug menace" still had major battles looming in the years ahead.

Nevertheless, whatever the difficulties that lay ahead, the seventies had produced a public debate on the nation's gravest domestic problem, after the casual apathy of the sixties. More first-rate minds had been drawn into the debate over the final solution and more professionalism had been injected into the federal, state and local law enforcement forces charged with tracking down and prosecuting the offenders. Customs and BNDD seizures had increased in every year since 1968, and the relatively new Drug Abuse and Law Enforcement Office, with its mixed corps of lawyers and hard-bitten narcotics agents, made a whopping 2,000-plus arrests in the first nine months since its establishment in the spring of 1972. All this was not enough, but it was—at last—progress, and the foundations had been laid for more of the same. The problem was still there, destroying lives and enriching international scoundrels beyond their wildest ambitions, but the problem had been officially acknowledged, national outrage had been kindled, and across the land thousands of men and women had enlisted in something like a crusade to excise this moral, social, and financial cancer from the national body.

# INDEX